IMAGES
*of America*

# RIVERBOATS OF NORTHERN CALIFORNIA

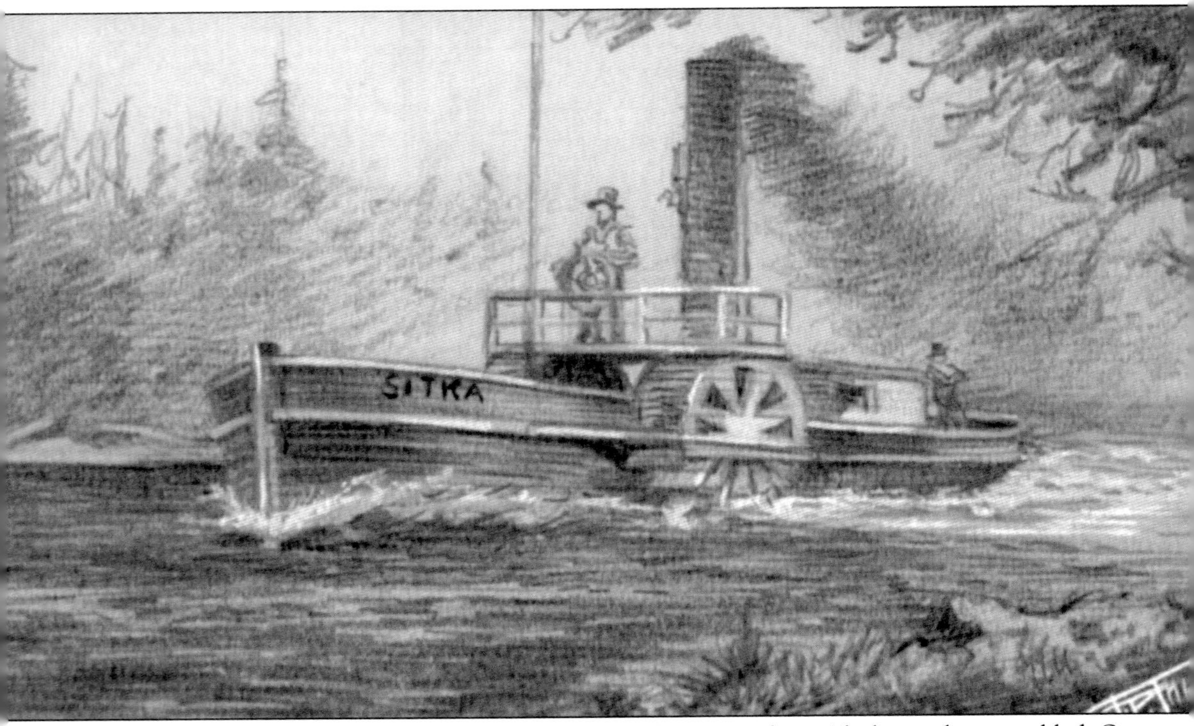


The *Sitka* was dismantled in 1847, shipped to San Francisco from Alaska, and reassembled. On November 29, 1847, the underpowered, 37-foot-long *Sitka* became the Sacramento River's first steamboat, arriving at New Helvetia six days and seven hours later. Without photographs of her, there are only artists' sketches. The art is not accurate (an unconnected steering wheel), but *Sitka*'s place in history warrants inclusion. (Author's collection.)

**On the Cover:** In this bucolic scene on the upper Sacramento River c. 1910, the Farmers' Transportation Co. riverboat *Valletta* is working a charter for an Independent Order of Odd Fellows (IOOF) picnic. Her passengers, dressed in their Sunday best, have crowded the maindeck, cabin deck, texas deck, and even the hurricane deck, an area usually forbidden to passengers. (Courtesy San Francisco Maritime National Historical Park, No. P84-064n.)

IMAGES
*of America*

# RIVERBOATS OF NORTHERN CALIFORNIA

Paul C. Trimble

ARCADIA
PUBLISHING

ISBN 978-0-7385-7496-7

Published by Arcadia Publishing
Charleston, South Carolina

Printed in the United States of America

Library of Congress Control Number: 2010941983

For all general information, please contact Arcadia Publishing:
Telephone 843-853-2070
Fax 843-853-0044
E-mail sales@arcadiapublishing.com
For customer service and orders:
Toll-Free 1-888-313-2665

Visit us on the Internet at www.arcadiapublishing.com

*This book is dedicated to my grandson, Alexander Michael Mackechnie*

# Contents

# ACKNOWLEDGMENTS

This book was a team effort, although many of the people with whom credit must be shared may not even be acquainted with each other. If anyone has been omitted, my apologies. Thanks go to Allan Fisher, Harry C. Aitken, and Grant Ute of the Western Railway Museum Archives. Grant also made available photographs from the collection of the late Richard Schlaich. James C. Scott at the Sacramento Public Library went beyond the proverbial extra mile, as did Ed LeBlanc and Ted Miles at the J. Porter Shaw Library of the San Francisco Maritime National Historical Park. Thanks also go to the California State Library in Sacramento, for without their invaluable collections, this book could not have become what it is, as well as to Michael Dolgushkin and all of the librarians in the California State Library's California History Room; fellow Arcadia author John Schmale, who was most generous in making photographs from his collection; longtime rail photographer Tom Gray; Kristie Shepard and the staff at the Napa County Historical Society's museum; fellow Arcadian Dianne Moll Smith, curator at the Sonoma Valley Museum, for her efforts to secure the use of that rare and priceless picture on page 106; and Sonoma Valley historian Robert D. Parmelee for information about the Sonoma Creek's riverboats.

The Vallejo Naval and Historical Museum and the Northwestern Pacific Railroad Historical Society allowed the use of photographs that I obtained from them while researching for a previous Arcadia work about the San Francisco Bay ferryboats. William C. Knorp, who collaborated with me on the ferryboats book, provided some of the photographs used in this book.

The Reference Desk at the Novato Branch of the Marin County Free Library located odd bits of information, as did Lisa Christiansen, librarian/archivist at the Stocklmeir Library of the California History Center at DeAnza College. Retired merchant marine officer Roger Bergmans offered technical explanations and advice.

It was a pleasure to have worked again with Arcadia editor John Poultney. John's unending encouragement and support are much appreciated. Special thanks go to Kevin Shields for his time, artistic talent, and skills in producing the maps for this book. Thanks once again to my daughter, Debbie Trimble, for her input and computer work. Thanks to the rest of my family for their encouragement.

Finally, thanks to the shipwrights, crews, mates, officers, pilots, and captains who made this history, for without them we would not have their history about which to write.

# INTRODUCTION

Why would a railroad historian write about Northern California riverboats? My riverboats interest began as a boy in San Francisco, fishing off the Municipal Pier at Aquatic Park and seeing the beached *Fort Sutter*. Too young to have ridden the river steamers, I do remember riding the San Francisco Bay ferryboats.

As I grew older and developed my interest in railroads, I learned that while no less than 11 California railroads operated ferryboats, two railroads operated riverboats. I also learned the differences between the two.

In 2007, I wrote *Ferries of San Francisco Bay* for Arcadia Publishing. This book is intended to be a companion to that work, and together they provide an overview of travel on Northern California's inland waterways. I have omitted the Colorado River riverboats since that history, while worthy of publication, goes beyond California itself. No slight is intended.

California's riverboat era began in 1847 and declined as publicly funded roads and bridges assumed a greater and greater share of the riverboats' business. Finally, on August 24, 1950, Capt. John H. Urton docked the *Petaluma* in her namesake city for the last time and closed the log on the last paddle wheel steamboat in the west.

Riverboats contributed to the growth and prosperity of the Golden State, moving people and freight from before the Gold Rush until the nuclear age. Considering that riverboating was done without such navigational aids as radar and sonar, they were relatively safe. While there were spectacular boiler explosions from time to time, they tended to disappear with the advent of steel (rather than iron) boilers and the owners' clampdown on the sport of racing.

How many riverboats plied Northern California's rivers? Because of inadequate documentation before 1885, we will probably never know for sure, but the best estimate is that there were well over 300 of them, albeit not all at the same time. They came in all sizes and for different purposes. Some, such as the fabled *Chrysopolis*, were floating palaces. Some carried freight and passengers. Others made their best money towing barges.

Some were lost in explosions, some were lost in fires, and some hit underwater snags and sank. Indeed, even a few were rammed and sunk. Many were abandoned and left to rot. Sadly, of those hundreds of vessels, only one remains afloat today in California, and that is the *Delta King*, sister ship to the famed *Delta Queen*. The rest have to be preserved in memories, photographs, and as cherished artifacts in museums.

The purpose of this book, therefore, is to make their history available to those who never rode a riverboat, heard the sounds of their steam whistles, or witnessed the leisurely pace and the soft splash of water of a stern paddle wheeler.

The odds are against their return. As they burned soft coal, wood, or oil for fuel, they emitted a black ugly smoke that would never pass muster today with California's environmental laws. Moreover, the crew sizes needed to operate them make today's labor costs prohibitive. The result is that we have only photographs, a few printed words, and memories to tell us about this wonderful travel mode.

These riverboats were not the river packets of Mark Twain's day on the Mississippi. Only one California riverboat even resembled a Mississippi packet, yet they were as important to California as Twain's steamboats were to the Mississippi Valley.

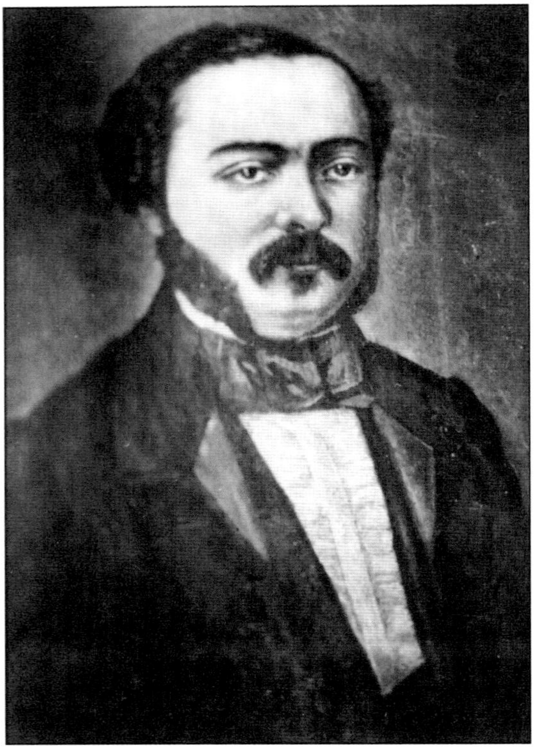

Swiss-born William Alexander Leidesdorf was a wealthy pioneer San Franciscan merchant and financier. In 1847, he acquired the *Sitka*, brought her to San Francisco, and initiated steamboat services to Sacramento. (Courtesy California State Library.)

This engraving of the 40-ton *Sitka* offers an idea of how she may have appeared. It was a time when steamers also utilized wind power to reduce fuel consumption, so having a foresail would not be out of place. (Courtesy California State Library.)

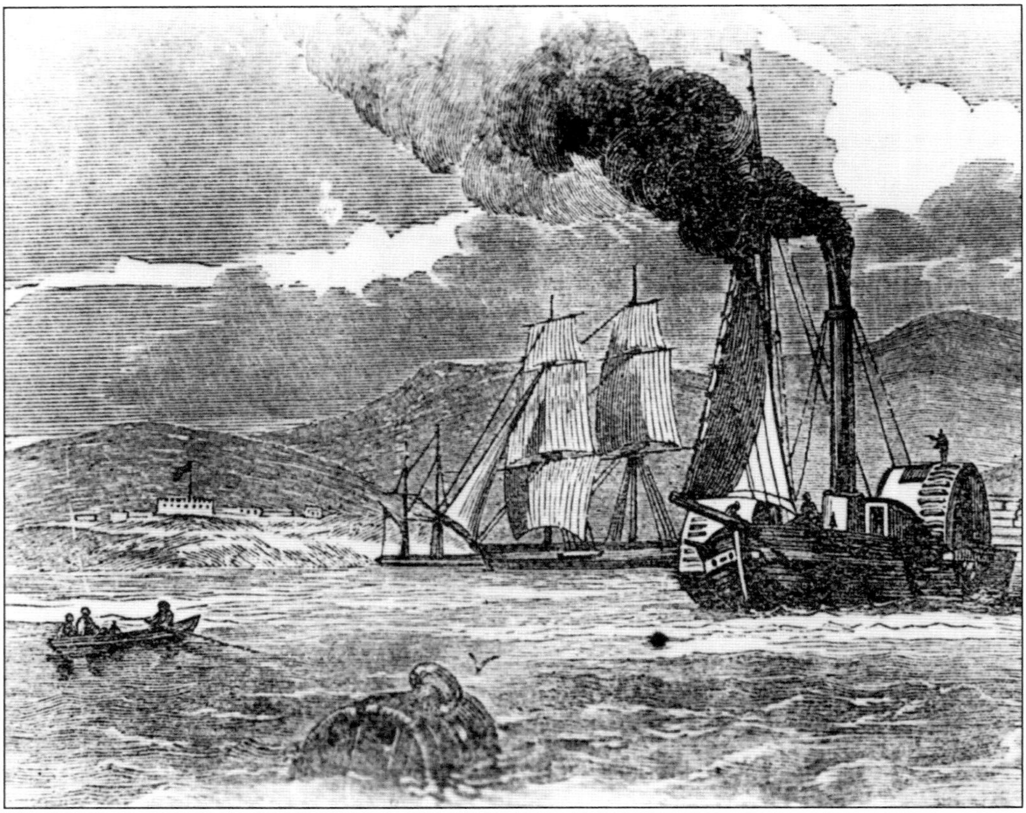

# *One*

# Riverboats and the Gold Rush

On January 19, 1849, James Marshall was inspecting the sawmill he was building on the American River near Coloma for John Sutter, an 1839 Swiss immigrant to California. Marshall's keen eye spotted something glittering in the millrace. He took a closer look. It was gold. Marshall informed Sutter, and they agreed to keep it a secret. However, somebody spilled the beans, and it was not long before the Gold Rush and the forty-niners changed California history. Roads to the goldfields were almost nonexistent, forcing the forty-niners to utilize the rivers, and for that, boats were needed. While hundreds of ships in San Francisco were abandoned by crews, mates, and captains alike in their own mad drives to get rich, some captains persuaded their crews to stay with their ships at least as far as Sacramento. Even if a captain could retain his crew, getting to Sacramento was not easy. From San Francisco to Sacramento, one had to sail into San Pablo Bay, the Carquinez Strait, Suisun Bay, Little Honker Bay, and the Delta with its numerous twists, turns, and many islands before getting it to the Sacramento River just below Rio Vista, 45 miles below Sacramento. These were barely charted waters, and underwater were snags, sandbars, and rollers that could beach or sink any ship. Finally, there were the matters of adverse tides and weather. The earliest Northern California steamboats were oceangoing sidewheelers. As local shipyards appeared, they were replaced by sternwheelers, which were more maneuverable due to having two or three rudders placed before the paddle wheels. The last sidewheeler on the Sacramento River was the ferryboat *Alameda*, bringing soldiers to Sacramento during an 1894 railroad strike.

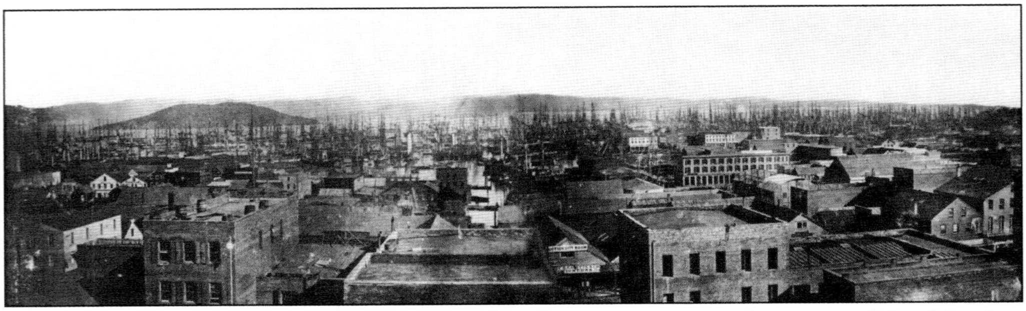

California gold not only lured the forty-niners but the crews, mates, and captains of the ships that brought them. As they anchored at San Francisco, crews jumped ship, heading for the goldfields. By 1851, they had left some 800 sailing ships abandoned, as most were too cumbersome to navigate the Delta and smaller rivers. (Author's collection.)

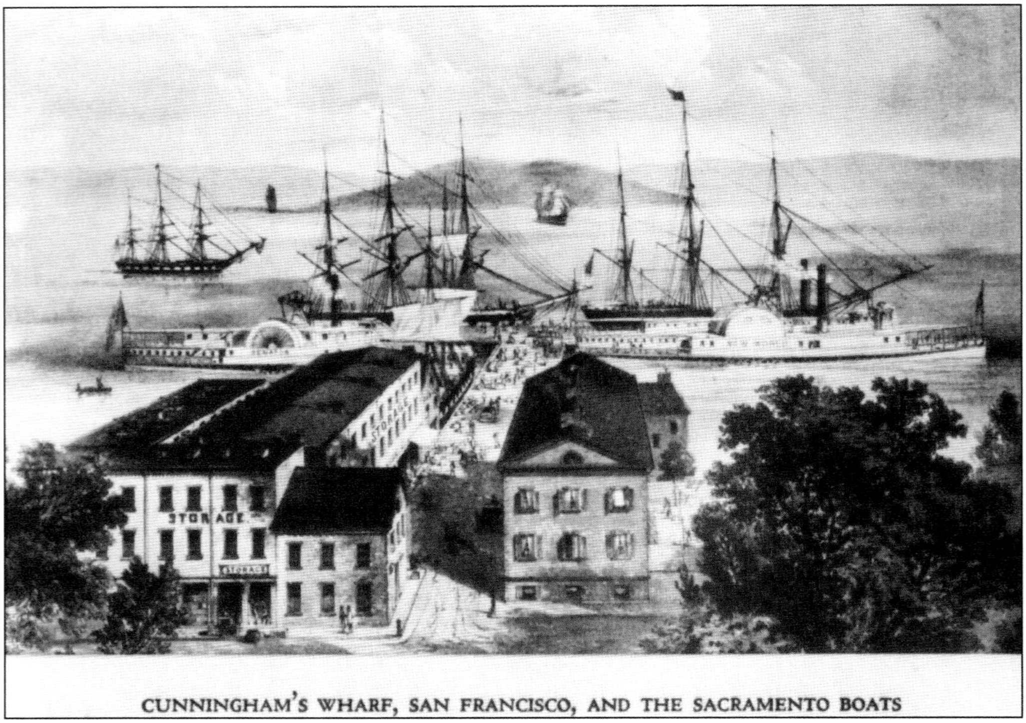


The *Senator* (1848) and *New World* (1850) were built on the East Coast and steamed around the Horn to California, cashing in on the Gold Rush trade on the Sacramento River. The 226-foot-long *Senator* was dismantled in 1882. Both ships are at Cunningham's Wharf in San Francisco. (Courtesy California State Library.)

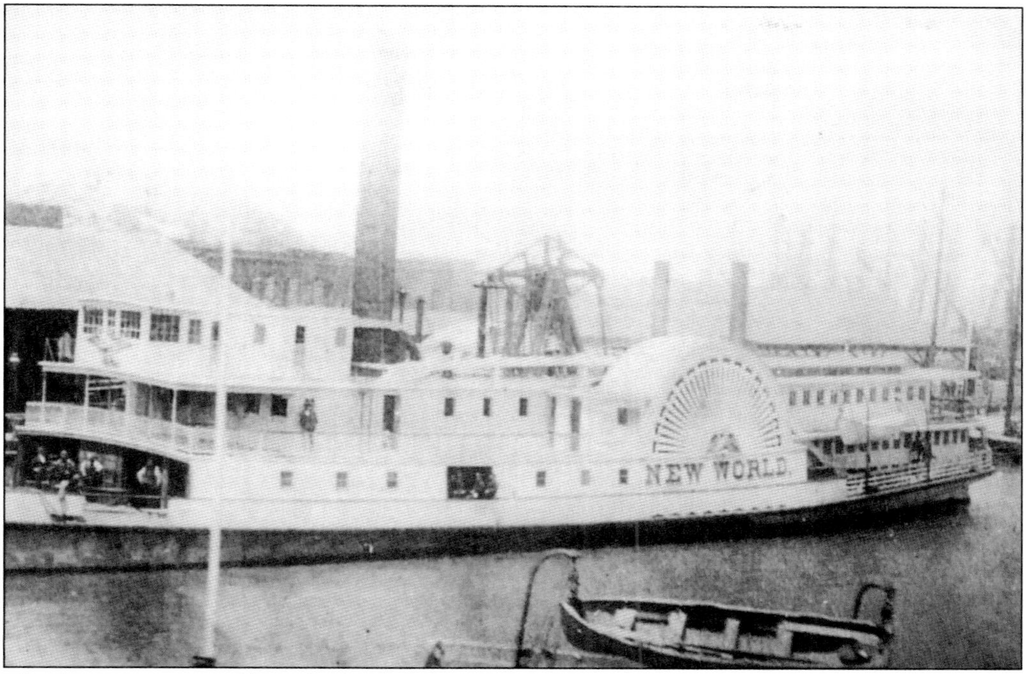


The 530-ton *New World* was built in 1850. As creditors were about to attach her, she escaped New York's sheriff and arrived in San Francisco three months later. She worked the Sacramento River until 1860, went to Puget Sound, and then returned to California, serving as a San Francisco-Vallejo ferryboat until retirement in 1879. (Courtesy Vallejo Naval and Historical Museum.)

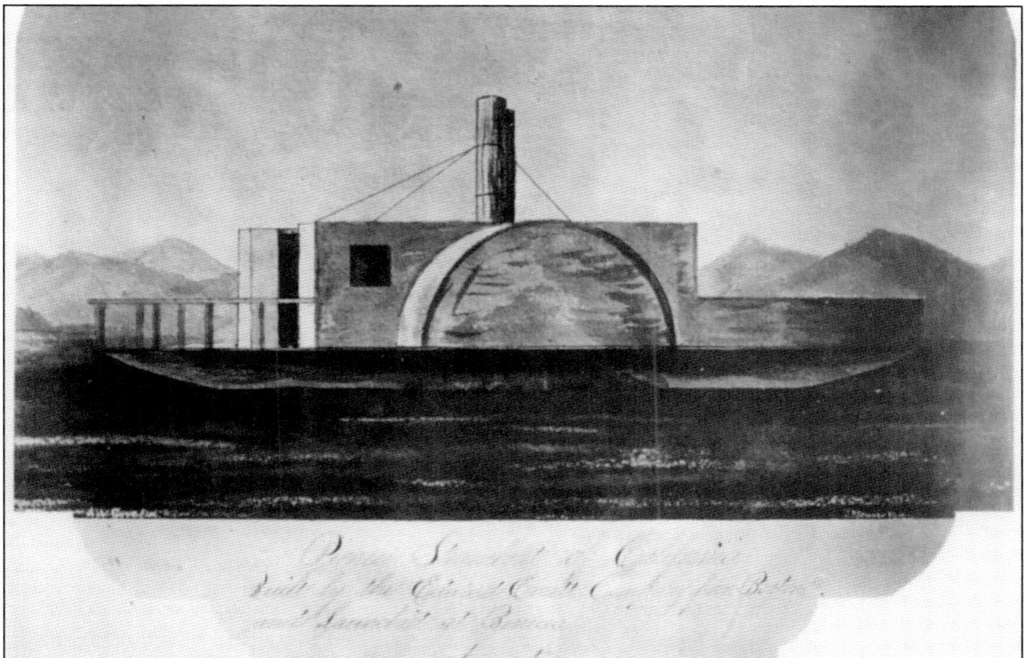

The sidewheeler *Pioneer*, first of two riverboats of the name in California, had a short but memorable career. Built at Benicia in 1849, she was snagged during that same year, but not before making several exploratory trips on Northern California rivers. (Courtesy California State Library.)

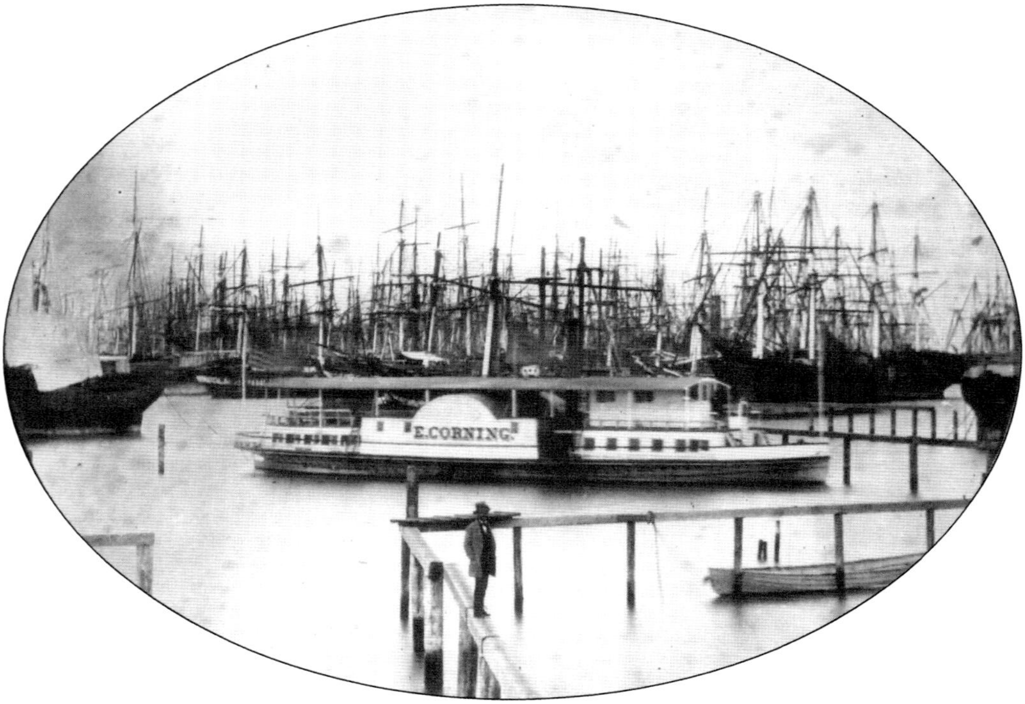


Before demarcation between ferryboats and riverboats, the *Erastus Corning* did both. She was built in 1850, and owner Charles Minturn, seen here, used her as a San Francisco-Oakland ferryboat. Her riverboat stints included the Petaluma Creek and the San Joaquin River before going off documentation by 1868. (Courtesy San Francisco Maritime National Historical Park, No. P81-010u.)

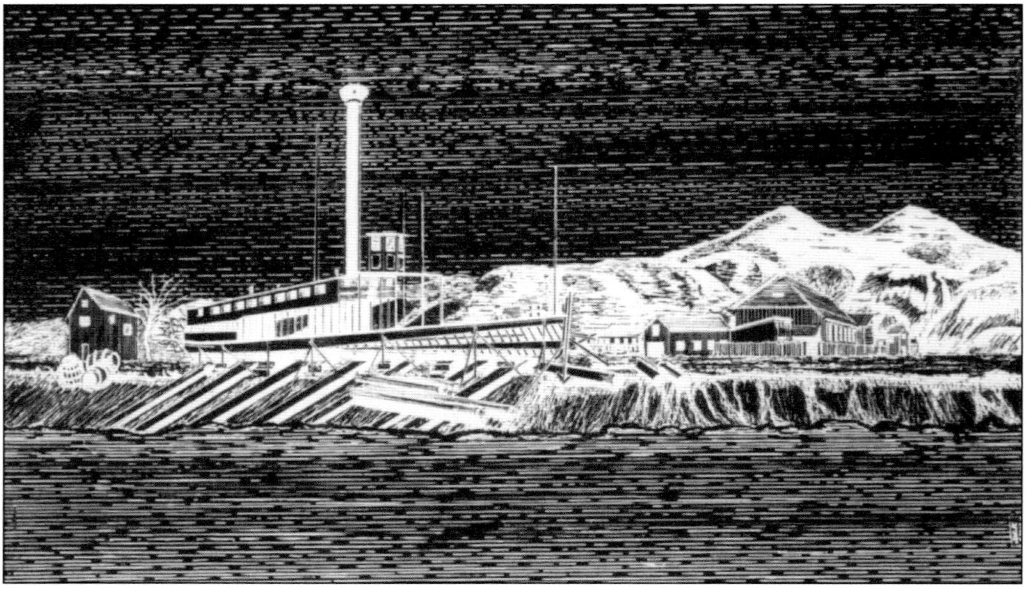

The *Governor Dana* was originally built in Maine for the upper Penobscot River. Instead, she was dismantled, placed aboard the sailing ship *Hartford*, and brought to California for reassembly around 1850. In this drawing by Jack Aiello, she is being reassembled at what is now Pittsburg, California. (Courtesy San Francisco Maritime National Historical Park, No. BH.30,984n1.)

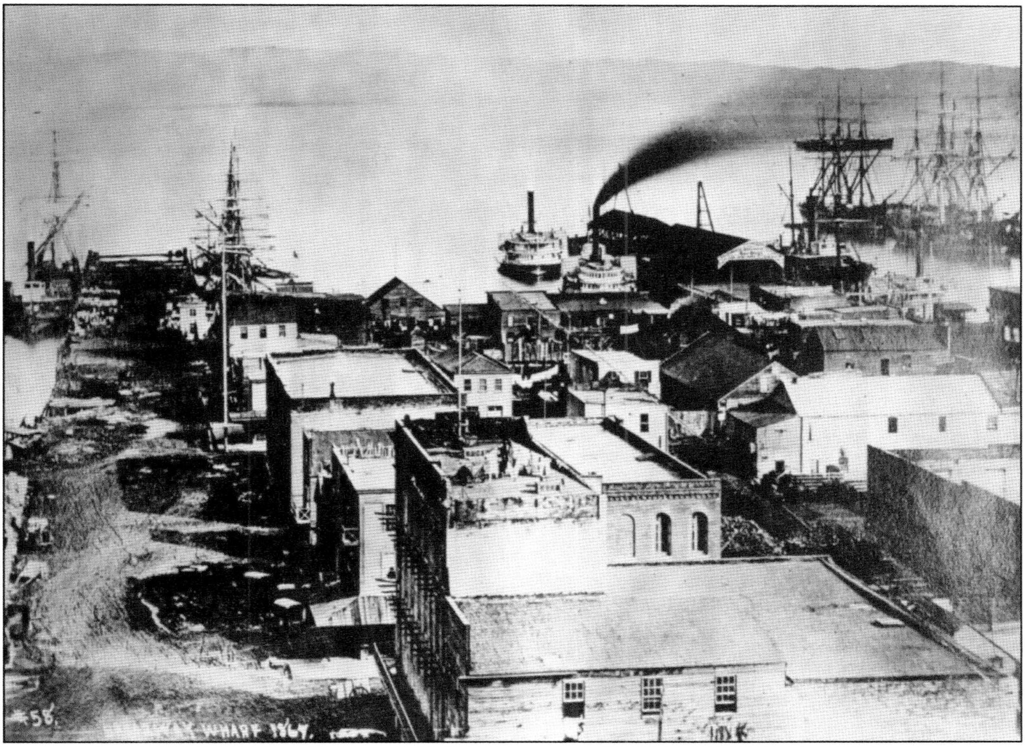

In 1864, San Francisco's Broadway Wharf was a busy place. Seen above are three white riverboats, two oceangoing steamships (one aided by sail), and three sailing ships. The streets are paved with mud well rutted from wagon wheels and puddles of water due to insufficient drainage. (Courtesy Western Railway Museum Archives, No. 49500.)

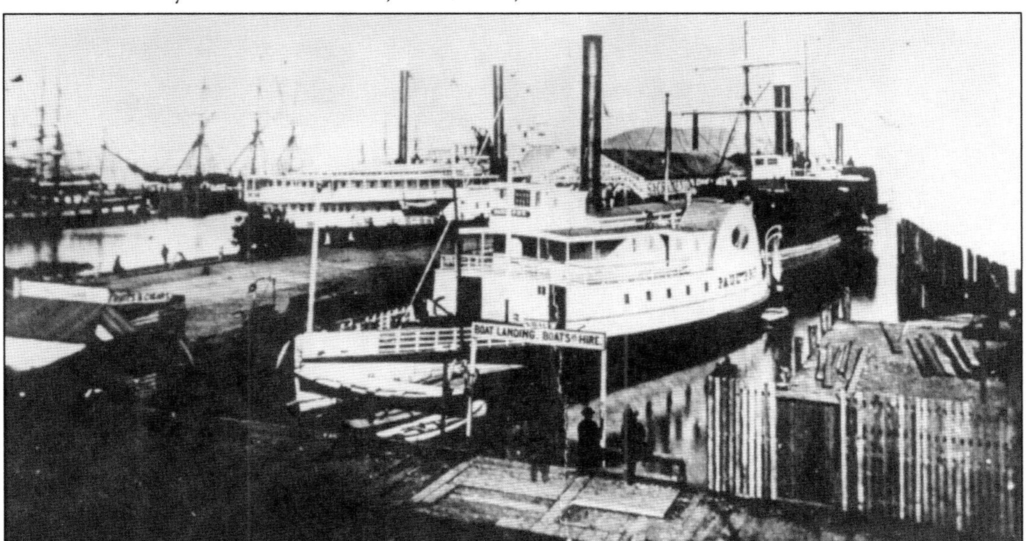

This 1865 view of San Francisco's Broadway Wharf shows the sidewheeler *Paul Pry*, a 330-ton ship built in December 1856. The much-traveled *Paul Pry* worked the Napa River to Sausalito and river service in the Sacramento Valley. She went off documentation by 1881. (Courtesy Western Railway Museum Archives, No. 49501.)

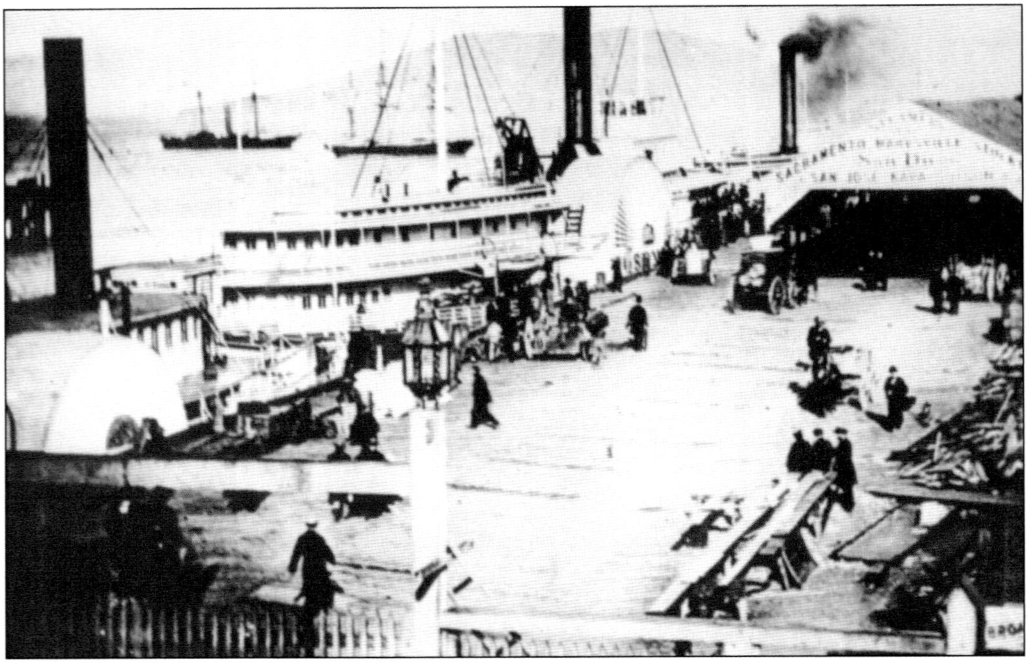

At Broadway Wharf in San Francisco in 1865, the 1862-built *Yosemite* is sandwiched between a brace of steamships. She offered luxury accommodations to Sacramento until sold in 1883 to the Canadian Pacific Railway for Puget Sound service. Her career ended when she was stranded at Bremerton, Washington. (Author's collection.)

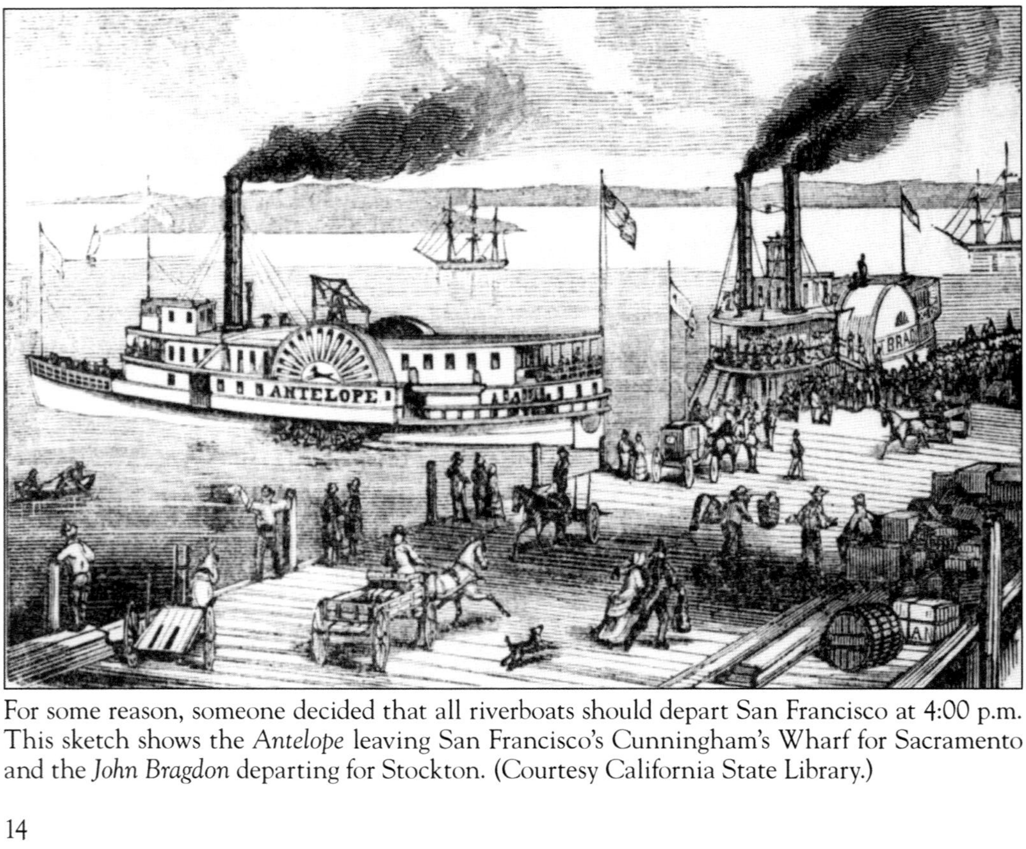


For some reason, someone decided that all riverboats should depart San Francisco at 4:00 p.m. This sketch shows the *Antelope* leaving San Francisco's Cunningham's Wharf for Sacramento and the *John Bragdon* departing for Stockton. (Courtesy California State Library.)

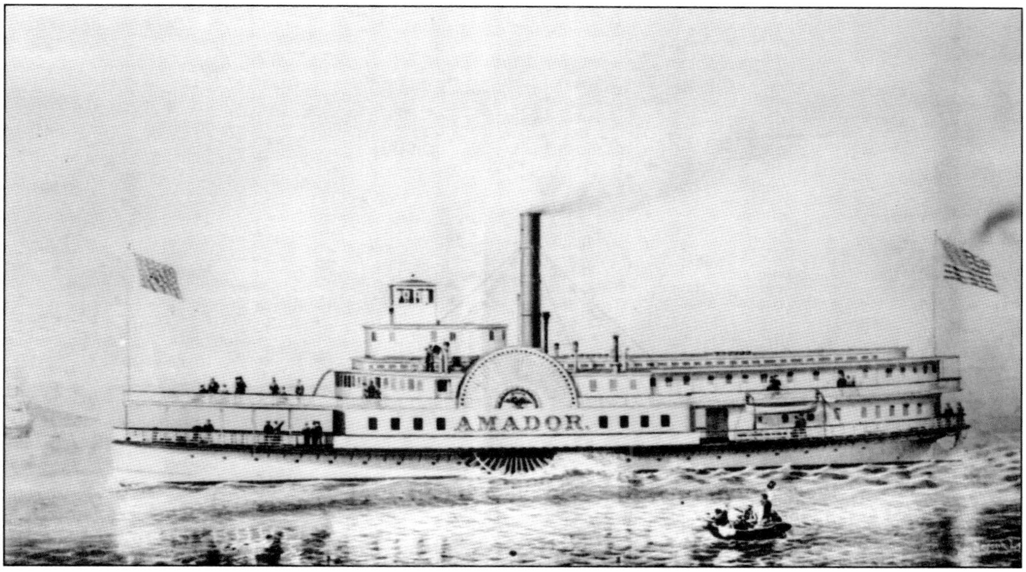


The 221-foot-long sidewheeler *Amador* was built as a riverboat in 1869 for the Central Pacific Railroad. In 1878, she was rebuilt into a double-ended ferryboat at the CPRR's Oakland shipyard while retaining her name. (Courtesy California State Library.)

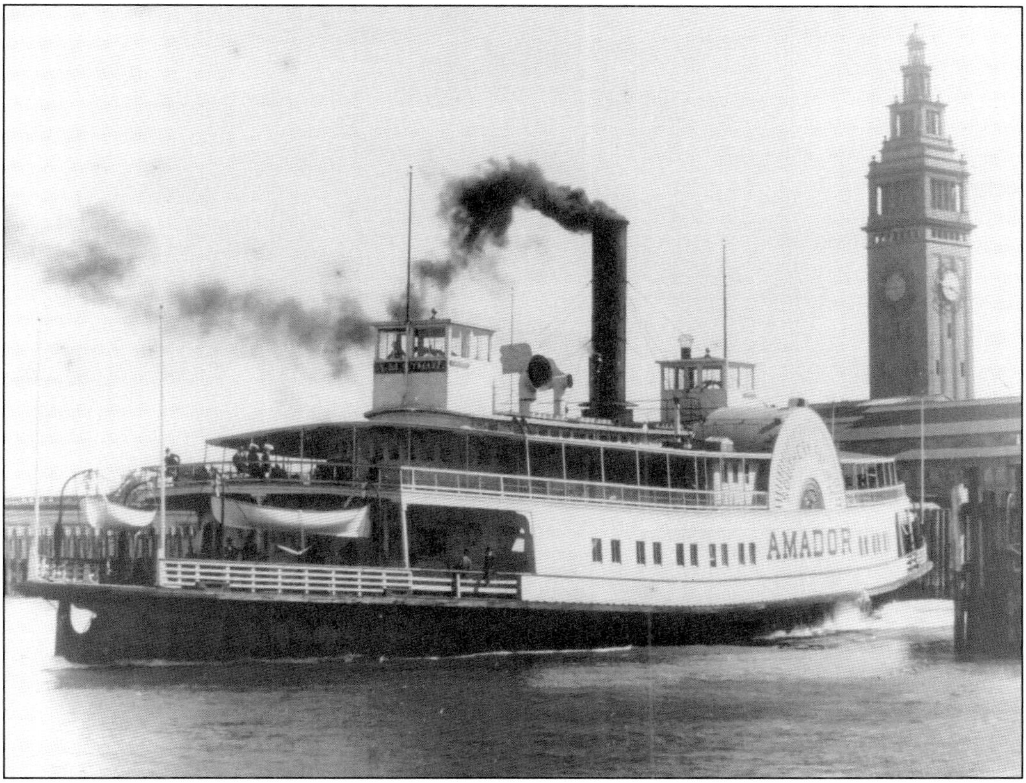


The *Amador* is seen here departing San Francisco's Ferry Building in 1904 with her hull lines showing her riverboat origins. In 1905, the *Amador* became a clubhouse for the University of California rowing team. In 1915, she was burned at the Panama-Pacific International Exposition in a fireboat demonstration. (Courtesy William Knorp Collection.)

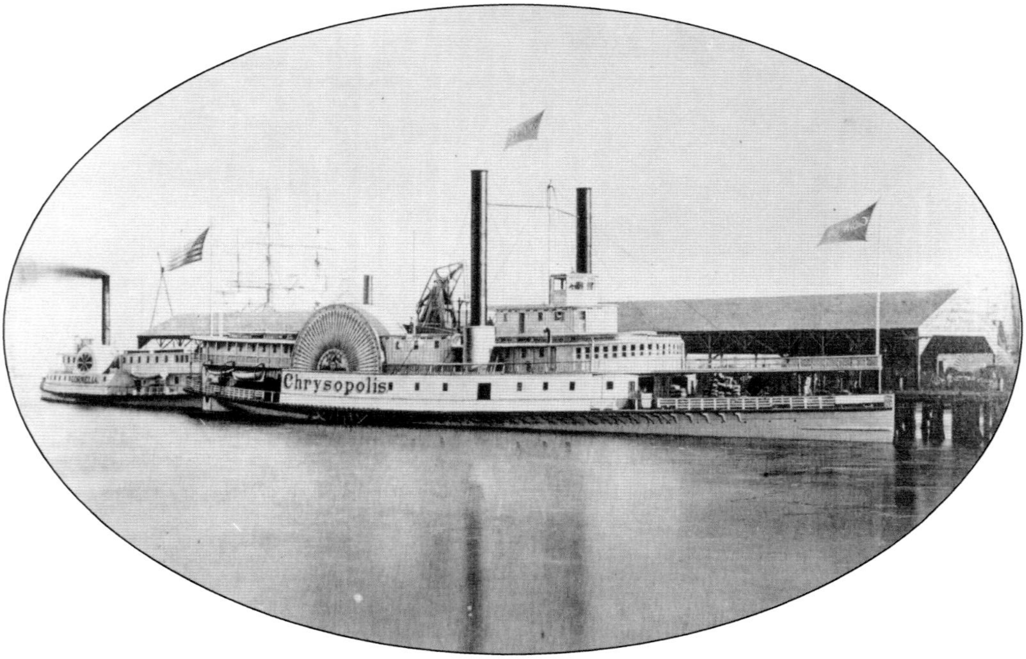


The palatial *Chrysopolis*, built in 1860 by John G. North of San Francisco, was second to none for elegance and speed. On December 31, 1861, the beloved *Chryssie* did 19.8 knots from Sacramento to San Francisco, arriving in 5 hours and 19 minutes, a still-standing record. Behind her is the *Cornelia*. (Courtesy Western Railway Museum Archives, No. 49498.)

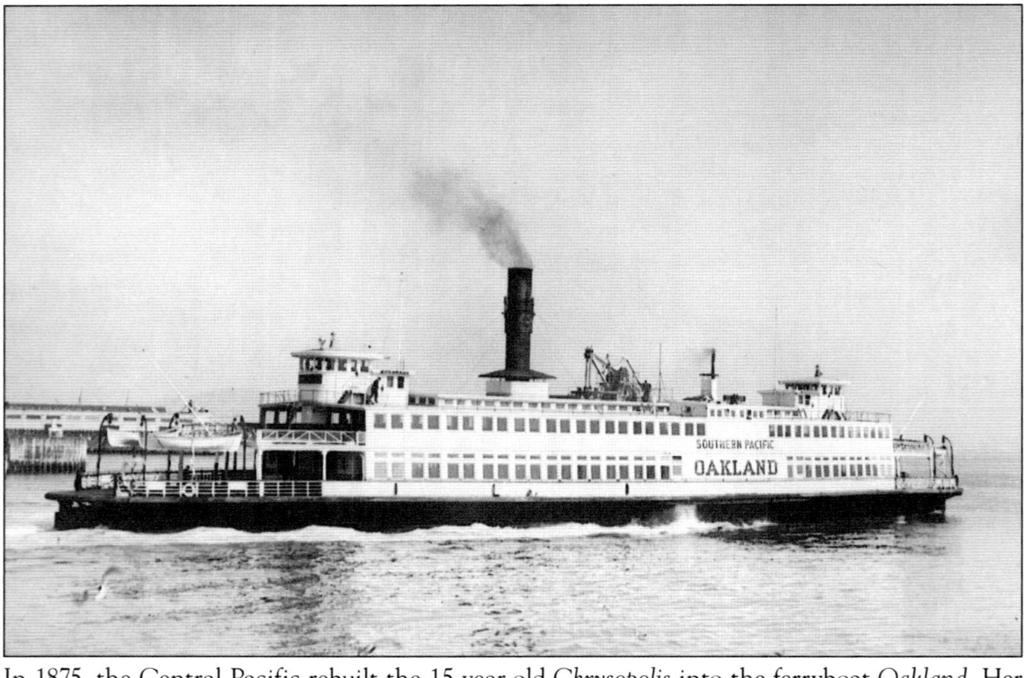


In 1875, the Central Pacific rebuilt the 15-year-old *Chrysopolis* into the ferryboat *Oakland*. Her hull was extended from 245 feet to 283 feet, her superstructure was torn down for the one shown here, and she became a double-ender. She retained her original engine until finally destroyed by fire in 1940. (Courtesy William Knorp Collection.)

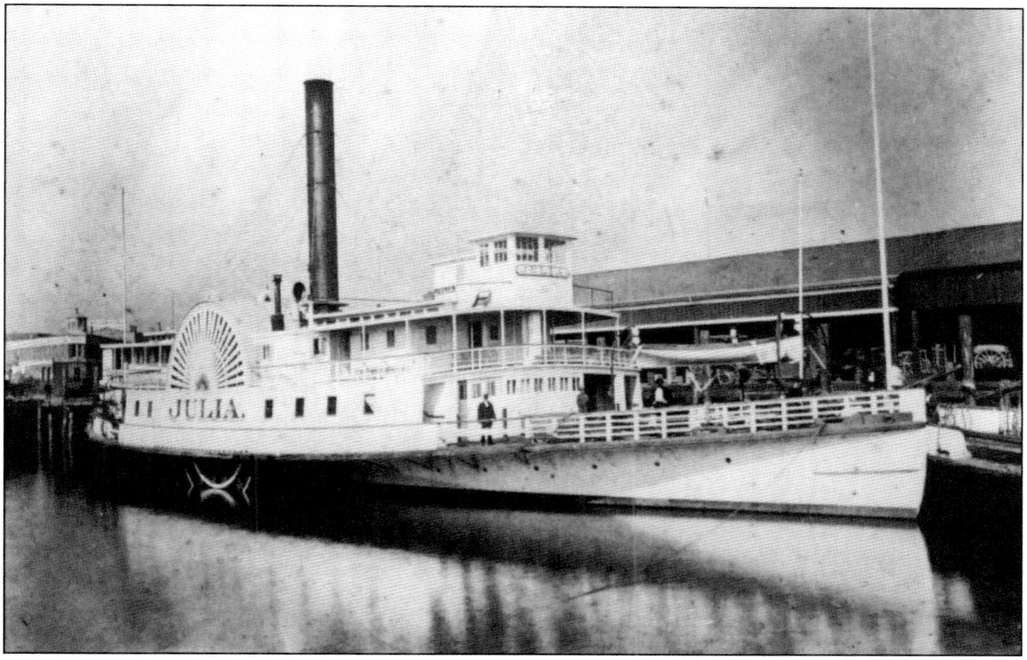


South of Courtland on the Sacramento River is the sidewheeler *Julia* in original configuration. Off Alcatraz Island on September 30, 1866, her boiler exploded, leaving five dead and 11 injured, some fatally. She was refitted and returned to work. In 1882, she was rebuilt into a double-ended ferryboat. (Courtesy California State Library.)

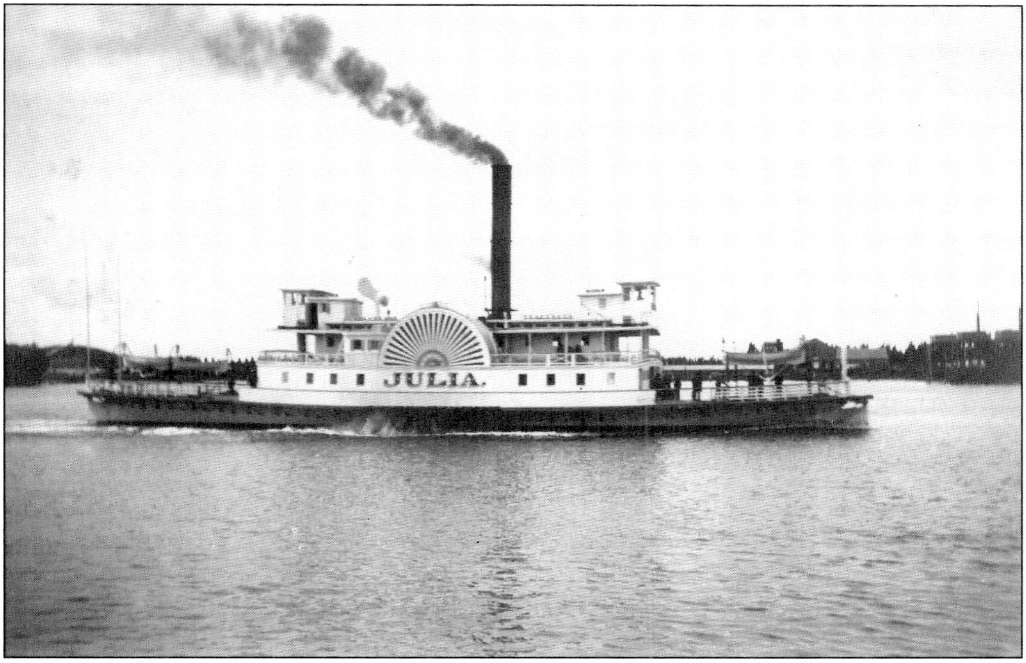


The *Julia* was rebuilt in 1882 from a riverboat into a double-ended ferryboat and in 1888 converted to burn oil. At South Vallejo on February 27, 1888, her boiler exploded, killing 30 of the 70 people aboard. Another decade would pass before oil burners would become acceptable. (Courtesy Vallejo Naval and Historical Museum.)

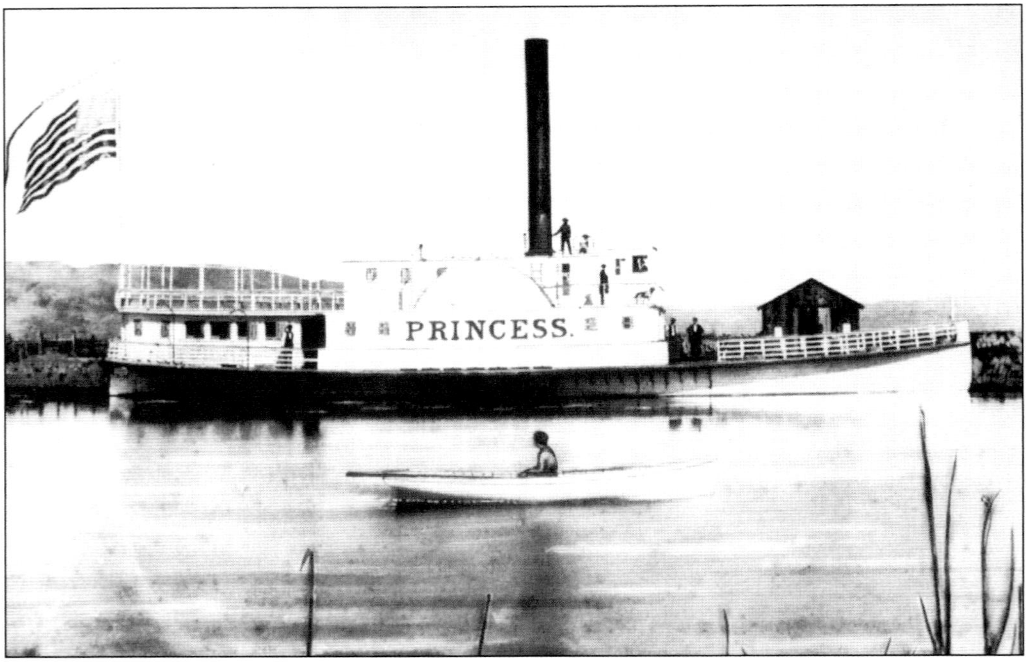


The 193-gross-ton *Princess* was suitable for navigating small creeks and rivers. Built sometime before 1859, she went to the Sausalito Land & Ferry Co. on May 10, 1868, bringing people from Sausalito's Princess Street to San Francisco's Meiggs Wharf. She was off documentation by 1881. (Courtesy Northwestern Pacific Railroad Historical Society Archives.)

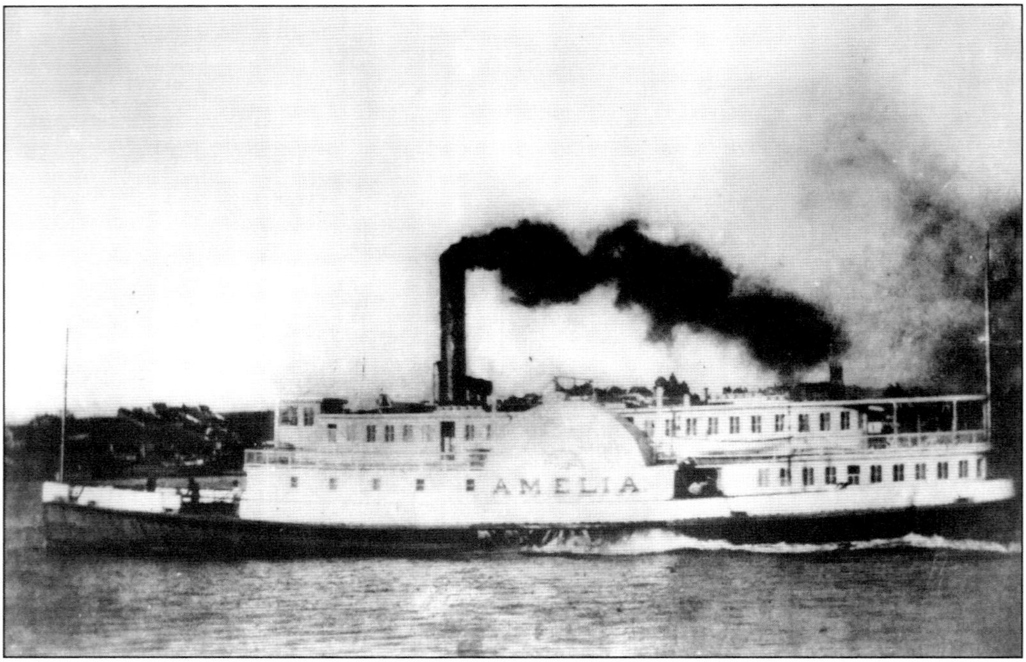


The 385.96-ton, 147-foot-long *Amelia*, built in 1863, linked the Napa Valley Railroad and the Napa River with San Francisco. In 1868, she went on the California Steam Navigation's San Francisco–Sacramento run. From 1879 until she was sold in 1882, she was a double-ended ferryboat for the Central Pacific Railroad. (Courtesy California State Library.)

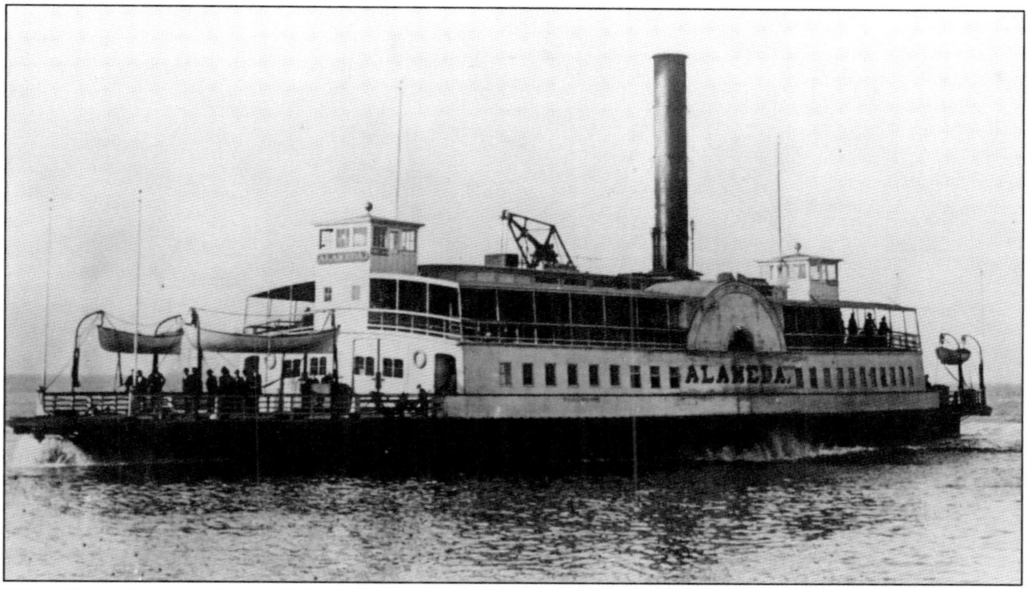


The *Alameda I* with her tall "jam factory" stack was built in 1866. She was the first San Francisco Bay double-ended ferryboat, eliminating turning around at each port, saving fuel and time. During the 1894 railroad strike, the Army commandeered her to bring troops to Sacramento, making her the last sidewheeler on the Sacramento River. (Author's collection.)

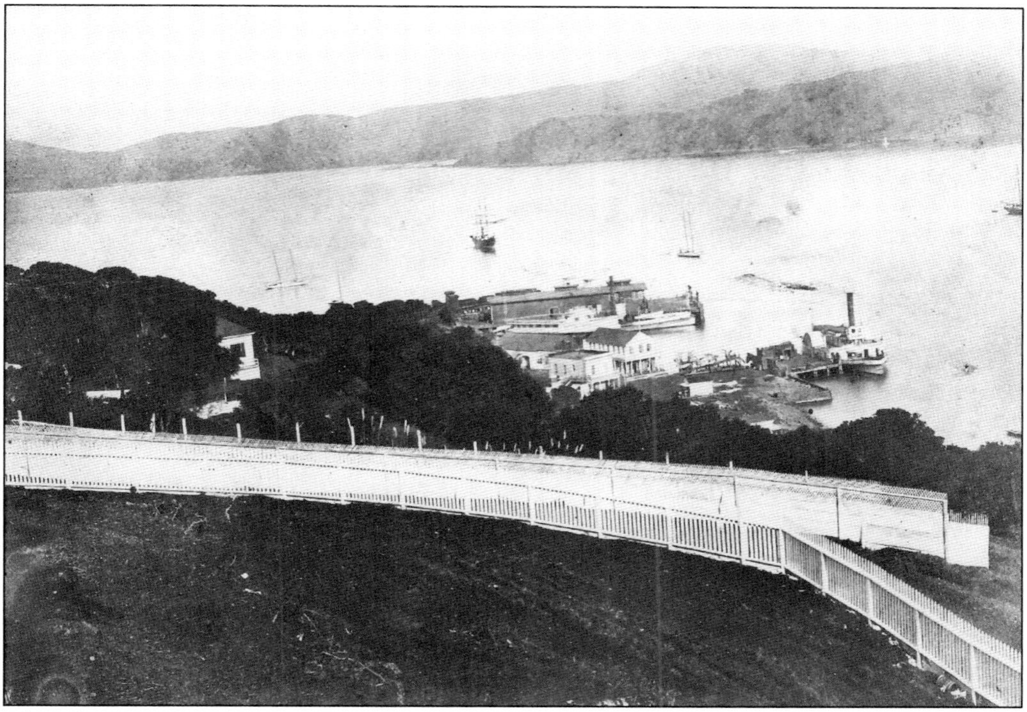

This photograph, taken at Sausalito in the 1870s when riverboats and ferryboats were usually lumped together as steamers, shows the *Contra Costa* (left) and the *Petaluma* (right). The *Petaluma* became the ferryboat *Petaluma of Saucelito* and, later, the *Tamalpais*. (Courtesy Northwestern Pacific Railroad Historical Society Archives.)

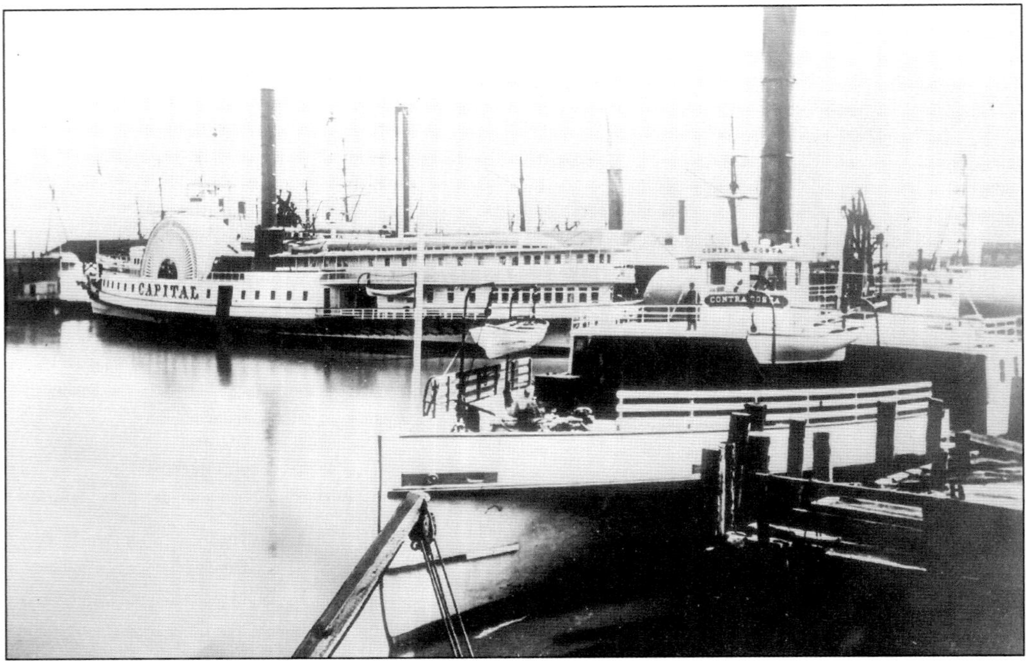

Tied up at the Davis Street Wharf in San Francisco in 1870 are the Contra Costa Steam Navigation Co.'s *Capital* and *Contra Costa*. These two steamers worked both as riverboats and ferryboats, simply going where business was to be had. (Courtesy Northwestern Pacific Railroad Historical Society Archives.)

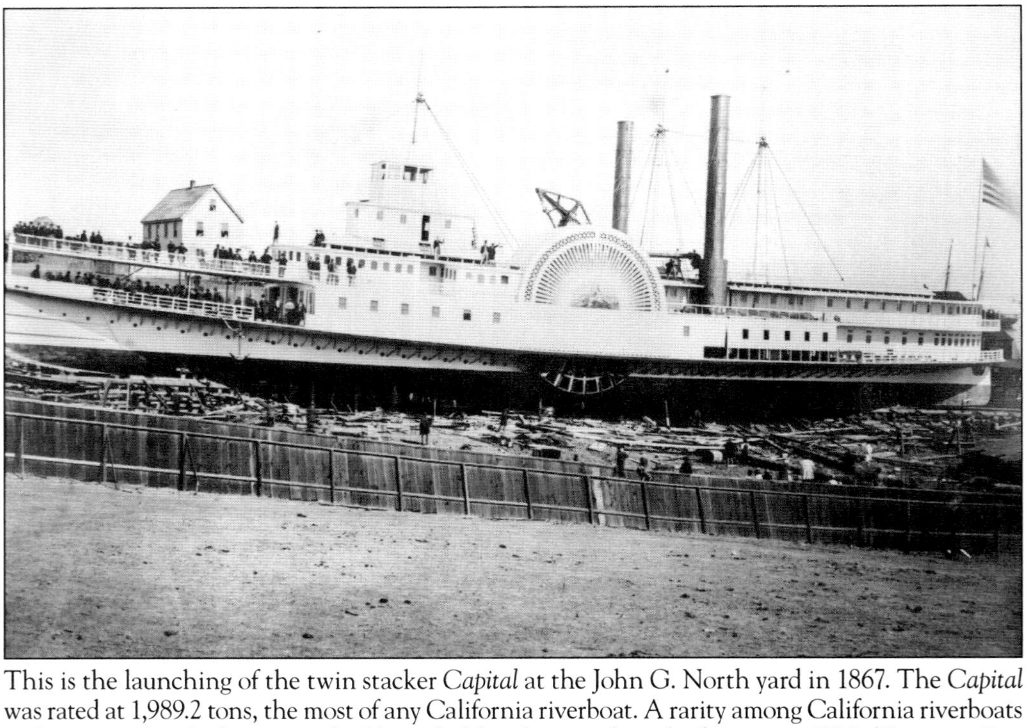
This is the launching of the twin stacker *Capital* at the John G. North yard in 1867. The *Capital* was rated at 1,989.2 tons, the most of any California riverboat. A rarity among California riverboats with two stacks, she became a double-ended ferryboat and was broken up in 1896. (Courtesy San Francisco Maritime National Historical Park, No. P82-0023.)

# *Two*

# San Francisco to Sacramento by Riverboat

Early riverboat captains and pilots were a crossbreed of shrewd entrepreneurs and flat-out daredevils who learned their trade through apprenticeship. After 1852, steamboat men had to be licensed. They were skilled at reading the waters, spotting any changes from a day or more before, and memorizing where the sandbars, snags, shifting channels, and other water hazards were. Most early riverboats were independently owned, and such men were needed to meet the dog-eat-dog competition. To prove their mettle and which were faster boats, the dangerous sport of racing went on, sometimes with disaster as iron boilers exploded from excessive steam pressures (steel boilers came into use in the 1870s). It has been said that a captain caught racing was fined five demerits—10 if he lost the race. By the end of 1850, there were some 28 riverboats on the Sacramento and Feather Rivers alone, not to mention cluttering the waters. Pilots had to tie up their riverboats alongside others when dock space was not to be had, and passengers walked across other vessels to reach shore or to board. The public put up with this because of gold. In 1848, California's gold mining yielded $245,301, in 1849, $10,151,360; in 1850, $41,273,106; in 1851, $75,938,232; and in 1852, an all-time high of $81,294,700. For that kind of money, people took chances. In March 1854, major riverboat owners got together and formed the California Steam Navigation Co. Soon, others joined in and tariffs were fixed: per person from San Francisco to Marysville, $12; to Sacramento, $10; and to Stockton, $8. Freight was $15 per ton to Marysville, $8 per ton to Sacramento, $6 per ton to Stockton; and to Red Bluff, $50 per ton. Price fixing it was, but it brought stability and probably saved lives.

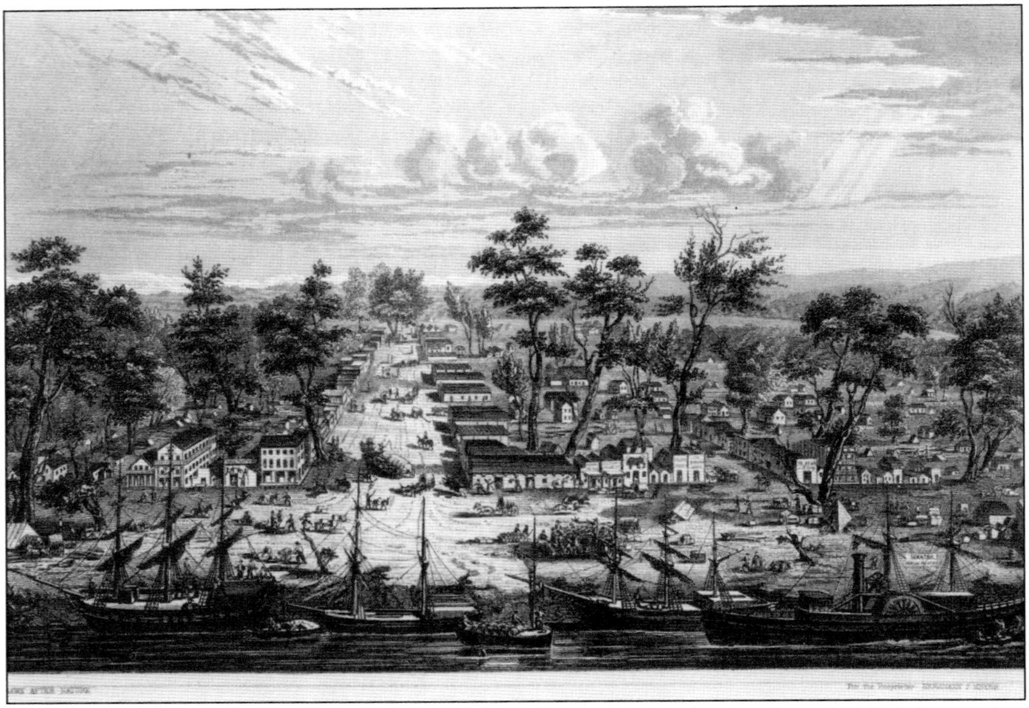

This much reproduced 1850 lithograph of Sacramento's riverfront essentially shows a town growing up fast, thanks to the Gold Rush. Three shallow draft sailing ships and one oceangoing sidewheeler reveal that Sacramento was as much a port city as anything else. (Courtesy Western Railway Museum Archives.)

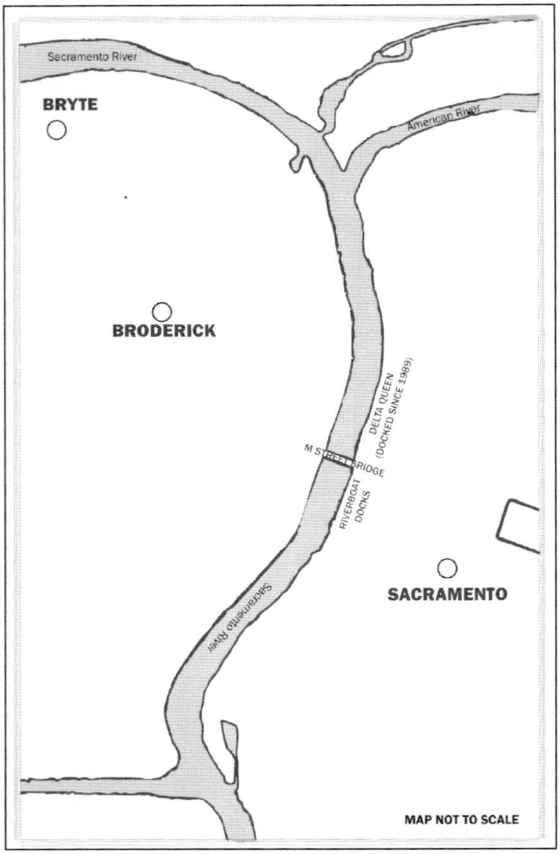


This shows the confluence of the American and Sacramento Rivers at Sacramento and the locations of Bryte and Broderick, part of today's West Sacramento. Bryte was where the *Alviso* and the *Weitchpec* were lost in the December 18, 1920, fire. (Map by Kevin Shields.)

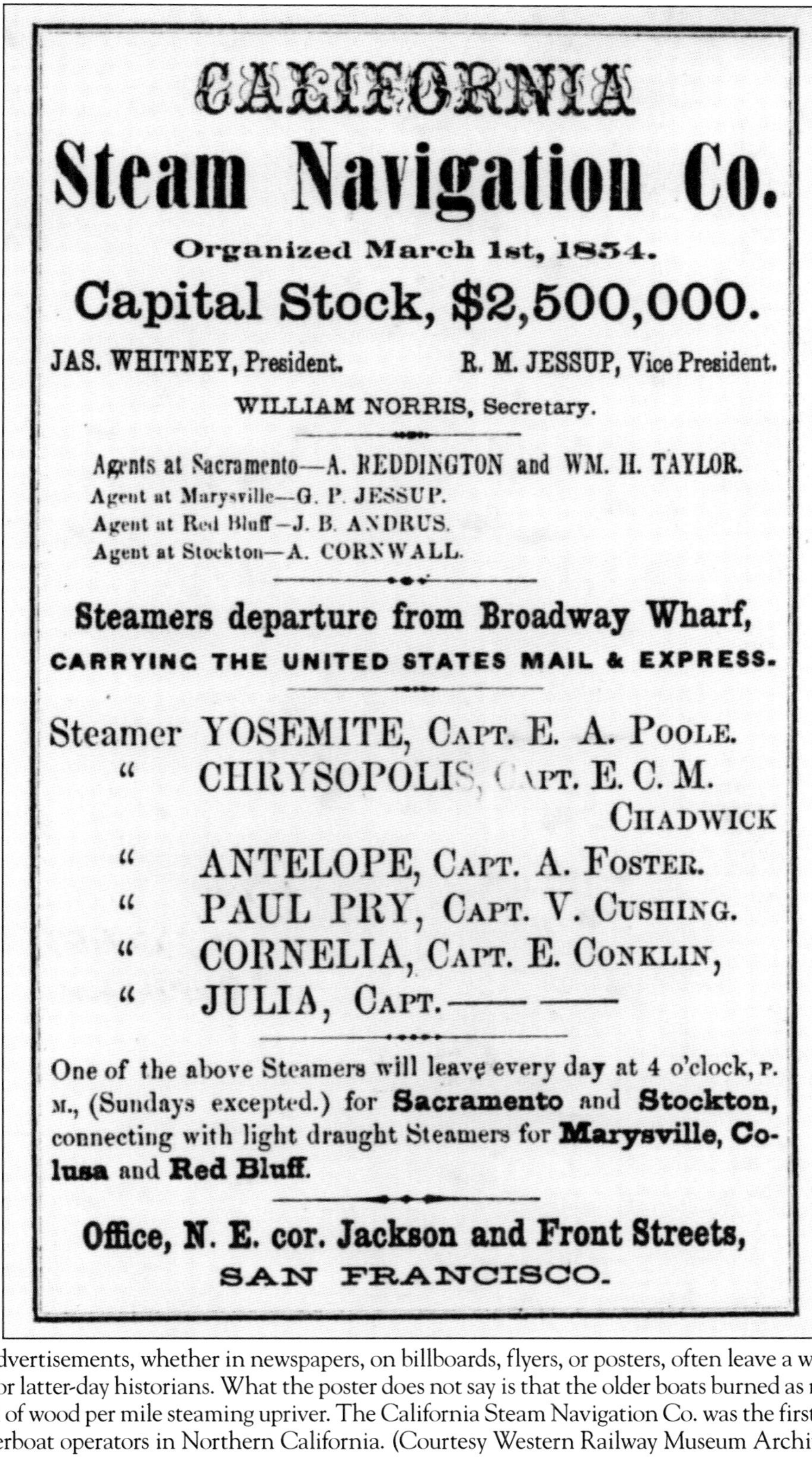


Old advertisements, whether in newspapers, on billboards, flyers, or posters, often leave a wealth of data for latter-day historians. What the poster does not say is that the older boats burned as much as a cord of wood per mile steaming upriver. The California Steam Navigation Co. was the first merger of riverboat operators in Northern California. (Courtesy Western Railway Museum Archives.)

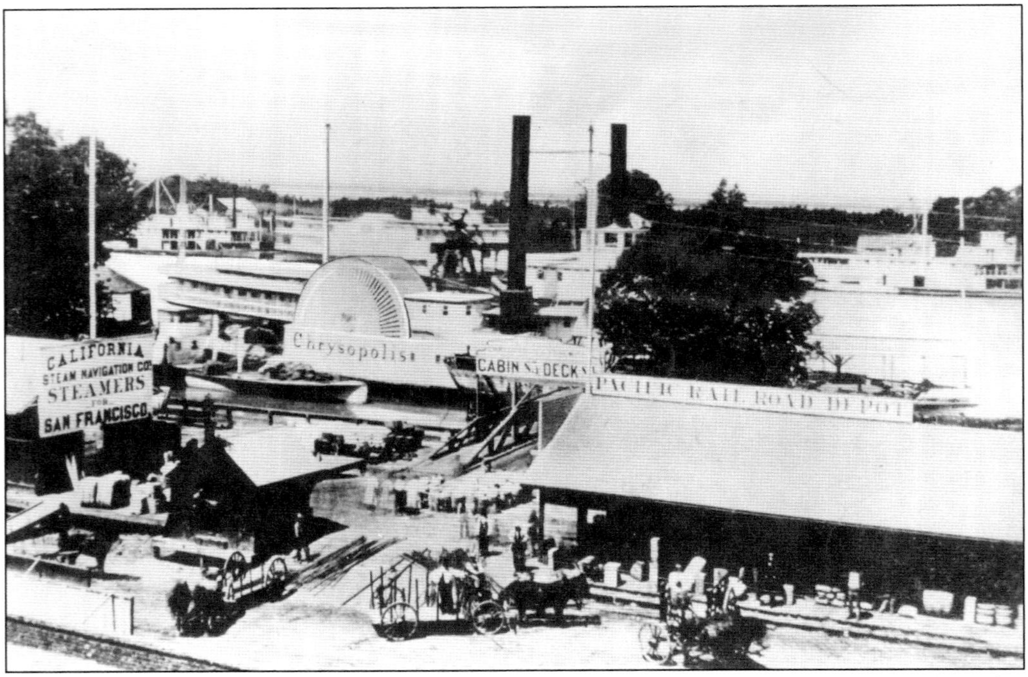


The twin stacker *Chrysopolis* of the California Steam Navigation Co. was built by master builder John G. North of San Francisco, using specially selected timbers from Northern California's forests. The location is where the restored *Delta King* resides as a floating hotel today. (Author's collection.)

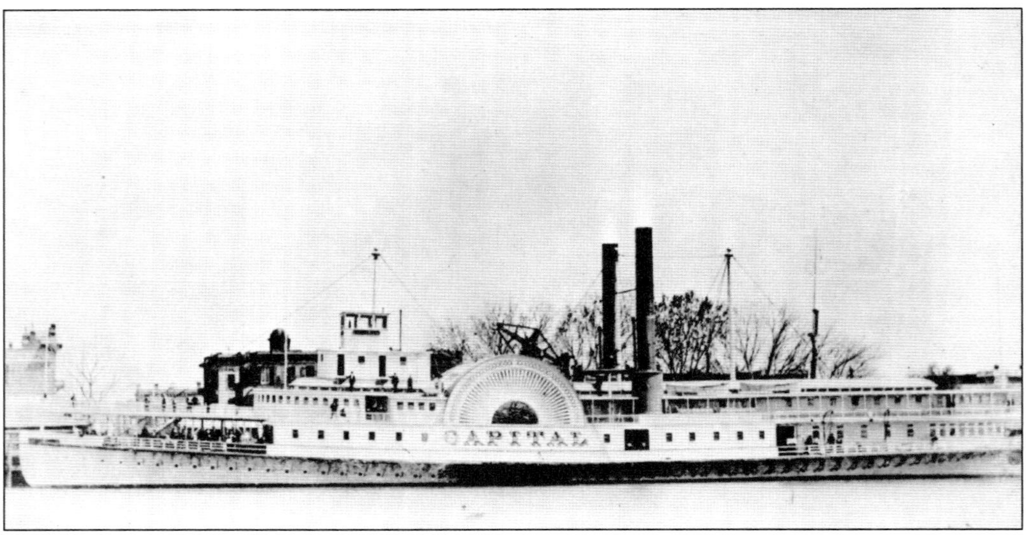


The *Capital* is tied up at the foot of K Street in Sacramento, adjacent to today's Old Sacramento State Historic Park. Besides her huge size, the *Capital* was also unusual in being a twin stacker, a rarity among California's riverboats. Later, she was rebuilt into a double-ended ferryboat. (Courtesy California State Library.)

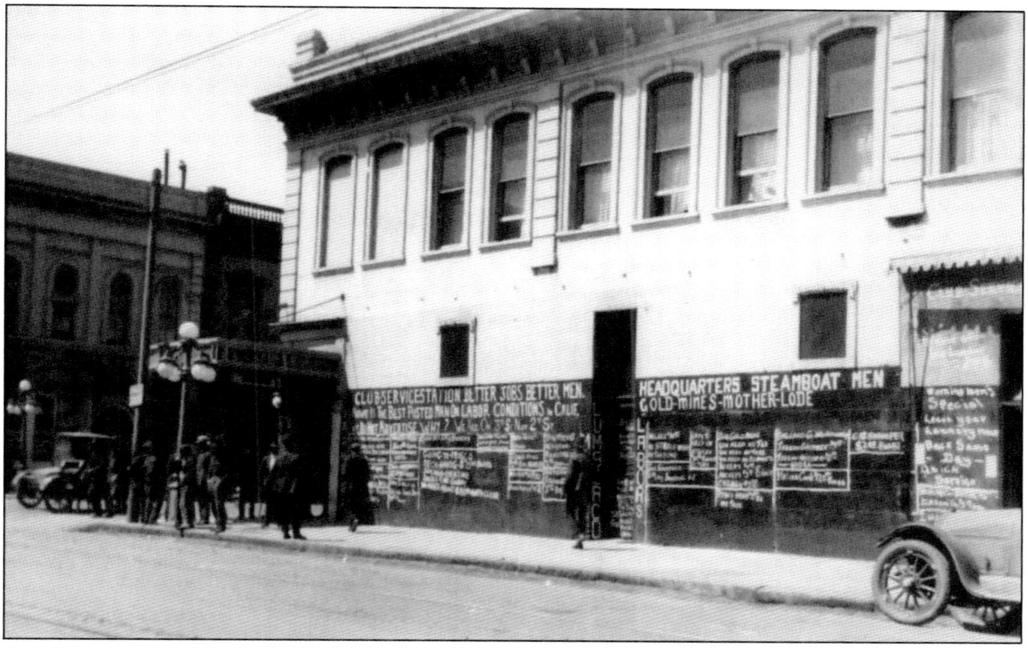


At the corner of K and Third Streets in Sacramento in 1913, a workingmen's club had handwritten advertisements for job openings. Germane to this book is the advertisement reading: "GOING-TO-FRISCO/DECK-HANDS—$75°° BOARD/50¢ HOUR-OVER-TIME/DOUBLE-TIME SUNDAY/YOU-MAKE-ABOUT-$85°°—MONTH-CLEAR." [sic] (Courtesy Western Railway Museum Archives.)

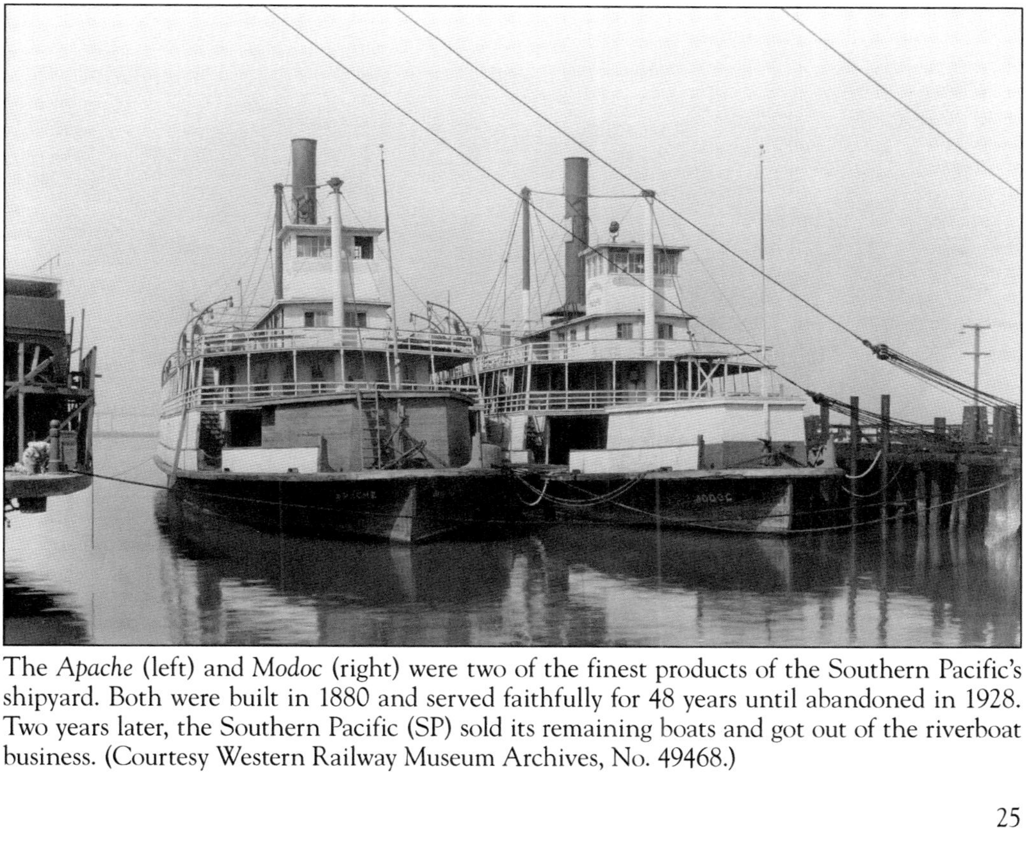

The *Apache* (left) and *Modoc* (right) were two of the finest products of the Southern Pacific's shipyard. Both were built in 1880 and served faithfully for 48 years until abandoned in 1928. Two years later, the Southern Pacific (SP) sold its remaining boats and got out of the riverboat business. (Courtesy Western Railway Museum Archives, No. 49468.)

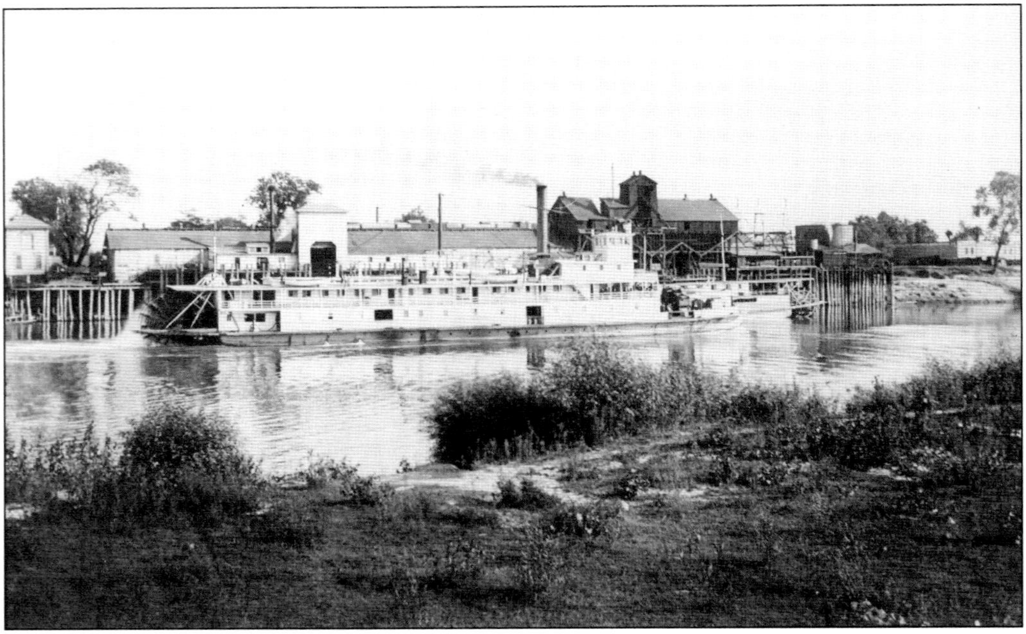

There was a time when a ticket to a sternwheeler up or down the Sacramento River meant a leisurely ride, well-prepared and reasonably priced meals while aboard, and a chance to enjoy the scenery. Here, the SP's *Modoc* is offering such an experience. (Courtesy Western Railway Museum Archives, No. 49463.)

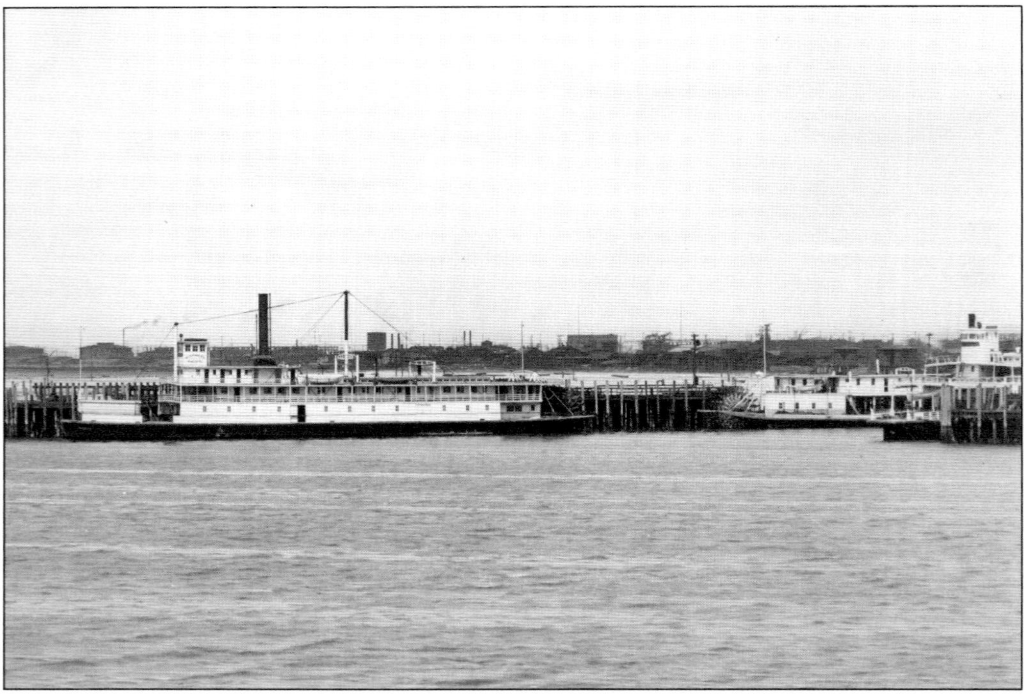

In 1926, Americans were dancing the Charleston and drinking bathtub gin while the stock market was climbing. Yet the Sacramento River's riverboat business was already in decline—within two decades they would be gone. During that time, the *Modoc* (left), *Fruto* (center), and another riverboat awaited their next call to duty. (Courtesy Western Railway Museum Archives, No. 49461.)

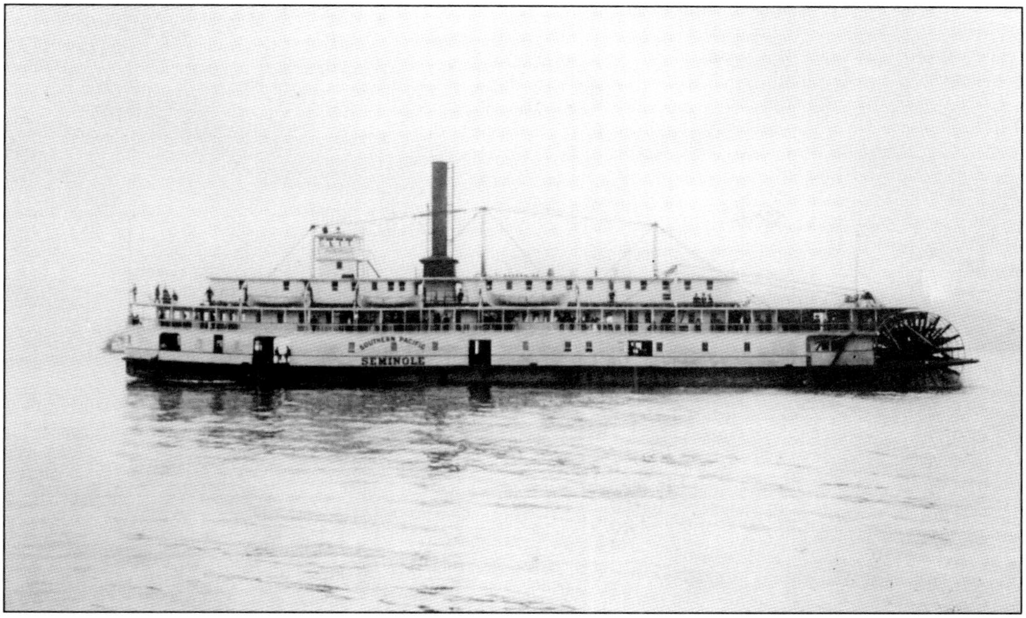


The *Seminole* was built in 1911 at the SP yards. Two years later in a dense fog off Angel Island, she was rammed and sunk by the *H. J. Corcoran*. Unusual for riverboats, her forward maindeck was fully enclosed, offering additional passenger space as well as a longer texas deck. (Courtesy Western Railway Museum Archives, No. 49467.)

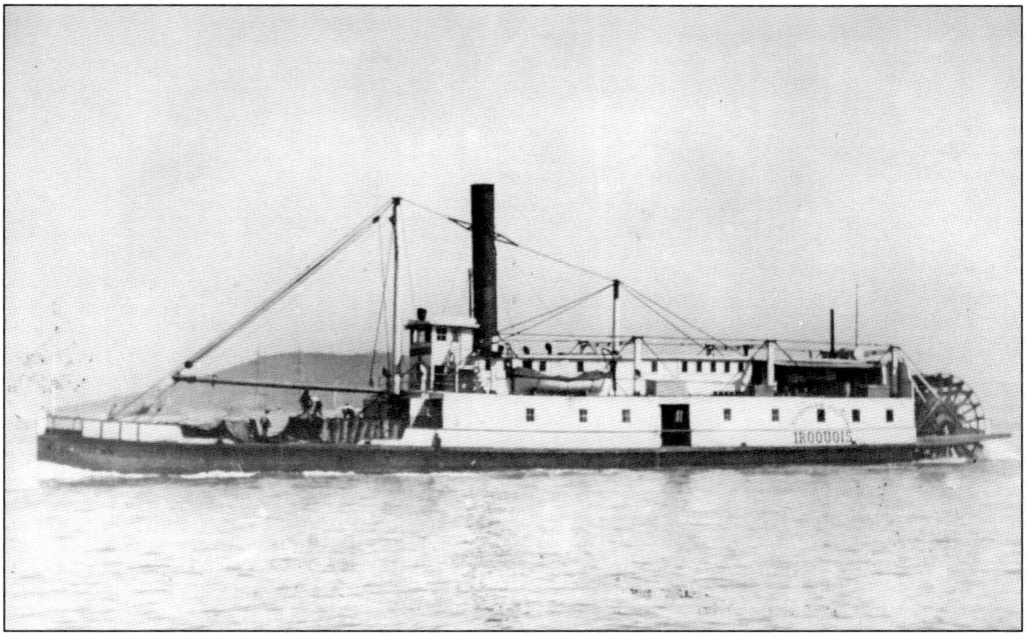


The *Iroquois* was built at Alameda in 1927 and went to work for the Southern Pacific. She carried a 10-man crew, rated 437 gross tons, and measured 153.3 by 38.2 by 6.6 feet. She went off documentation in 1920, but records do not indicate why. (Courtesy Western Railway Museum Archives, No. 49459.)

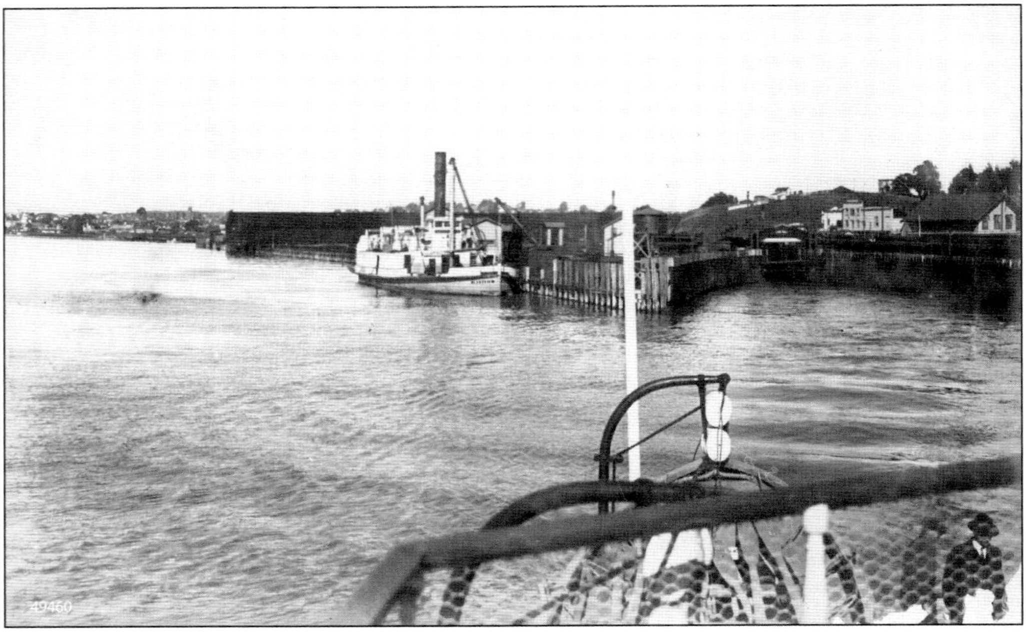

It would not have been out of place for the Southern Pacific's *Iroquois* to have been tied up at South Vallejo, as seen in this 1907 photograph taken from the cabin deck of the ferryboat *Bay City*. Note the dock being next to the ferryboat slip. (Courtesy Western Railway Museum Archives, No. 49460.)

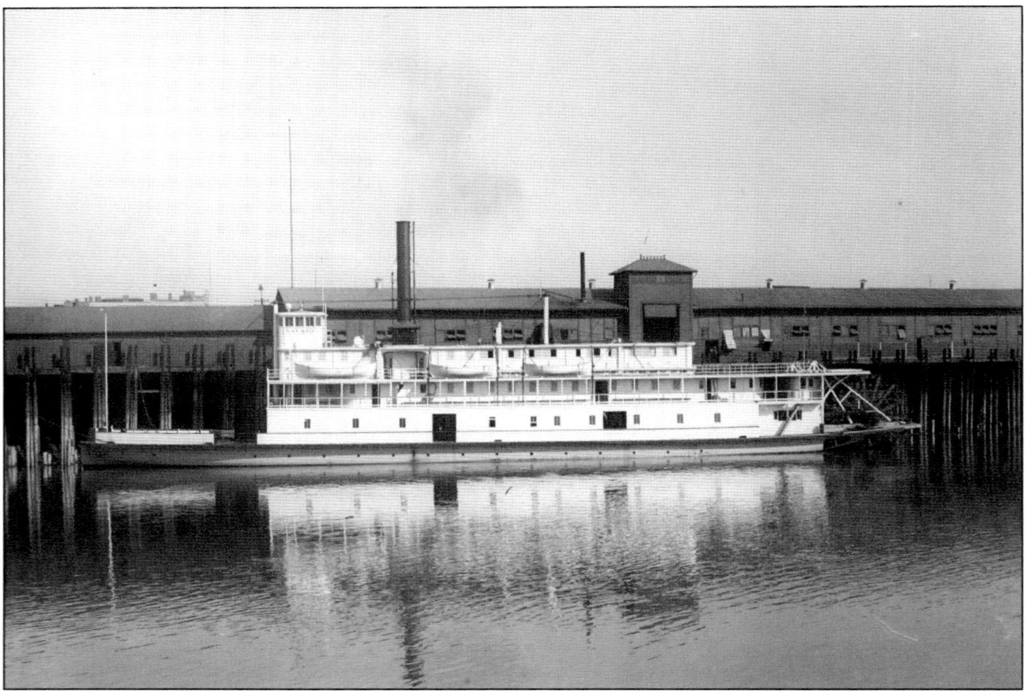

On September 8, 1909, historian-photographer David L. Joslyn photographed the SP's new *Navajo* at Sacramento. Later, her forward maindeck would become enclosed, providing more room for freight, open space for passengers, and a longer texas deck. (David L. Joslyn photograph; from William Knorp.)

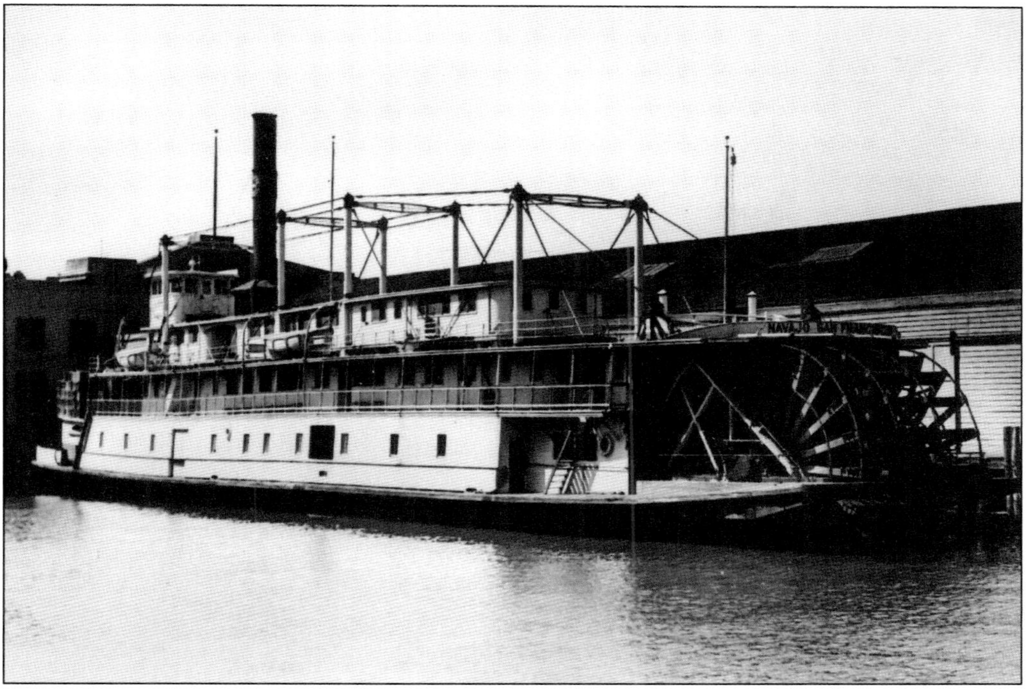

The 252-foot-long, 1,122-ton riverboat *Navajo*, built at the SP shipyard in Oakland in 1909, was a mainstay among SP riverboats for 20 years. When the Espee got out of the riverboat business on January 2, 1930, *Navajo* went to the California Transportation Co. (Courtesy San Francisco Maritime National Historical Park, No. P82-019a.1957pl.)

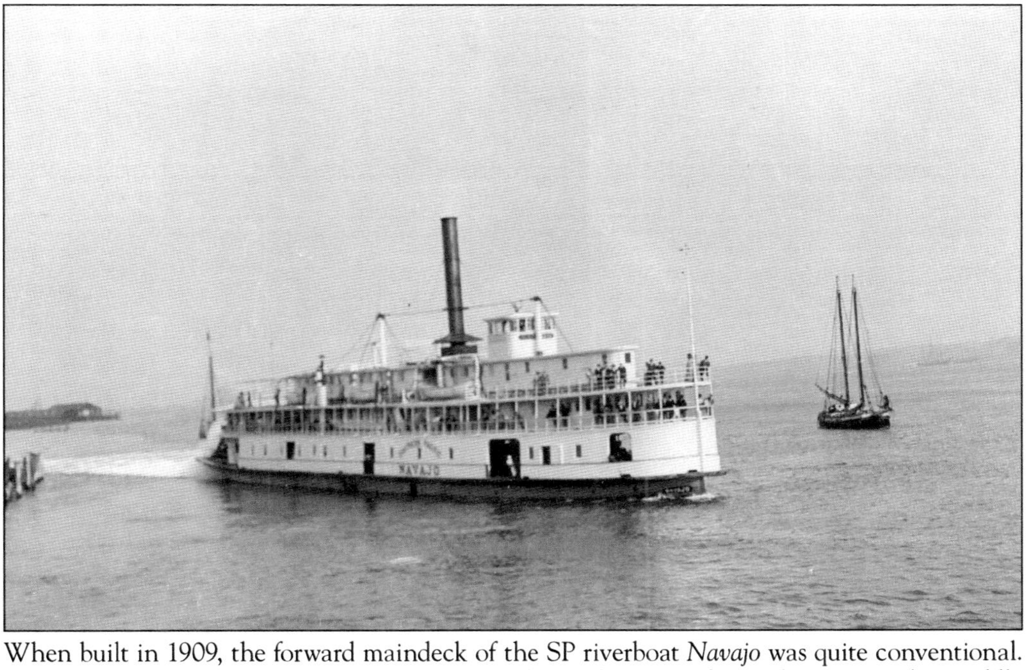

When built in 1909, the forward maindeck of the SP riverboat *Navajo* was quite conventional. Shortly after, she was rebuilt more closely resembling the *Seminole*. In this picture, her paddle wheel is creating plenty of white foam, while her stack is giving out almost no exhaust at all. (Courtesy Western Railway Museum Archives, No. 49466.)

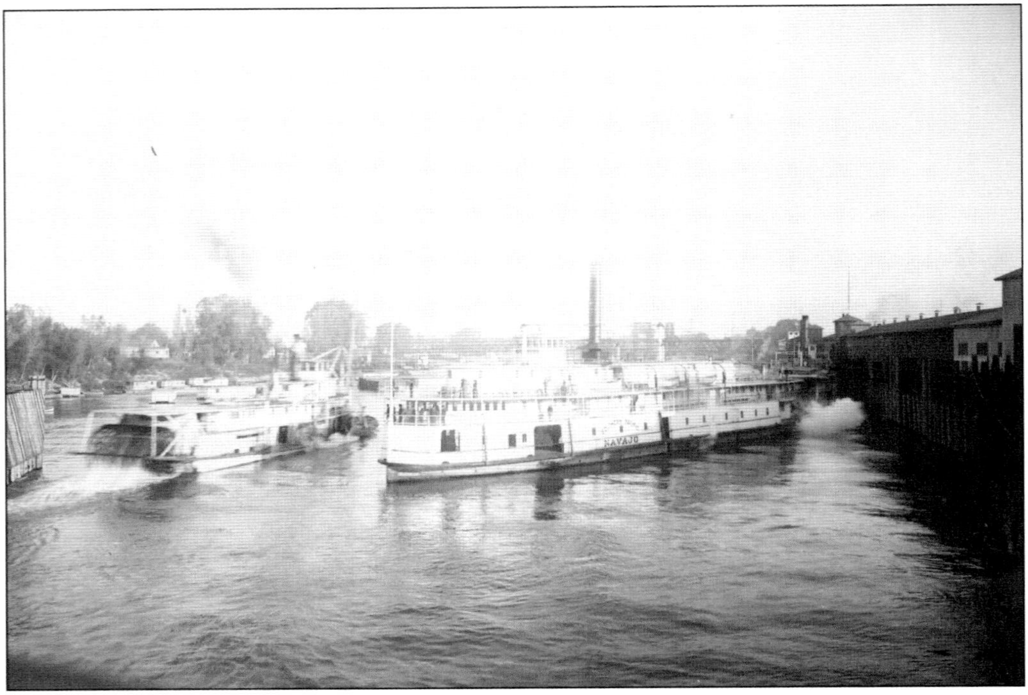

Busy times on the Sacramento riverfront have the Southern Pacific riverboat *Navajo* beginning another trip to San Francisco as an unidentified riverboat steams past her. Photographic quality shows the water being churned by two paddle wheels working at the same time. (Courtesy Western Railway Museum Archives, No. 49464.)

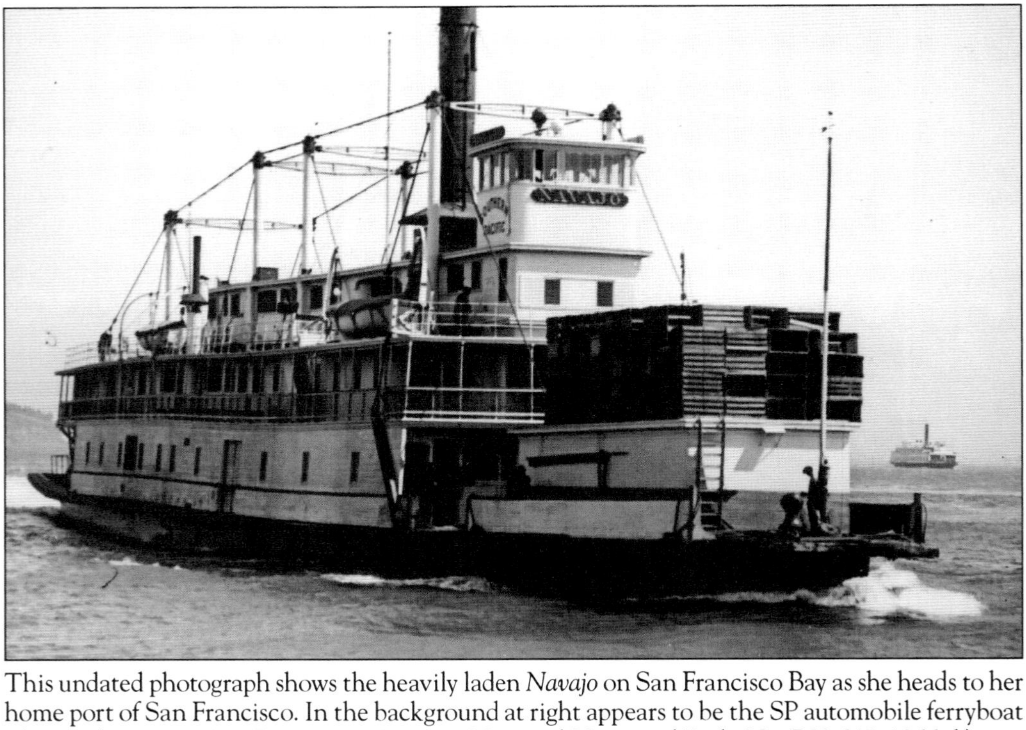


This undated photograph shows the heavily laden *Navajo* on San Francisco Bay as she heads to her home port of San Francisco. In the background at right appears to be the SP automobile ferryboat *El Paso.* (Courtesy San Francisco Maritime National Historical Park, No. P82-019a1966pl.)

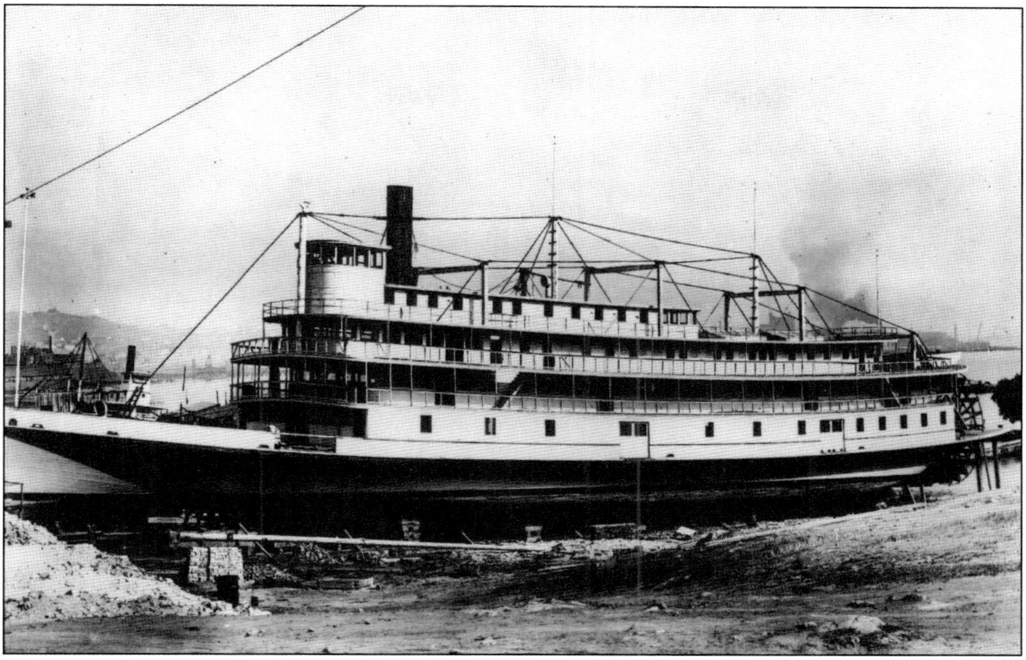

On her ways and nearing launching in 1910 is the *Capital City* in the yard of James Robertson of San Francisco. Robertson also built the *Fort Sutter* and several ferryboats, including the *City of San Rafael* in 1924, the last sidewheeler to be built on San Francisco Bay. (Courtesy San Francisco Maritime National Historical Park, No. P79-139.15pl.)

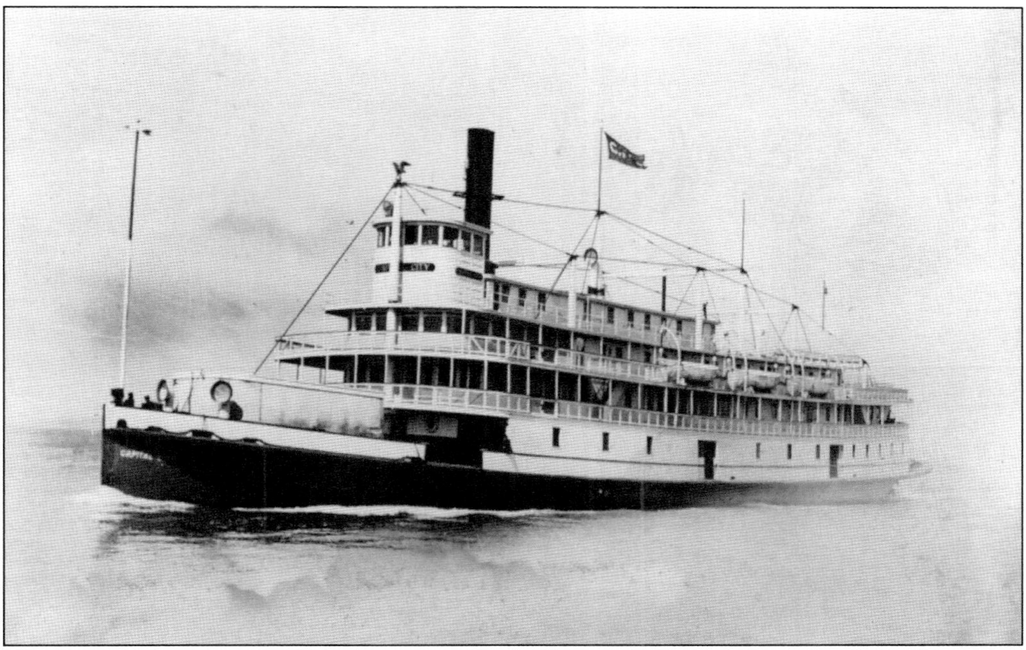

There was a time when postcards cost a nickel or less, plus a 1¢ stamp. Transportation companies often sold them with images of their railroads, ferryboats, and, in this case, their riverboats. Thus, this image shows the *Capital City* under steam. (Courtesy John Schmale Collection.)

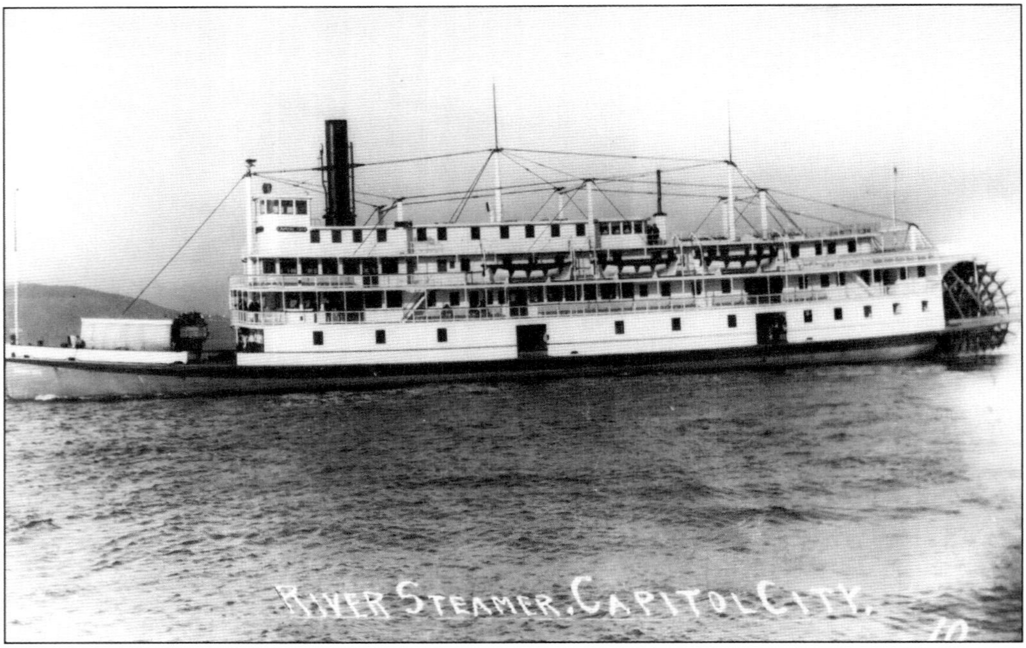


The 1,142-ton *Capital City* measured 220 by 42.6 by 9.3 feet and was built in 1910 by John G. North in San Francisco for the San Francisco–Sacramento runs. In 1927, she was put on the San Francisco–Stockton route and was renamed *Port of Stockton* in 1932. (Courtesy Bancroft Library, University of California, Berkeley.)

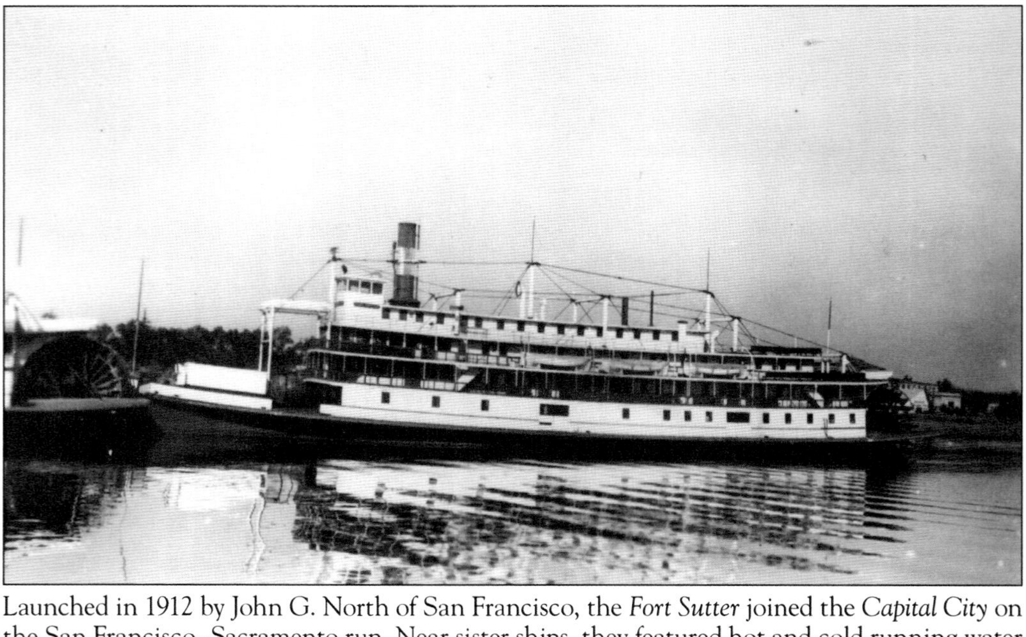

Launched in 1912 by John G. North of San Francisco, the *Fort Sutter* joined the *Capital City* on the San Francisco–Sacramento run. Near sister ships, they featured hot and cold running water in their staterooms. Both went into government service during World War II and had sad endings. (Courtesy Bancroft Library, University of California, Berkeley.)

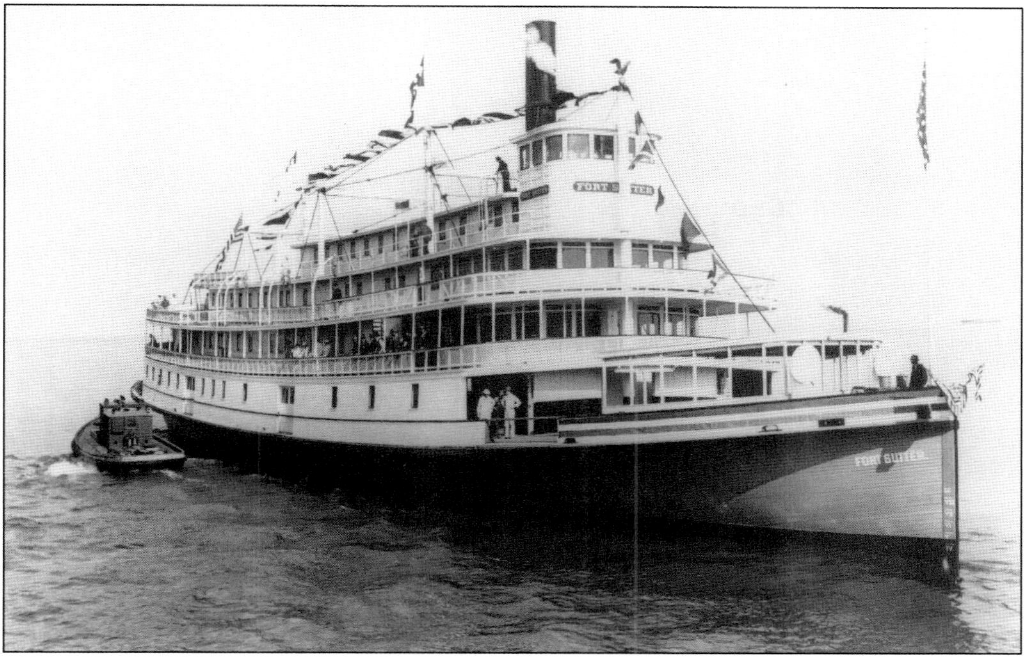

The *Fort Sutter* made her debut in 1912, well before the construction of high-speed highways and bridges over San Francisco Bay and its tributaries. The future then looked bright for the sumptuous *Fort Sutter*, but rising motor vehicle use eventually doomed the riverboats altogether. (McCurry photograph; courtesy Tom Gray collection.)

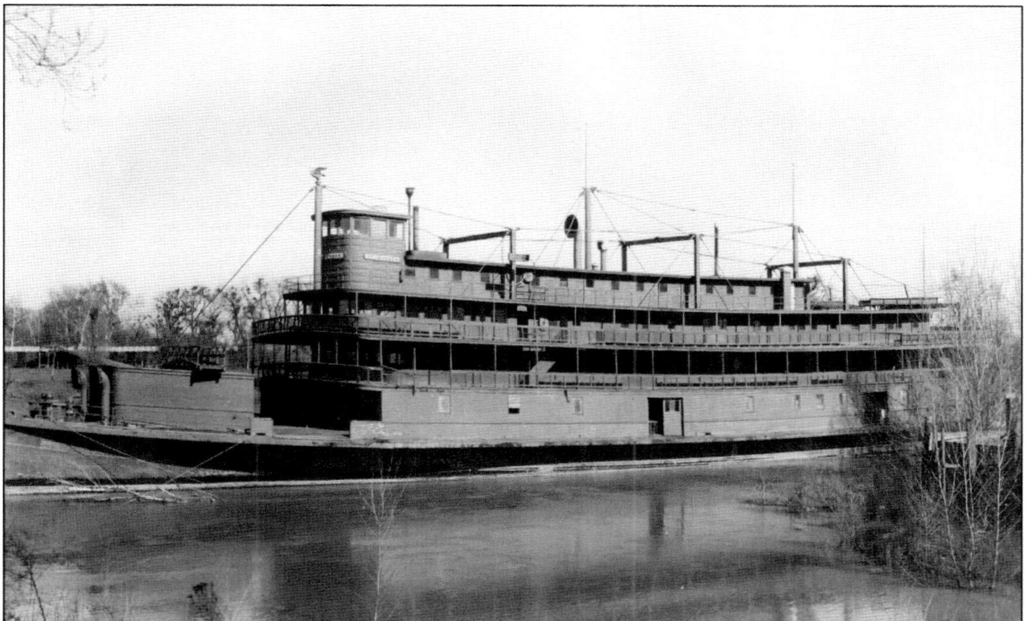

The *Fort Sutter* was once resplendent in white paint. Wartime duty called, and as young men exchanged zoot suits for service uniforms, the *Fort Sutter* donned Navy gray. She is moored on March 13, 1947, at Three Mile Slough, still in Navy livery, never to return to passenger service. (Courtesy Sacramento Public Library.)

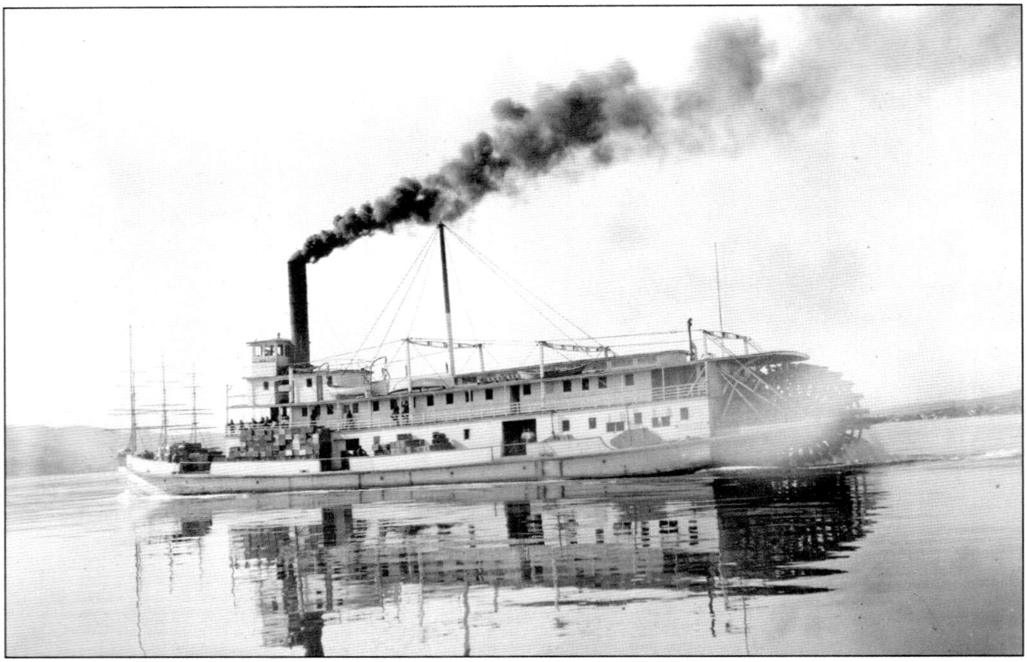

The 619.15-ton *Pride of the River* was just that—a pride of the river. Built in 1878, she served the California Transportation Co. well until 1942 when she was abandoned after 64 years, including a stint for Hollywood in the film *Steamboat Round the Bend* (1935). (Courtesy Western Railway Museum Archives, No. 49673.)

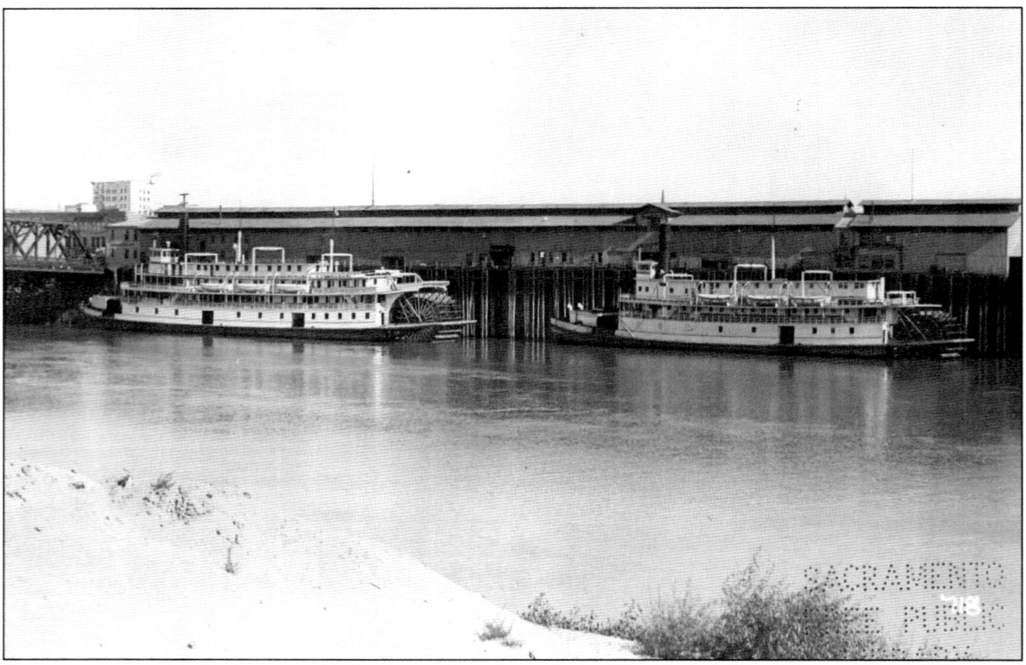

In this c. 1930 scene, the *Pride of the River* is tied up at Sacramento with the *Captain Weber* behind her. These two vessels would star in the 1935 movie *Steamboat Round the Bend*, along with Will Rogers (his last film), Anne Shirley, Irvin S. Cobb, and four other riverboats. (Courtesy Sacramento Public Library.)

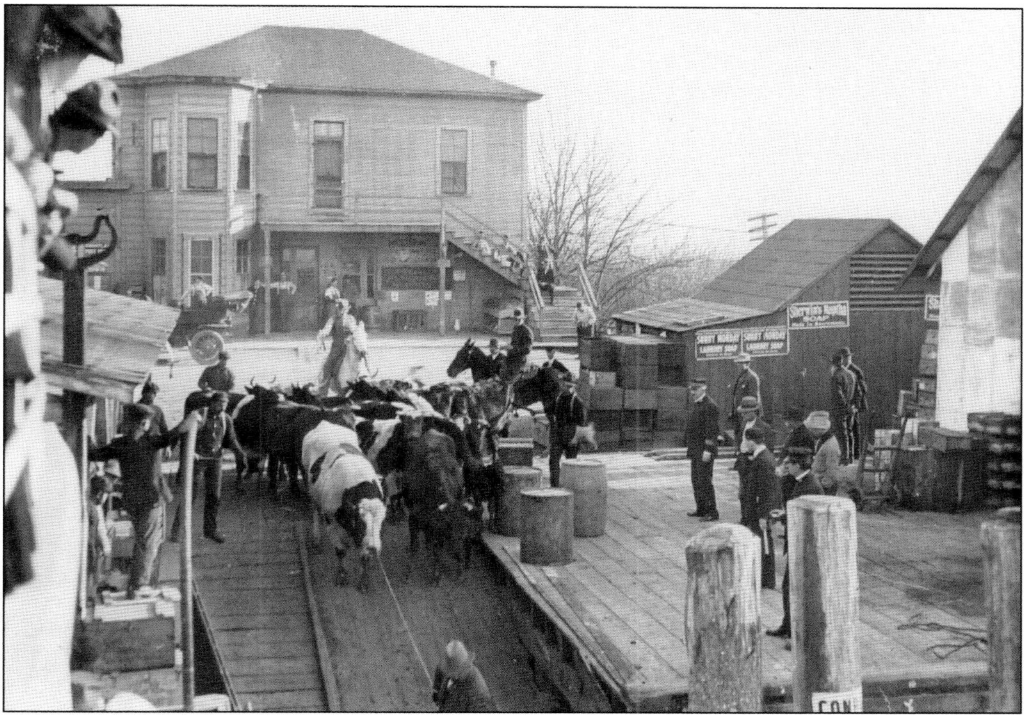

The maindecks of Northern California riverboats carried all types of cargo, from manufactured goods to livestock. Here, a small herd of bovines is being driven aboard a riverboat at Courtland c. 1918. For people, a riverboat trip could be exciting, but for cattle, it could mean a one-way ride. (Courtesy John Schmale collection.)

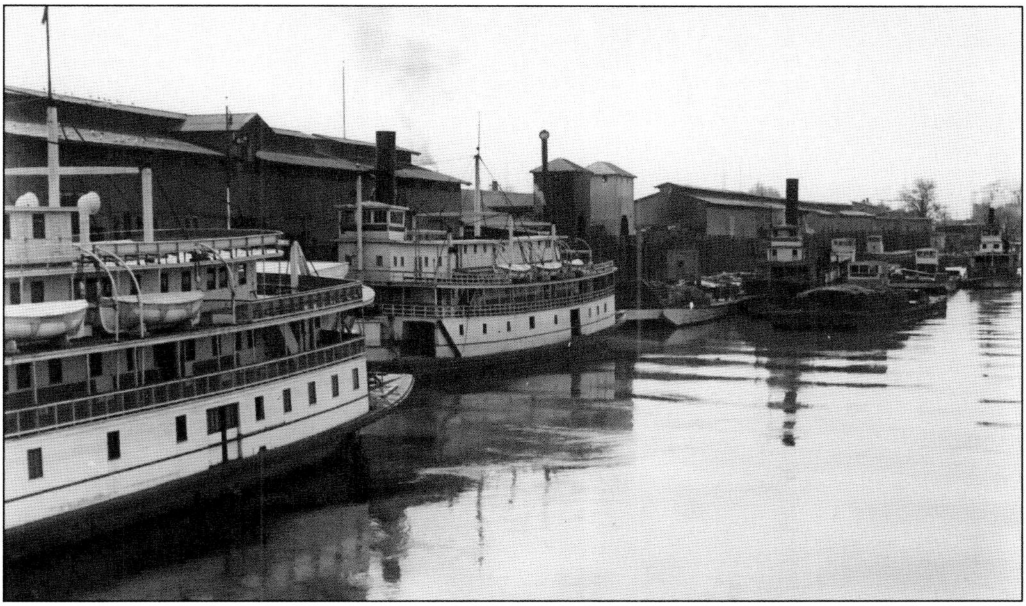

This photograph was taken around 1930 in Sacramento. From left to right are an unidentified riverboat, *Captain Weber*, *San Joaquin No. 4*, six barges, and another unidentified riverboat. Smoke is coming only from the stack of the boat at far right, indicating the others may be idled, victims of the Great Depression and changing travel modes. (Courtesy Sacramento Public Library.)

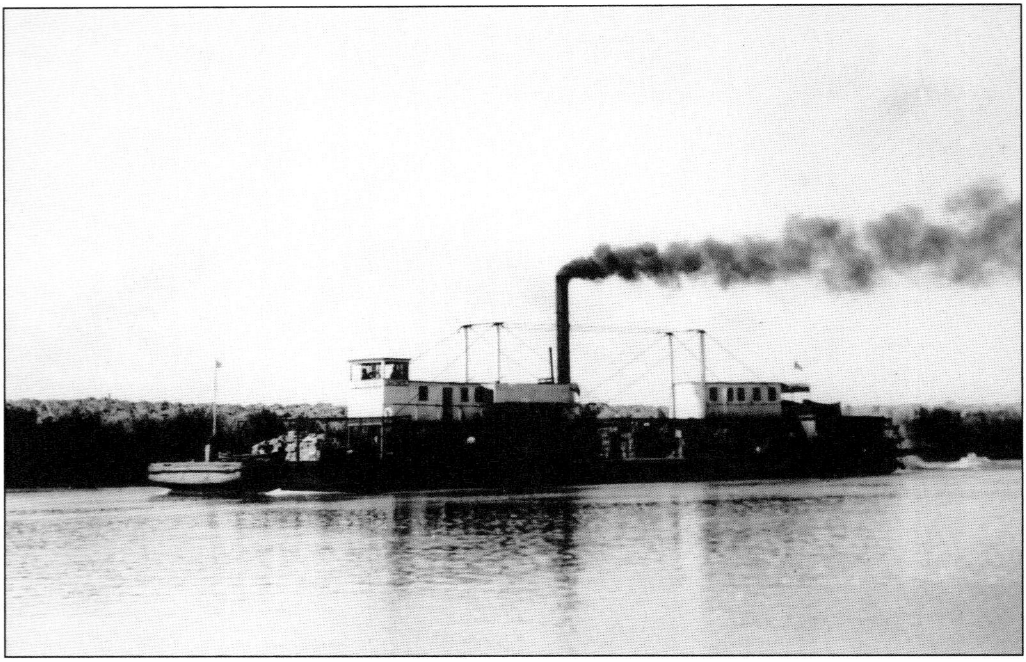

The sternwheeler *Acme* was 177.5 feet long and had a 294-ton rating. She was built in 1889 and was broken up in 1911. Other than working on the Sacramento River and an unusual design, comparatively little is known about her. (Courtesy San Francisco Maritime National Historical Park, No. C7-4, 714PL.)

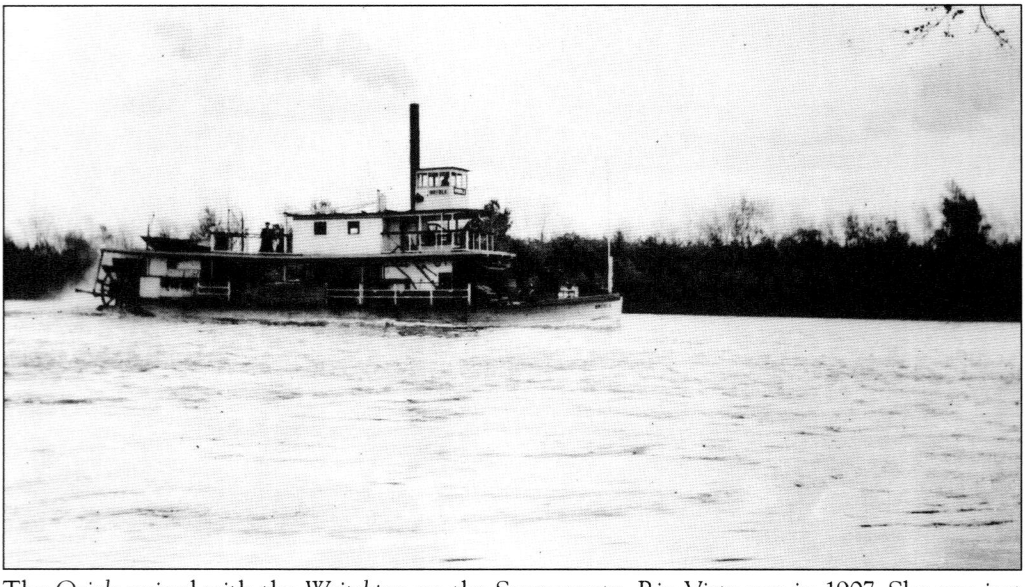

The *Oriole* paired with the *Weitchpec* on the Sacramento–Rio Vista run in 1907. She was just an ordinary get-the-job-done riverboat. Built in 1905 at Sacramento, she rated only 68.1 tons, measuring 81.5 by 17.8 by 3.9 feet. Old time riverboat men recalled that she burned up in 1921. (Courtesy San Francisco Maritime National Historical Park, No. P82-110.4n.)

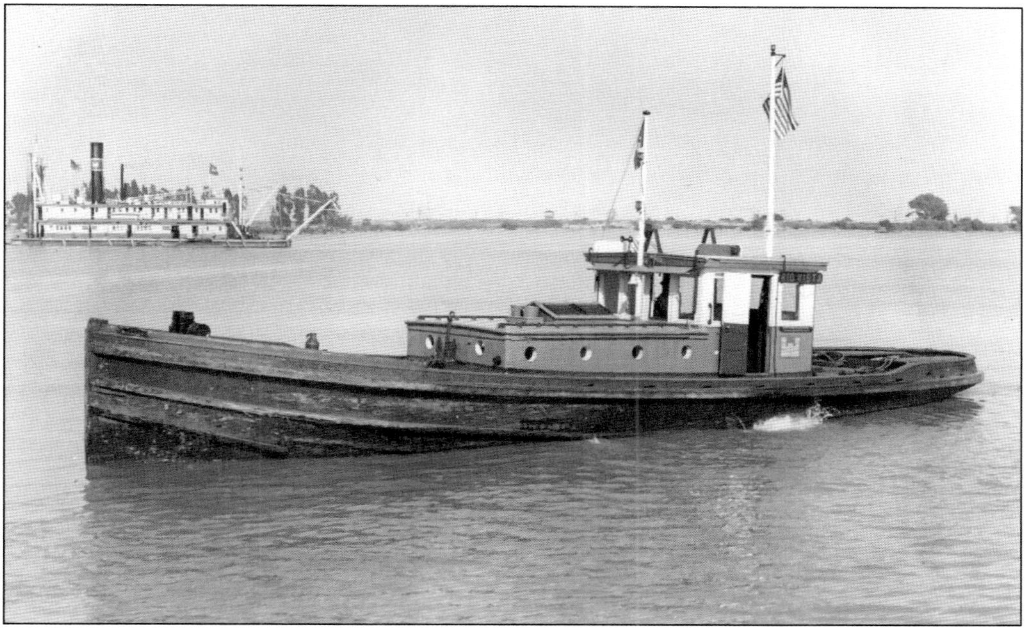

The riverboats' safety and continued existence depended upon Army Corps of Engineers' dredges and snagboats keeping the channels deep enough and clear for navigation. In the foreground of this c. 1936 image is the snagboat *Rio Vista*, and in the background is a river dredge. (Courtesy Sacramento Public Library.)

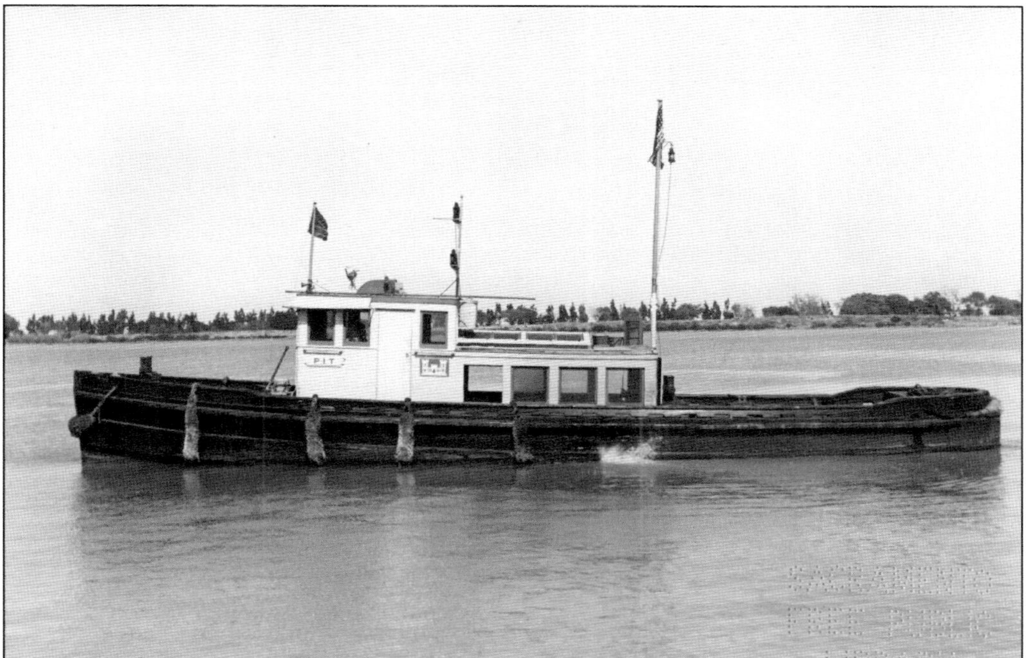


This 1930 photograph shows the Army Corps of Engineers' snagboat *Pit* on the Sacramento River. Snags (underwater objects such as fallen trees or logs stuck in the mud) could stove a hole in the hull of a riverboat, resulting in sinkings, financial loss, and sometimes losing the vessels themselves. (Courtesy Sacramento Public Library.)

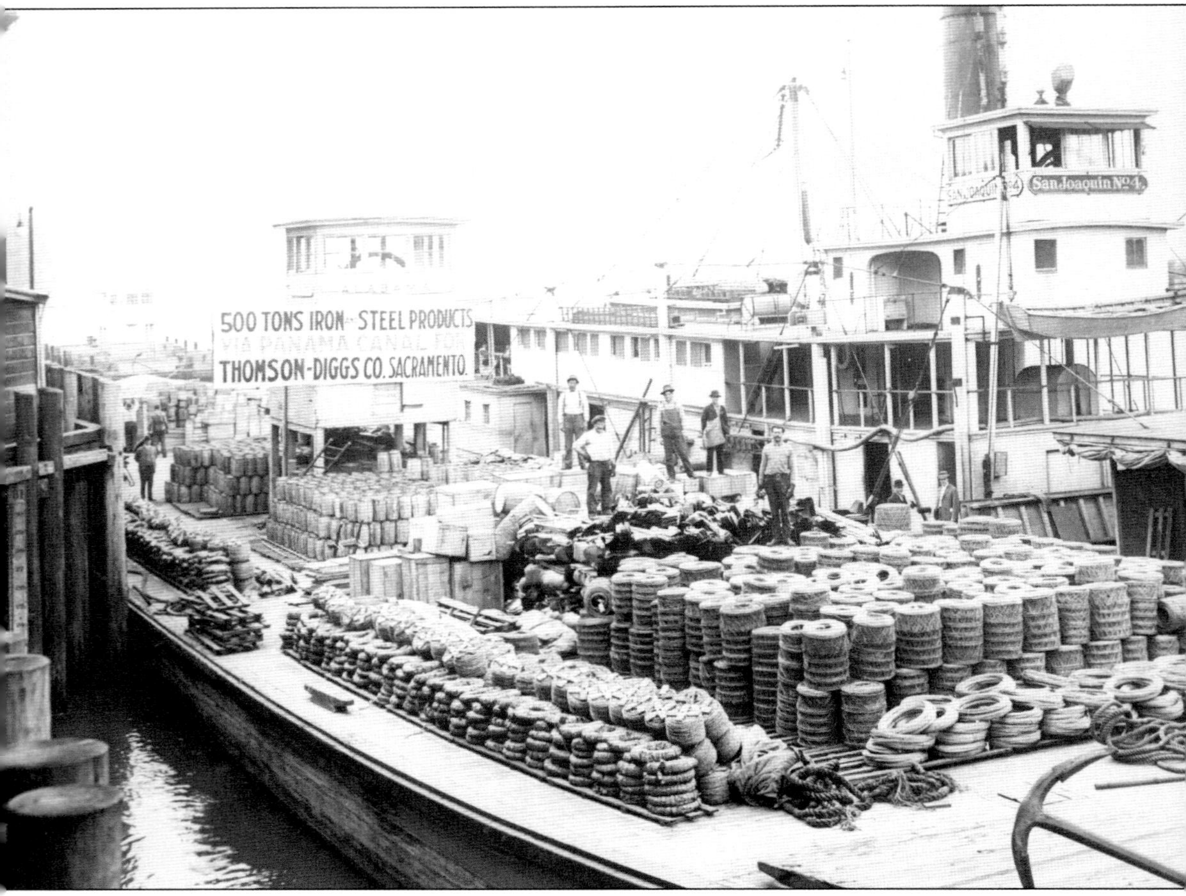


For those unfamiliar with mathematics or physics, it must seem mind boggling that the *Alabama*, a flat-bottom barge, could carry 500 tons of iron and steel products and not sink. The *Alabama* has probably been towed by the riverboat *San Joaquin No. 4*. Behind the *Alabama* is the barge *Rio Vista*. (Courtesy Western Railway Museum Archives, No. 49518.)

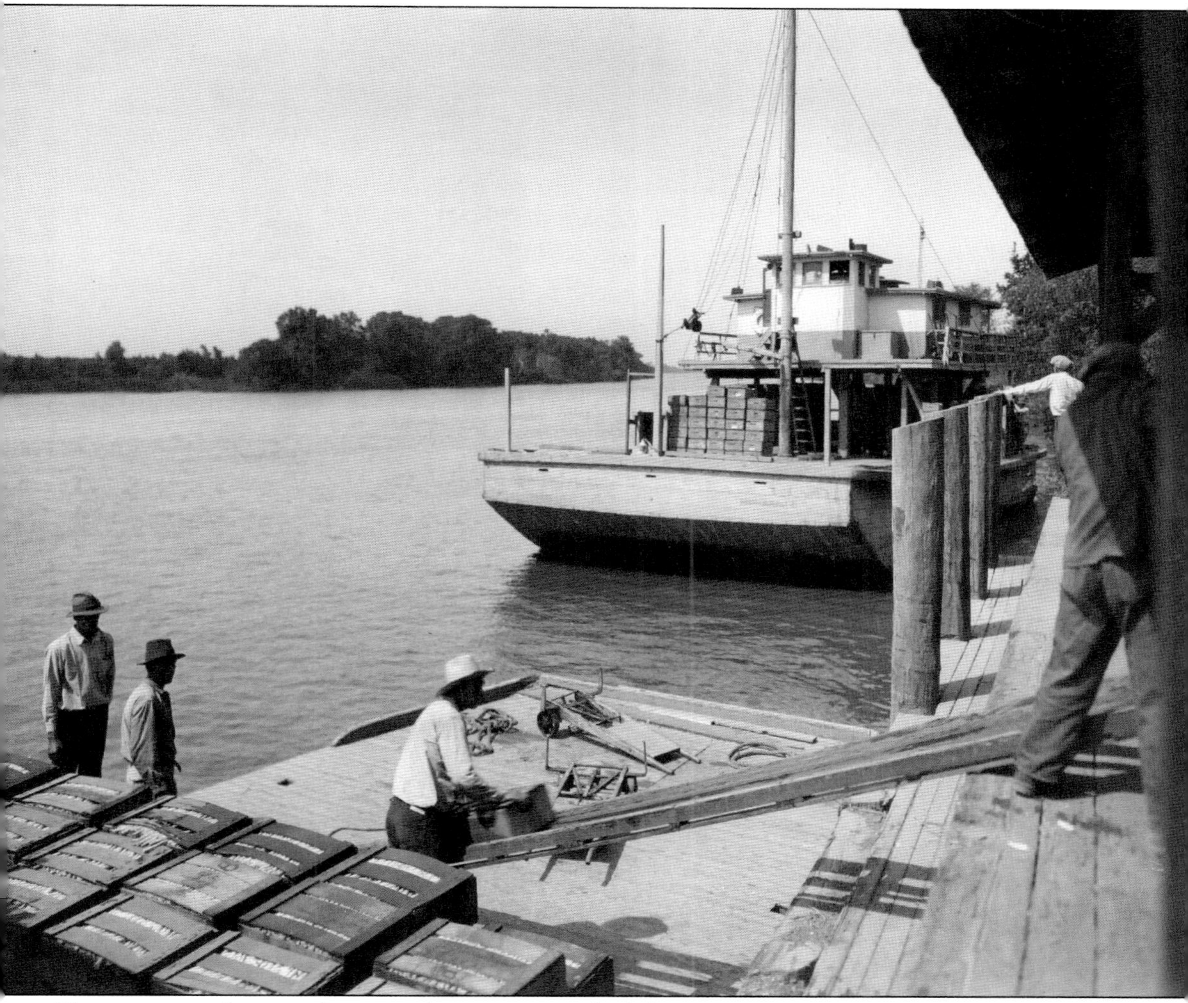

The square-toed, ungainly scow schooners once plied their ways on San Francisco Bay and its various tributaries and, in the case seen above, on the Sacramento River. Economically competitive with riverboats, they were dependent upon the winds and tides. Here, a pair of scow schooners are taking on crates of celery. (Courtesy Western Railway Museum Archives, No. 50340.)

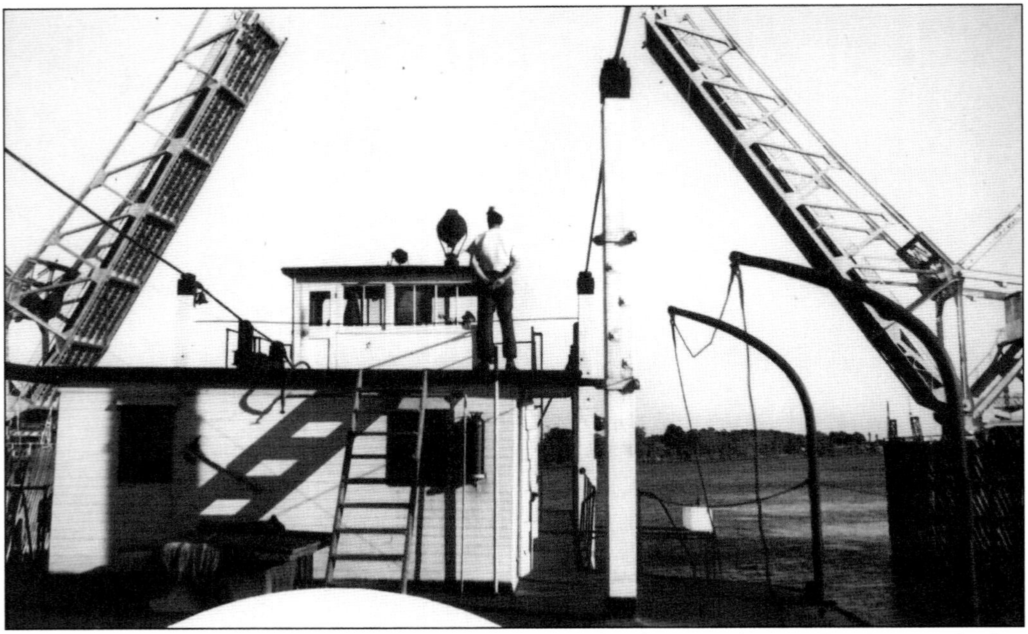

In 1938, the steamer *Dauntless* was rebuilt and motorized to become the MV *San Joaquin*. In this view from her hurricane deck, she is passing under a drawbridge on the Sacramento River in August 1948. (Courtesy San Francisco Maritime National Historical Park, San Francisco *Call-Bulletin* Collection, No. P82-019a2049PL.)

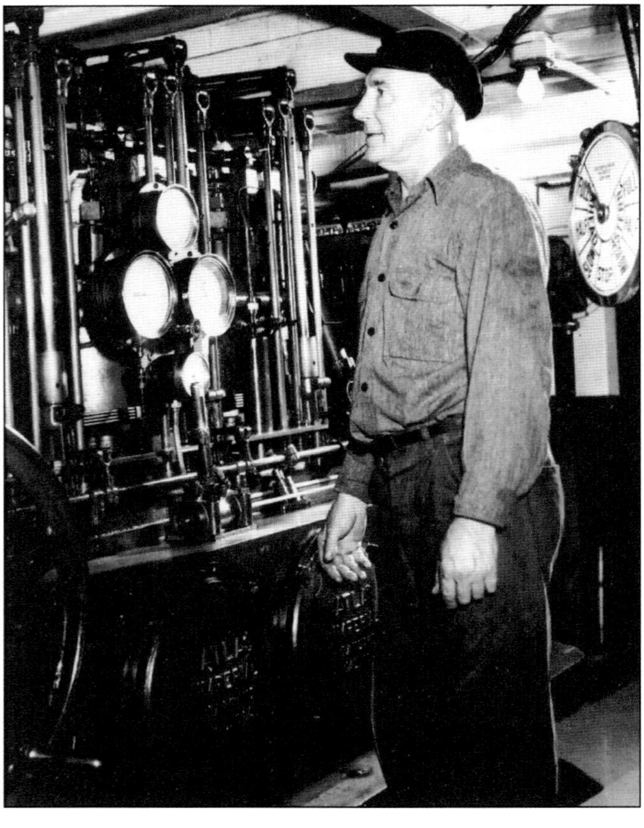

Capt. Herbert A. "Barkey" Kunzelman is in the MV *San Joaquin*'s engine room wearing neither starched whites nor dress blues, for the *San Joaquin* is a workhorse—a blue-collar workingman's vessel. Behind the "Old Man" is the telegraph for receiving orders from the pilot to the chief engineer. (Courtesy San Francisco Maritime National Historical Park, No. P82-019a.2052PL.)

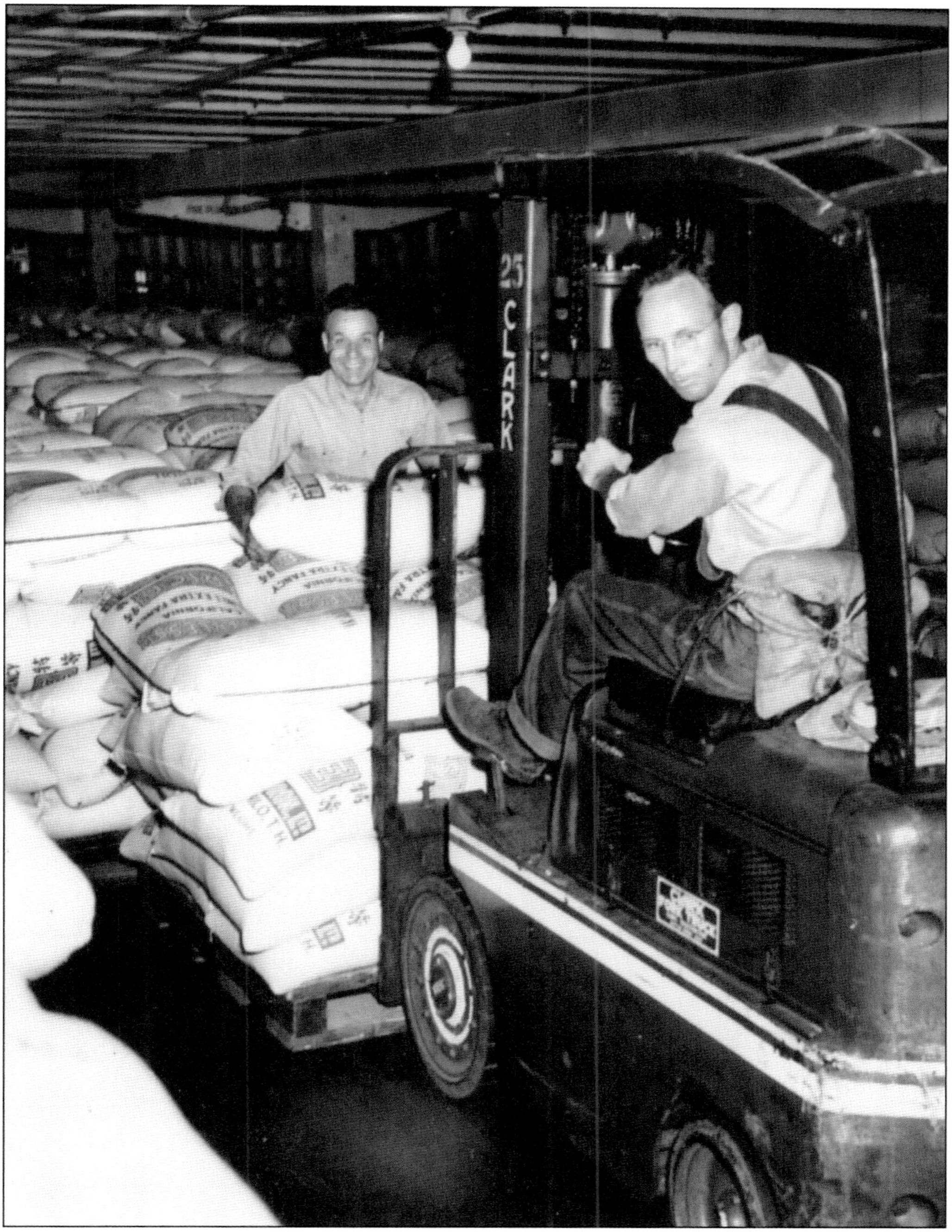


This photograph, taken in August 1948, shows thousands of sacks filled with Northern California rice being off-loaded from the maindeck of the MV *San Joaquin*, ex-steamer *Dauntless*. Rice remains a major crop in California's agricultural economy. (Courtesy San Francisco Maritime National Historical Park, No. P82-019a.PL.)

# STEAMERS DE LUXE

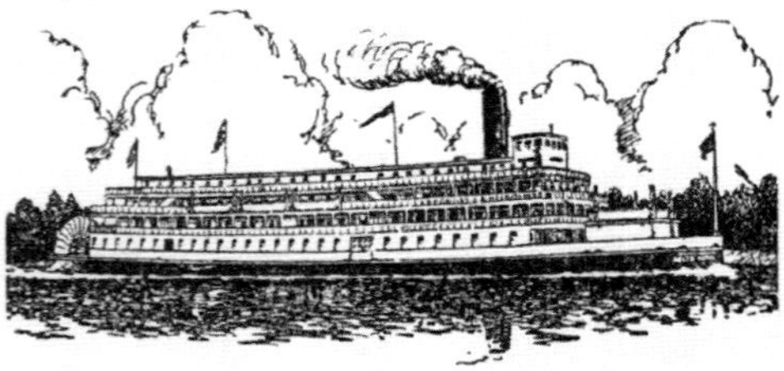

**"Delta King" — "Delta Queen"**
(Sister Ships—1838 tons)
*Between*
SAN FRANCISCO — SACRAMENTO
Leave 6:30 P. M. — Arrive 5:30 A. M.

## At Your Service

HOT AND COLD RUNNING WATER IN EVERY STATEROOM AND SUITES OF TWO AND THREE ROOMS WITH PRIVATE BATH OR SHOWER

Special Advantages for Automobile Parties

*The*
**California Transportation Company**

"Steamers De Luxe" says it all on a card advertising the *Delta King* and *Delta Queen*. Note that passengers could still enjoy breakfast aboard the *Deltas* well after their boat had docked. (Courtesy Western Railway Museum Archives.)

STEAMERS DE LUXE

## DINING ROOM SERVICE

*Table d'Hote and a la Carte*

| DINNER *From* | BREAKFAST *From* |
|---|---|
| 6:30 to 8:30 P. M. | 6:00 to 9:00 A. M. |

## MAIN LOBBY

PURSER'S OFFICE - NEWS STAND
BARBER SHOP

## SMOKING ROOM AND BAR OFF MAIN LOBBY

SOFT DRINKS - COFFEE - SANDWICHES
Served *from* 6:30 P. M. to 1:00 A. M.

## SOCIAL HALL ON SALOON DECK

STEWARDESS IN ATTENDANCE

Main saloons and staterooms are served with washed air, cooled in summer and warmed in winter. Passengers regulate volume of air desired by chain control of air register in staterooms.

STEAMERS DE LUXE

## NEWS STAND

ALL CURRENT MAGAZINES - DAILY PAPERS
PLAYING CARDS

**Cigars - Cigarettes - Candies**

*The following Toilet Articles may be purchased at News Stand*

| | |
|---|---|
| Tooth Brushes | $0.50 |
| Tooth Pastes and Powders | 30c—.50 |
| Shaving Creams and Powders | 35c—.40 |
| Talcum Powder | .25 |
| Peroxide of Hydrogen | .25 |
| Listerine | .25 |
| Witch Hazel | .15 |
| New Skin | .15 |
| Styptic Stick | .10 |
| Asperin Tablets | .35 |

Combs, Shoe Laces and Collar Buttons.

## PERSONAL SERVICE

A call bell in every stateroom for convenience of passengers connects with Purser's office, and bell boys and boys in white coats are always in attendance to assist passengers on and off the boat with their luggage.

Under "personal service," note that it was a time when Filipino stewards were referred to as "bell boys" and "boys in white coats" with impunity, something not tolerated today. The prices on the advertising card also testify to a bygone era. (Courtesy Western Railway Museum Archives.)

STEAMERS DE LUXE

## PERSONAL SERVICE

BARBER SHOP — NEWS STAND

OPEN

*From* 5:00 P. M. to 11:00 P. M.

*Barber Shop—Men*

| | |
|---|---|
| Haircut | $0.50 |
| Shave | .25 |
| Beard Trimmed | .35 |
| Facial Massage | .50 |
| Facial Massage (Boncilla) | 1.00 |
| Hair Singe | .25 |
| Plain Shampoo | .50 |
| Shampoo (Egg, Oil or Tonic) | .75 |
| Hair Tonics | .25 |

*Barber Shop—Women*

| | |
|---|---|
| Hair Bob | $0.50 |
| Neck Clip | .25 |
| Plain Shampoo | 1.00 |
| Shampoo (Egg, Oil or Tonic) | 1.25 |
| Hair Tonics | .25 |

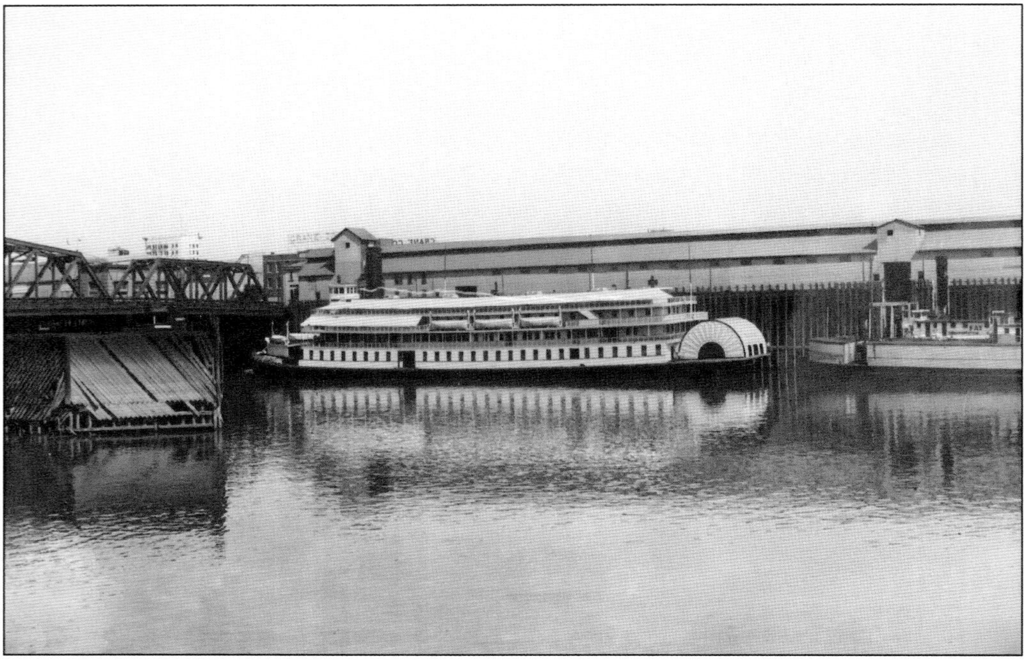

The *Delta King* is berthed at Sacramento near the old M Street Bridge. The vessel at the *Delta King*'s stern is hard to identify with her wheelhouse being rebuilt and missing signboards. She is property of the Fay Transportation Co., an operator of diesel-powered riverboats. (Courtesy San Francisco Maritime National Historical Park, No. P84-081.16pl.)

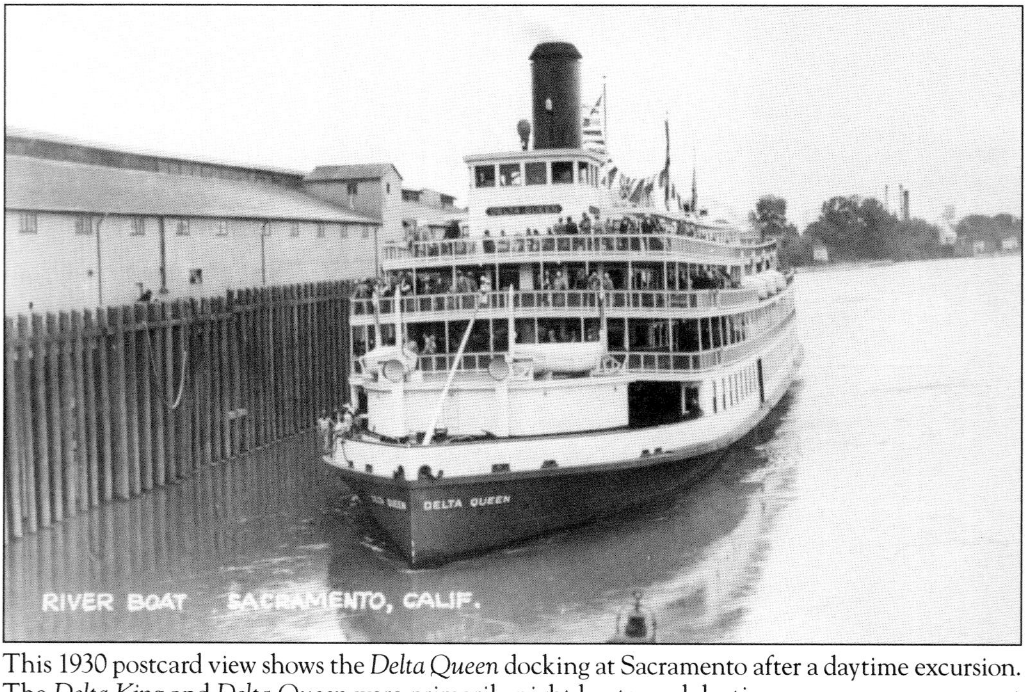


This 1930 postcard view shows the *Delta Queen* docking at Sacramento after a daytime excursion. The *Delta King* and *Delta Queen* were primarily night boats, and daytime runs were rare, except for the starting and ending of summer months. (Courtesy Sacramento Public Library.)

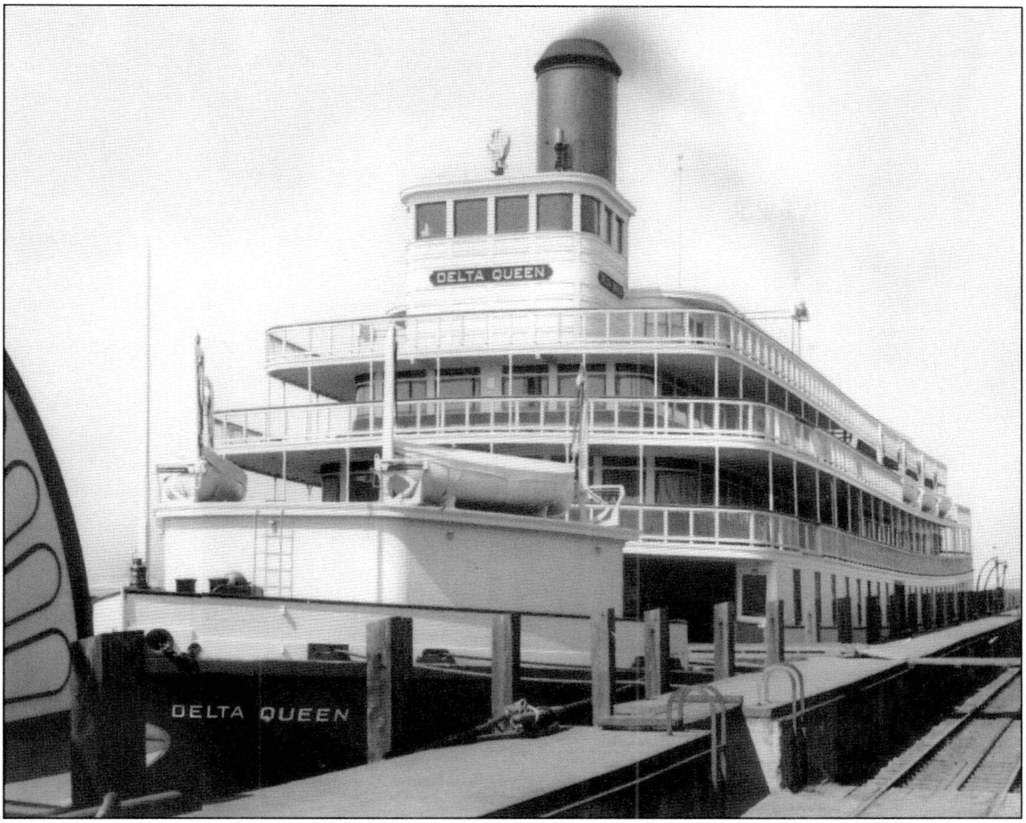


The *Delta King* and *Delta Queen* were built in 1926 as a last-gasp effort to stem the tide of increasing automobile use. While modern in every respect for their time, their interiors also fully reflected the opulent heritage of American riverboats. (Courtesy San Francisco Maritime National Historical Park, No. P82-019a.1852p1.)

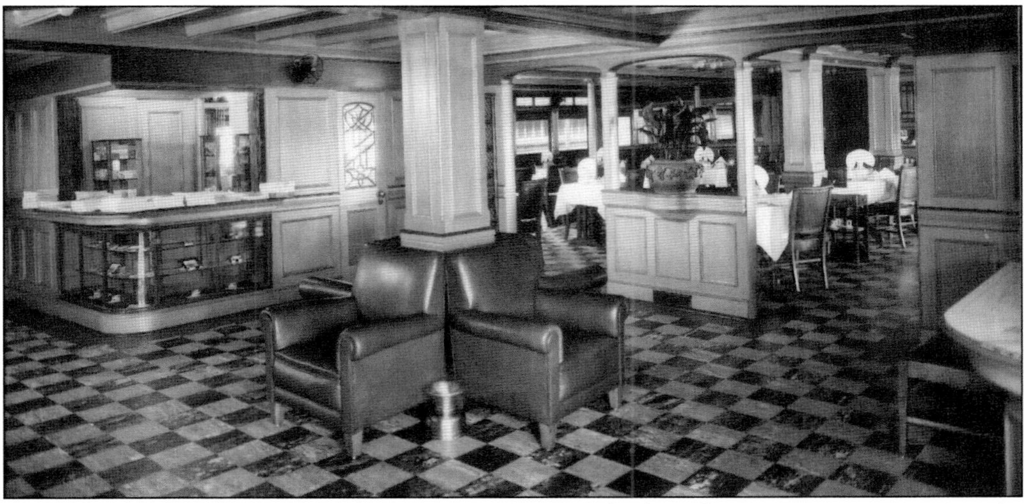

This is the main lobby of the *Delta Queen*'s Saloon Deck when she was new in 1927. Note the brass cuspidor on the floor between the two cushioned chairs. Today, it is hard to believe that expectoration of tobacco juice was once considered acceptable public behavior. (Courtesy San Francisco Maritime National Historical Park, No. P82-019a.1854pl.)

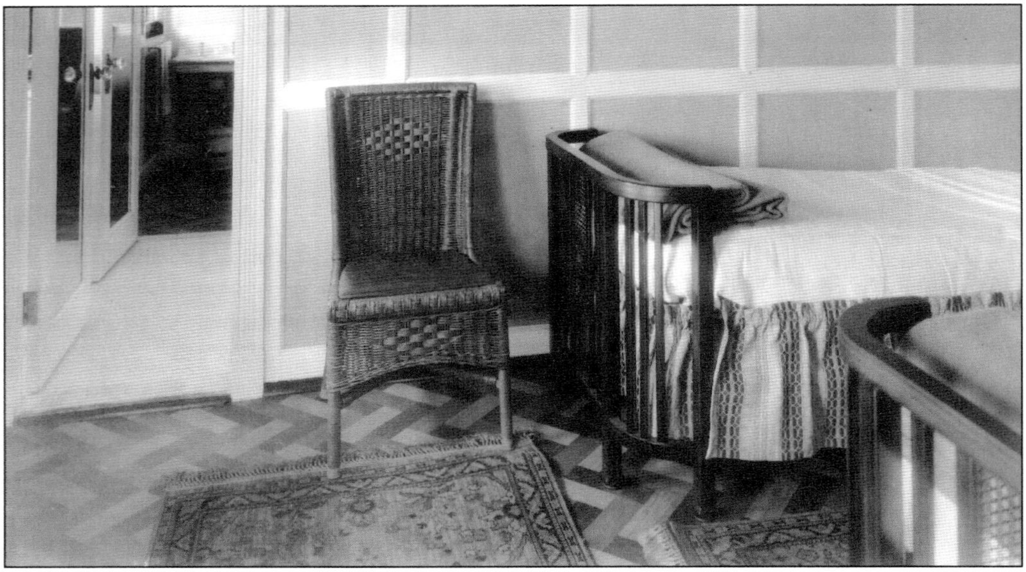

This suite aboard the *Delta Queen* was furnished with two twin beds, en suite bathroom, a wicker chair with seat cushion, and rugs on the deck or floor. The author will hear no puns regarding *queen*-size beds! (Courtesy San Francisco Maritime National Historical Park, No. P82-019a.1855pl.)

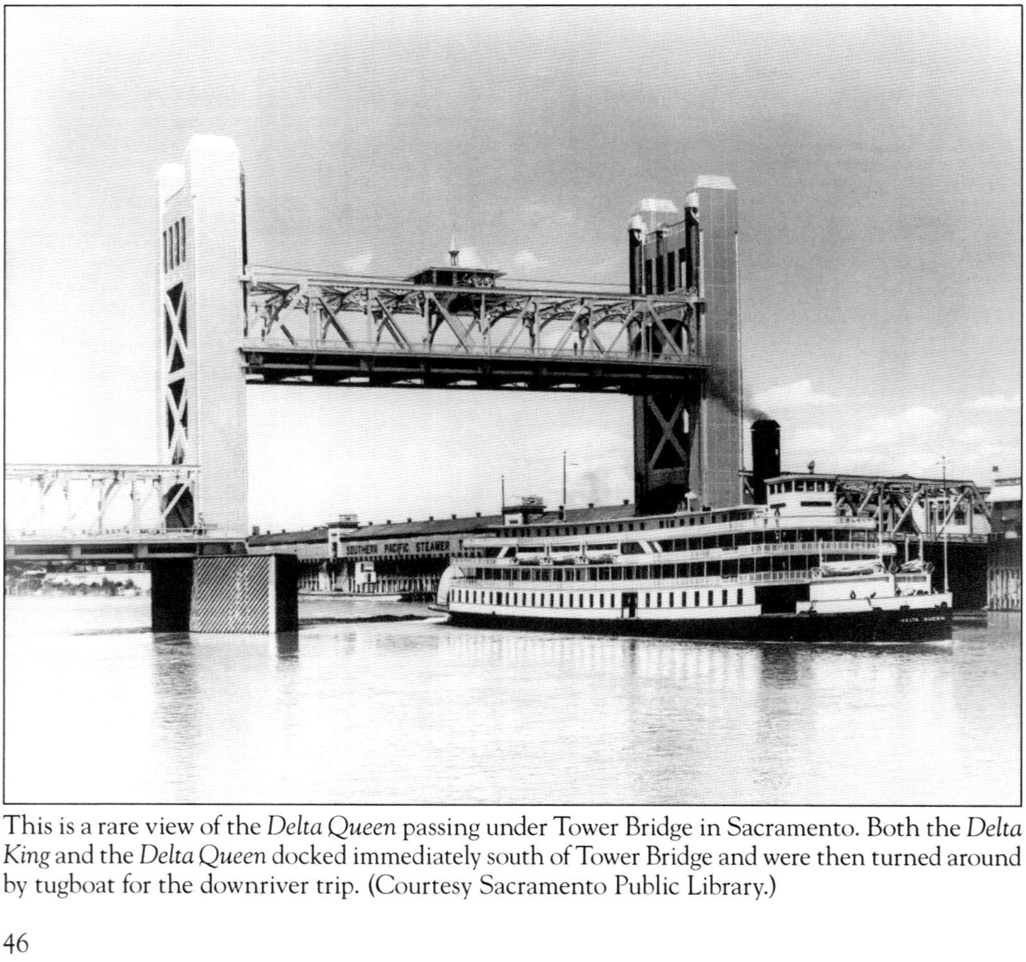


This is a rare view of the *Delta Queen* passing under Tower Bridge in Sacramento. Both the *Delta King* and the *Delta Queen* docked immediately south of Tower Bridge and were then turned around by tugboat for the downriver trip. (Courtesy Sacramento Public Library.)

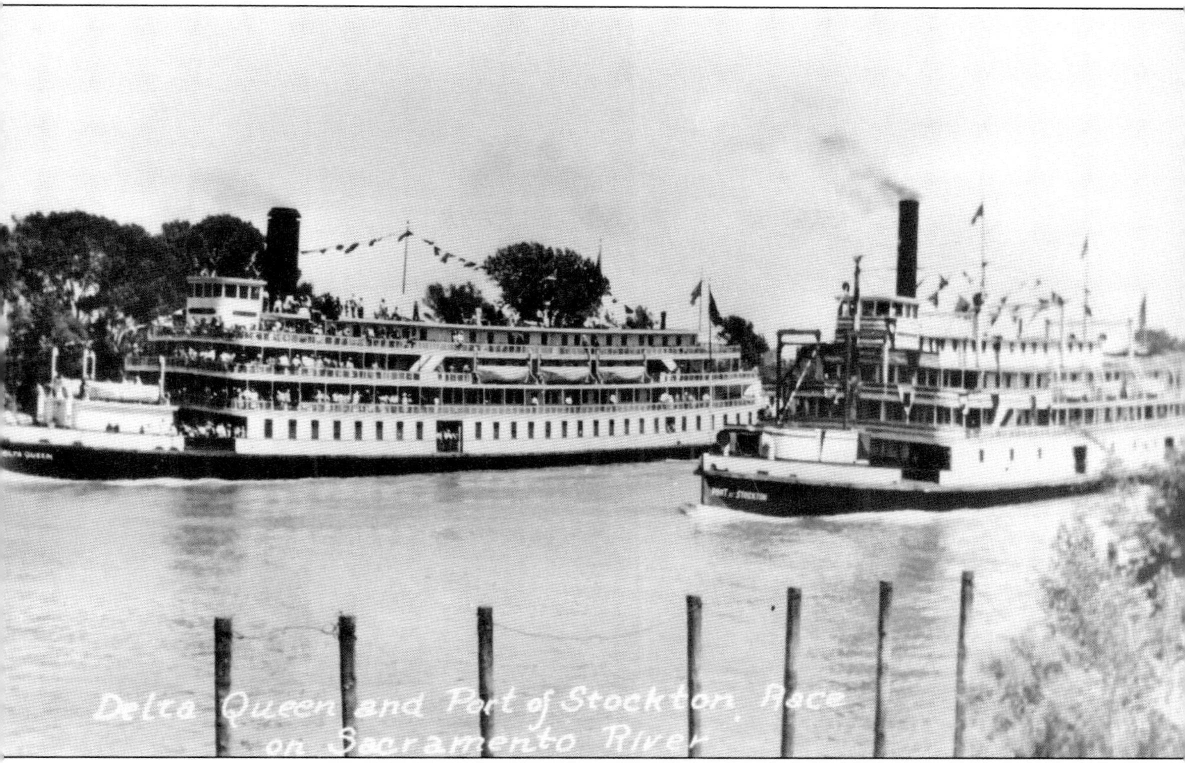


On June 25, 1938, Californians witnessed something not seen in decades: a steamboat race on the Sacramento River from Sacramento to Clarksburg. Contestants were the *Port of Stockton* and the *Delta Queen*. The *Port of Stockton* won by a whisker—so close that the judges initially declared a tie. (Courtesy Western Railway Museum Archives, No. 49517.)

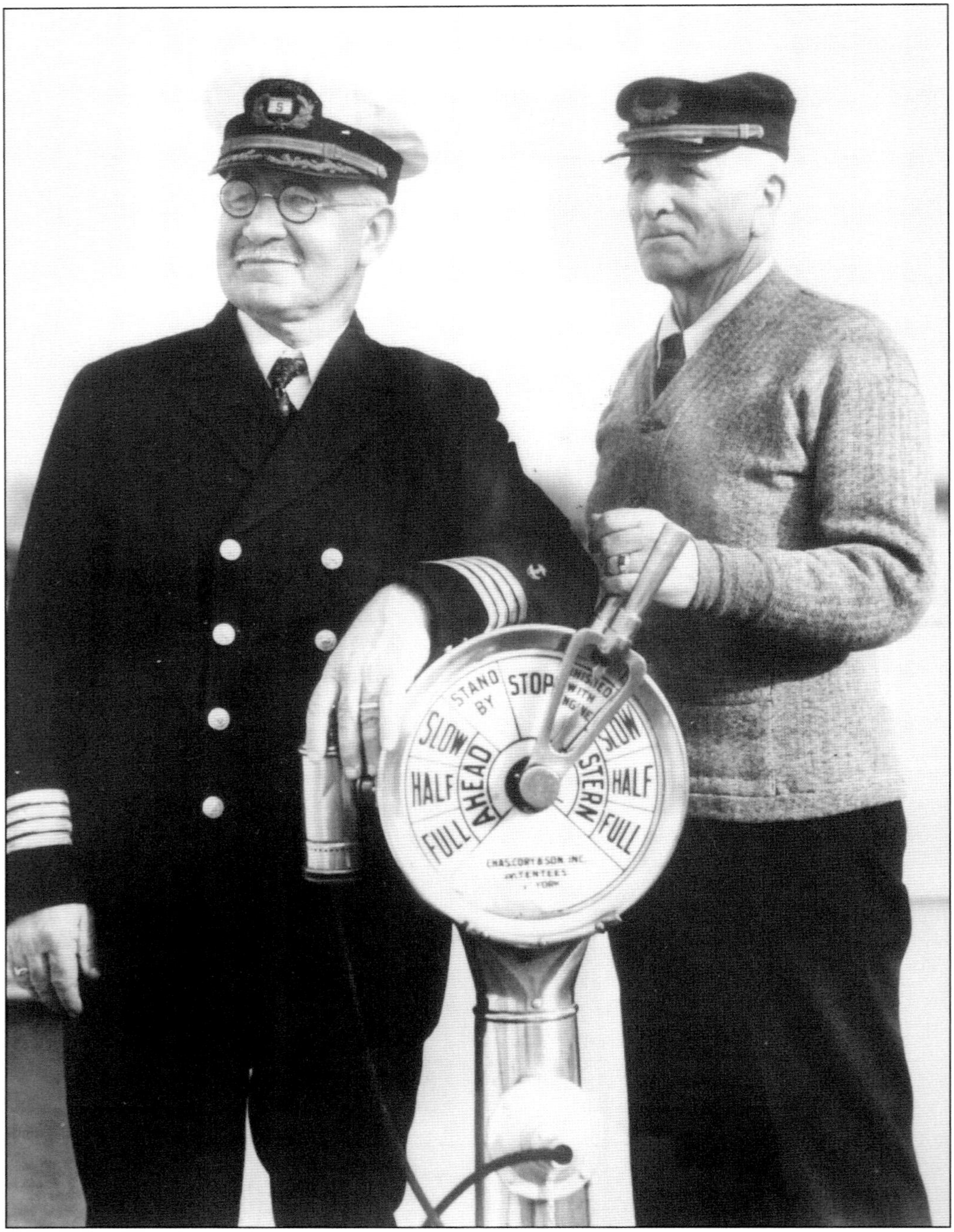


William Lester Cooley, at left in 1933, was relief captain of the *Delta King* when she was new and, later, became the captain of the *Delta Queen*. He was the last civilian captain of the *Delta Queen* before she went into US Navy service in World War II. (Courtesy California State Library.)

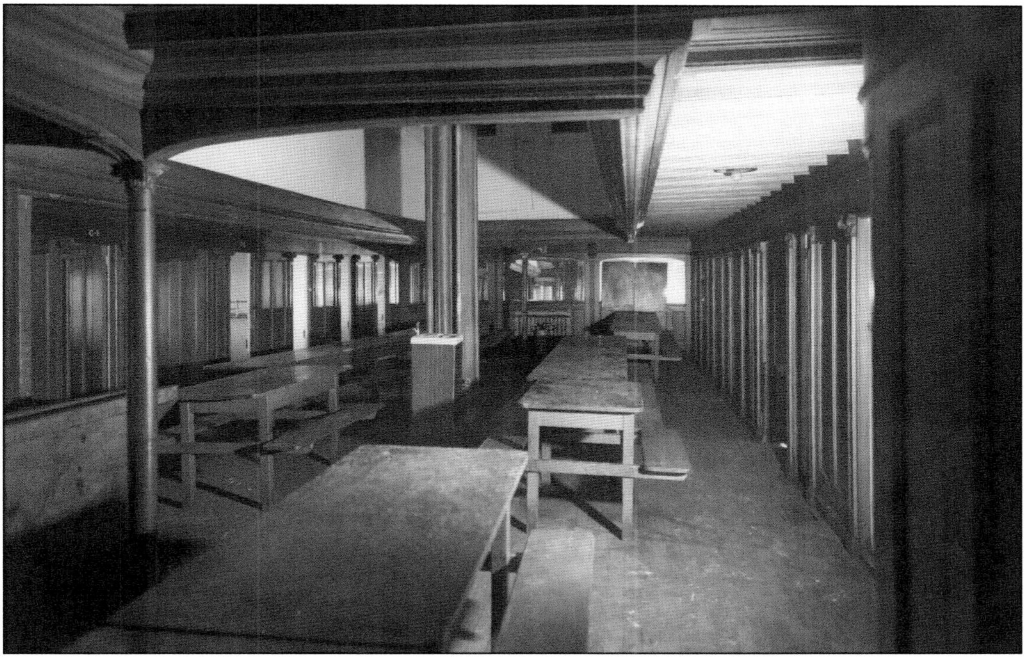

Following World War II, the *Delta King* and *Delta Queen* went to the US Maritime Commission, which moored them in Suisun Bay. In this image from March 13, 1947, what had once been the fashionable Saloon Deck of the *Delta King* was now a deserted floating barracks. (Courtesy Sacramento Public Library.)

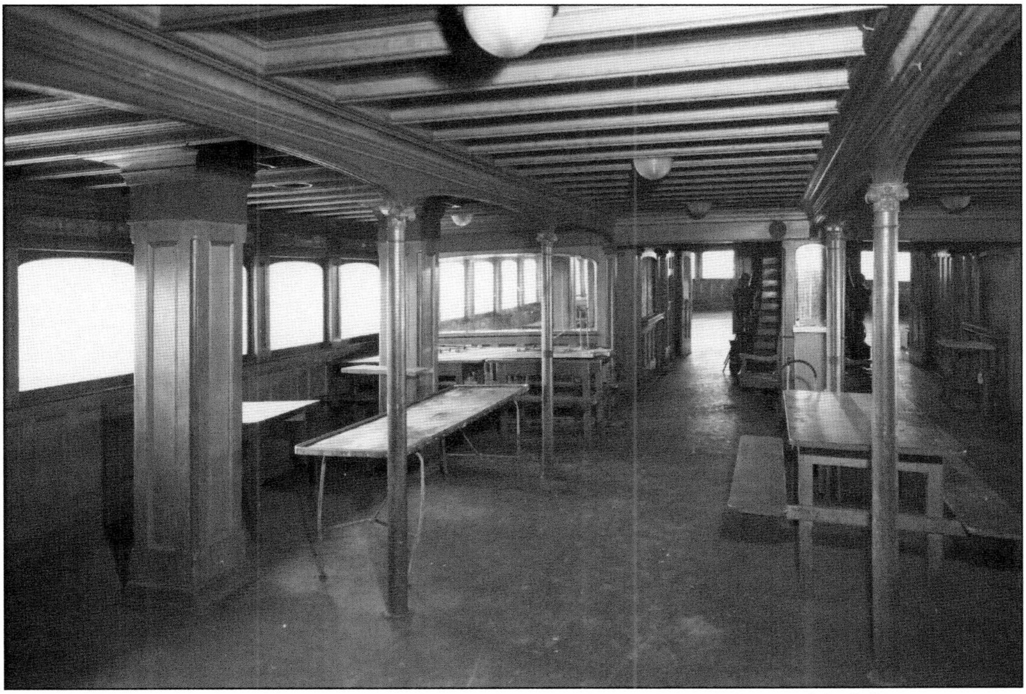

After US Navy service during World War II and 13 months as part of the mothball fleet on Suisun Bay, the *Delta King* needed a bit of sprucing up to be ready to resume civilian work. Times had changed, however, and she never steamed up again. (Courtesy Sacramento Public Library.)

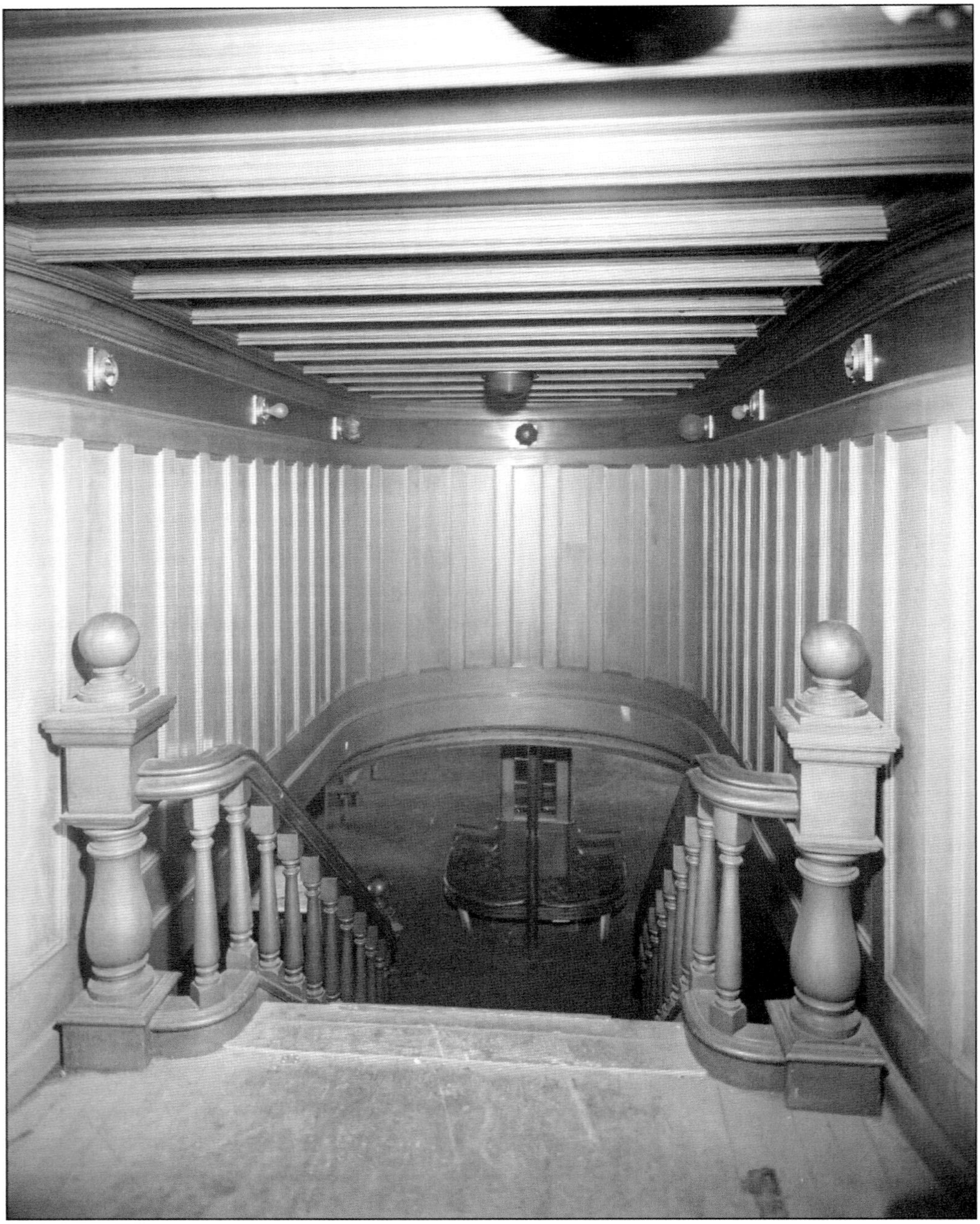

Navy gray paint could not mask the elegance of the *Delta King*'s staircase. Thirty-seven days had passed since the *Delta Queen* had begun her journey to the Mississippi River, and it would be another 42 years before the *Delta King* would have a permanent home at Sacramento. (Courtesy Sacramento Public Library.)

## *Three*

# Upriver from Sacramento

North of Sacramento and the confluence of the Sacramento and American Rivers, the Sacramento is fed by the Feather and Yuba Rivers. Above Colusa, the Sacramento has a meandering course with enough twists and turns to inflict lumbago on an eel. From Red Bluff north to Redding, there usually was not enough water depth, except after a rare snowmelt in the Cascade Range, to sustain riverboating on a regular basis. Therefore, for all practical purposes, Red Bluff remained the head of navigation on the Sacramento River. Upriver from Sacramento were found the smaller, more shallow draft sternwheelers that could better maneuver the river's course. They were also more able to go in and out of brush landings where trees served as dolphins and wooden planks reaching from the riverboat's bow to the levee served as gangplanks for loading and off-loading. Between Sacramento and Red Bluff, as well as on the San Joaquin upriver from Stockton (although to a lesser extent) were traders, or trader boats, which stopped just about anywhere on the river where there was a farm or town where trading was done. Trader boats were, in effect, miniature supermarkets on water where people could obtain just about anything from ploughs to cotton thread in exchange for farm products such as eggs, honey, hams, fruit, or vegetables, not to mention hides or wild animal pelts. The traders usually worked from Monday through Saturday. However, their captains were not always opposed to working on the Sabbath if a lodge, association, or any other group wanted to charter a boat for an excursion. One simply went where the money was. This also had the effect of providing recreation before the days of freeways speeding people to amusement parks, sports stadiums, or other diversions.

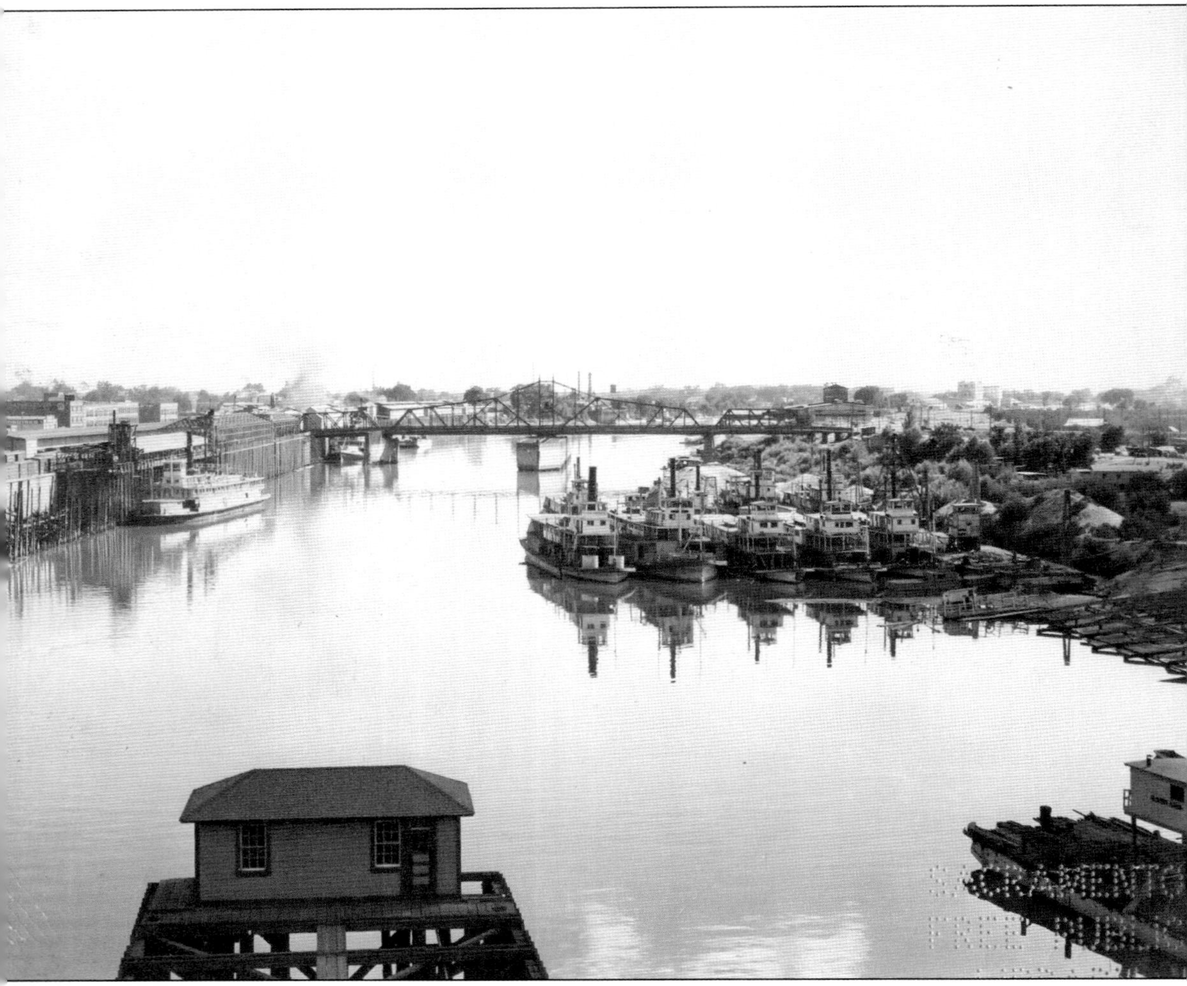

The photographer in 1904 was facing south on the Sacramento River, from around Sacramento's J to M Streets. At right, riverboats tied up at Broderick are, from left to right, *San Joaquin No. 2*, unidentified, *Dover*, unidentified, *Jacinto*, and a barge. In the lower right is the barge *Richland*. (Courtesy Sacramento Public Library.)

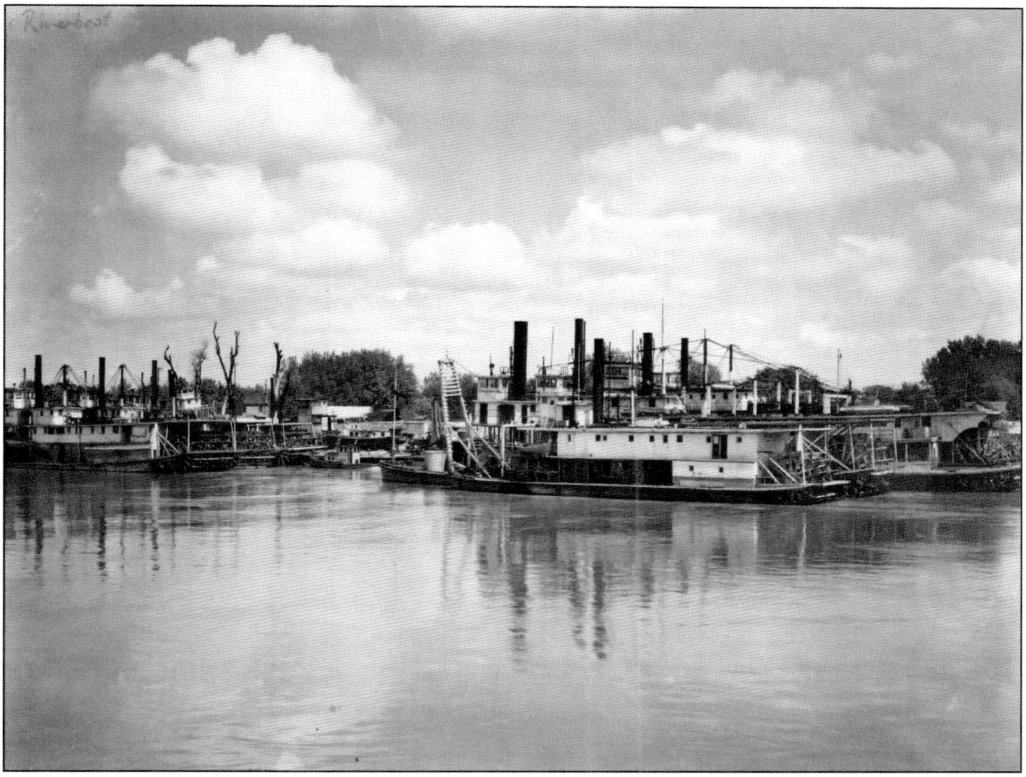

The 101-foot *San Jose* (left, front) was built in 1898 and served on the Sacramento and Napa Rivers. She was lost in the 1932 fire at Broderick. Also, seen here are *San Joaquin No. 2*, *Dover No. 2*, *Red Bluff*, a tugboat, barge *Montana*, and *Sentinel*, lost in a 1919 fire. (Courtesy California State Library.)

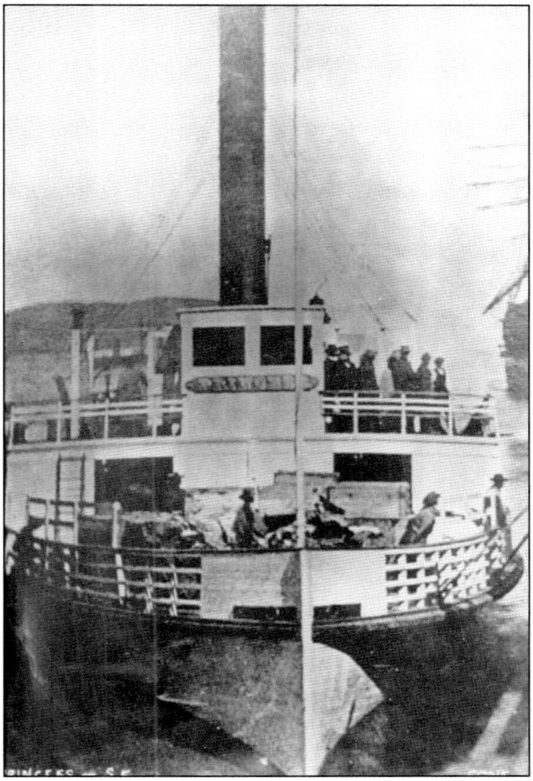

Most published pictures of the 1859-built *Princess* are on page 18. This rare image shows the *Princess*'s bow, looking aft. While better known for her ferryboat services between 1868 and 1875, she worked upriver from Sacramento when those days were over and was broken up in 1881. (Courtesy Western Railway Museum Archives, No. 49503.)

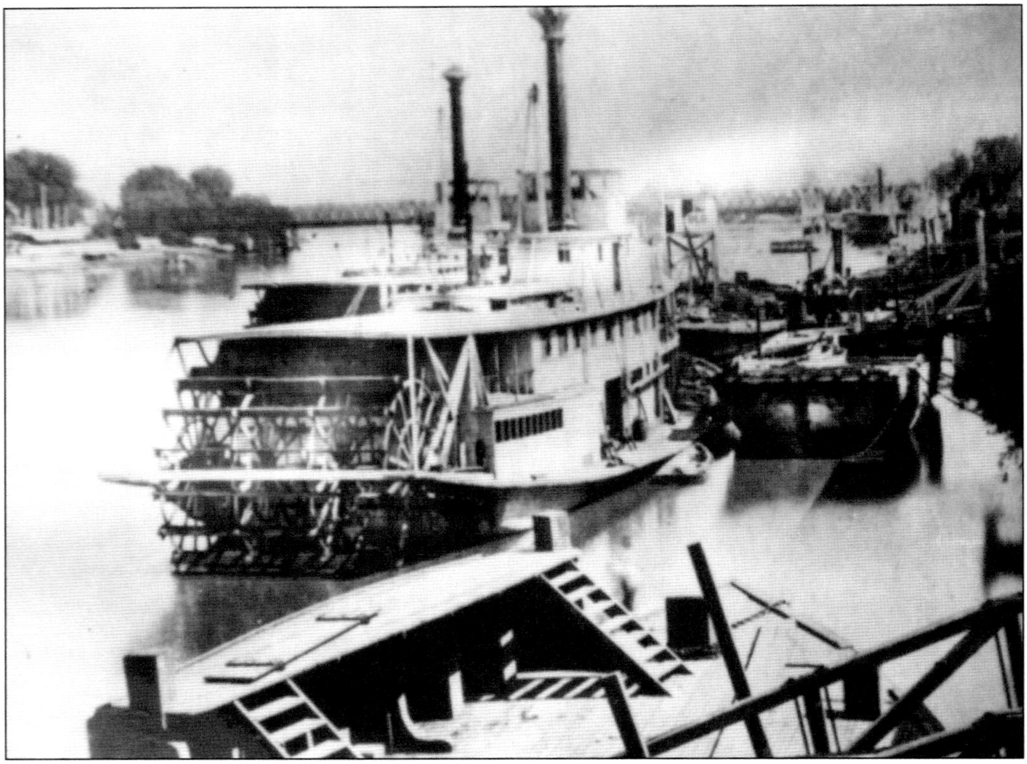

This view shows the *Dover I* tied up at Sacramento. Built in 1869, this 183.64-ton sternwheeler went off documentation prior to 1885. The large, bulb-like screen atop her stack is a spark arrester designed to prevent fires, particularly in the grain fields in summer. (Courtesy California State Library.)

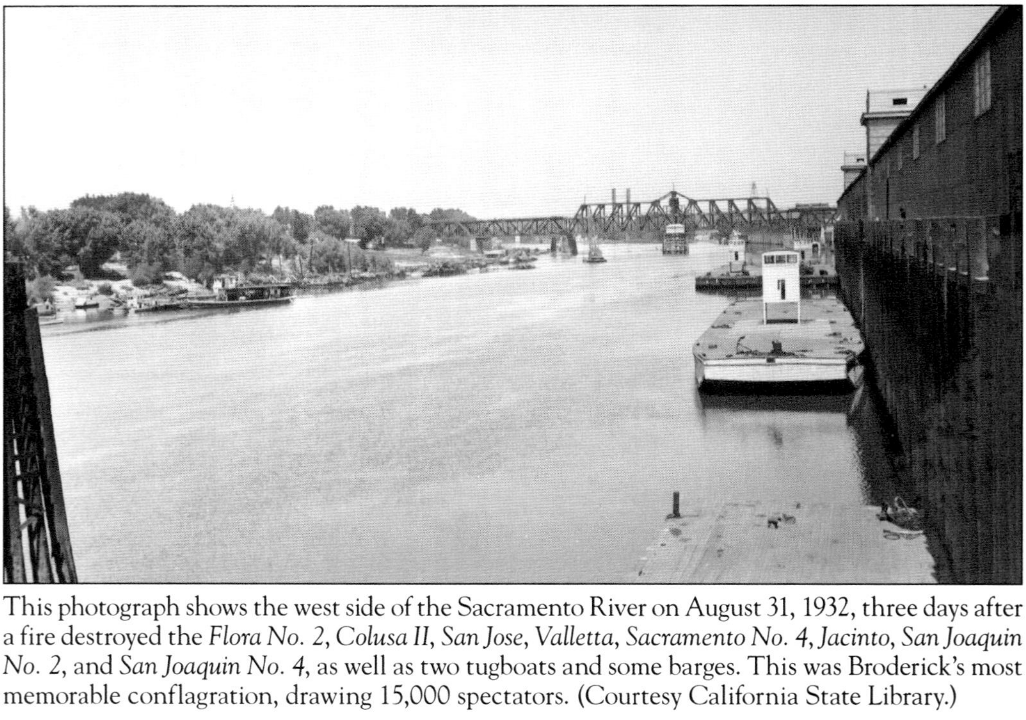

This photograph shows the west side of the Sacramento River on August 31, 1932, three days after a fire destroyed the *Flora No. 2*, *Colusa II*, *San Jose*, *Valletta*, *Sacramento No. 4*, *Jacinto*, *San Joaquin No. 2*, and *San Joaquin No. 4*, as well as two tugboats and some barges. This was Broderick's most memorable conflagration, drawing 15,000 spectators. (Courtesy California State Library.)

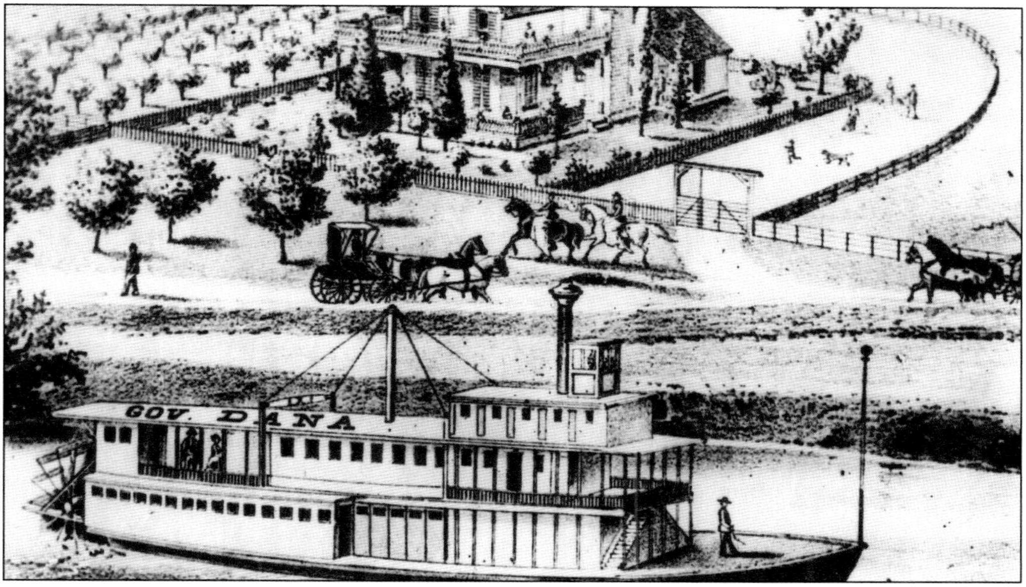


The *Governor Dana*, one of California's earliest riverboats, appears at the ranch of Joseph Gardner of Sutter County on the upper Sacramento River. Only 140 feet in length, she rated at 364 tons. She was built before 1850 and went off documentation before 1885. (Courtesy San Francisco Maritime National Historical Park, No. P83-013.2p.)

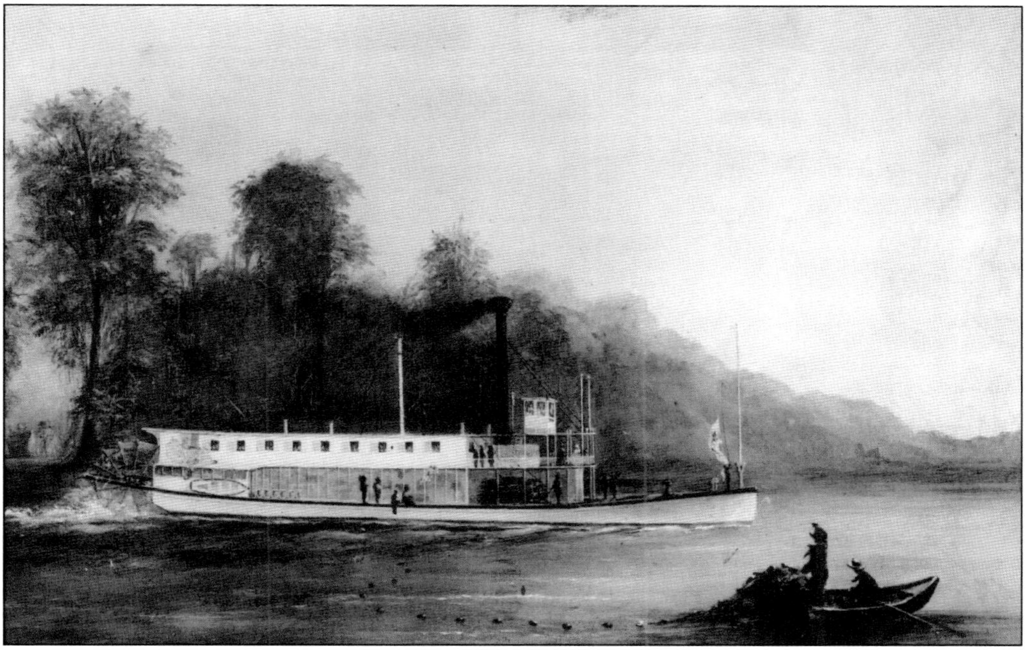

The sternwheeler *Governor Dana* was a 140-foot-long, 364.5 tonner that worked the upper Sacramento River, going off documentation sometime prior to 1885. In 1853, she was racing the *R.K. Page* on the Sacramento when the *R.K. Page*'s fireman "supplemented" her fuel with coal oil, precipitating another riverboat explosion. (Courtesy San Francisco Maritime National Historical Park, No. C7.14,657p1.)

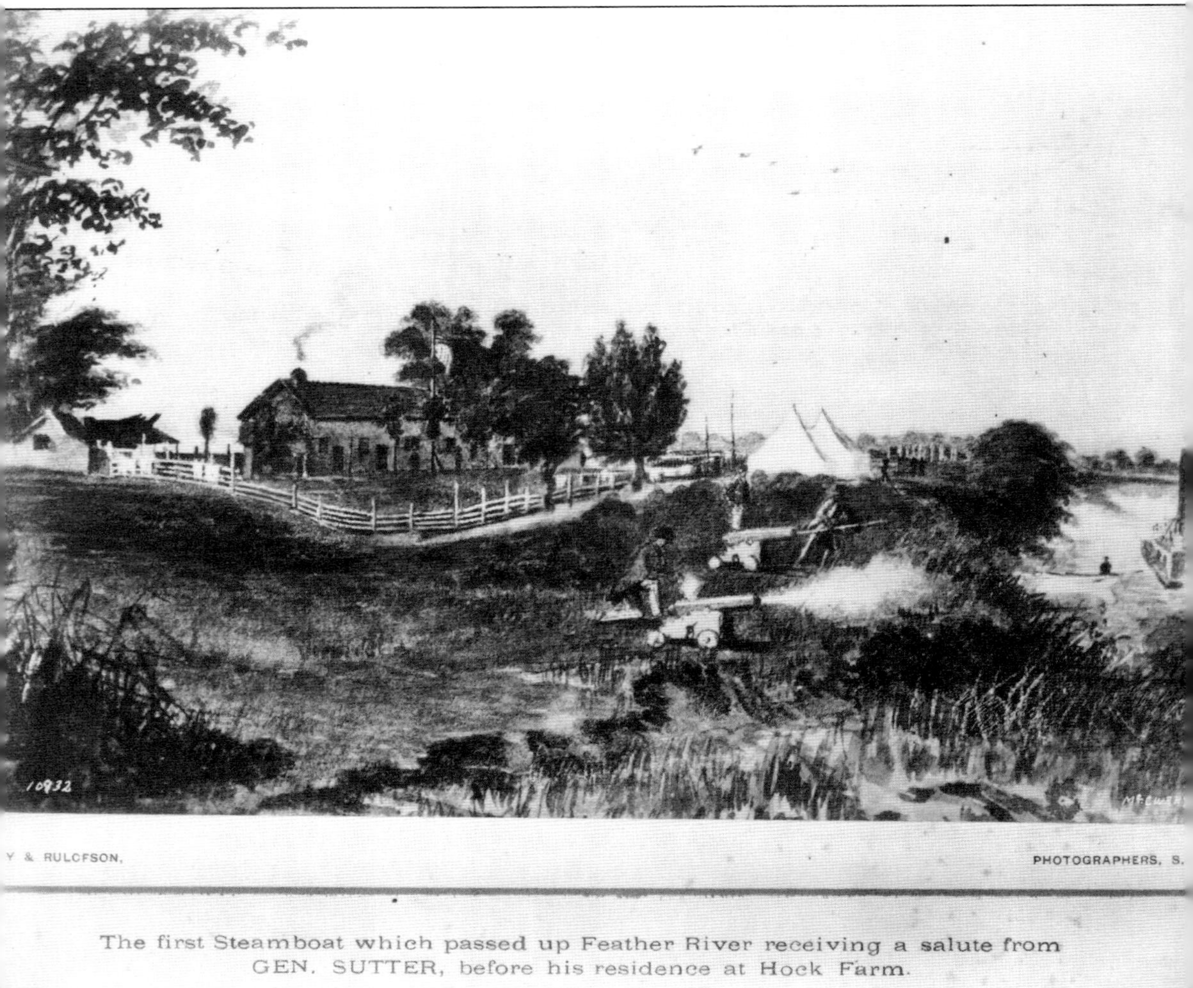


This is an artist's conception of the first steamboat on the Feather River, passing by John A. Sutter's Hock Farm, about eight miles south of Yuba City. The boat appears as a sternwheeler, but accounts attest her to have been the sidewheeler *Pioneer* (see page 8). The vessel may have been the sternwheeler *Lady Washington*, another pioneer riverboat. Either way, she is taking a salute from General Sutter for her contribution to California history. (Courtesy California State Library.)

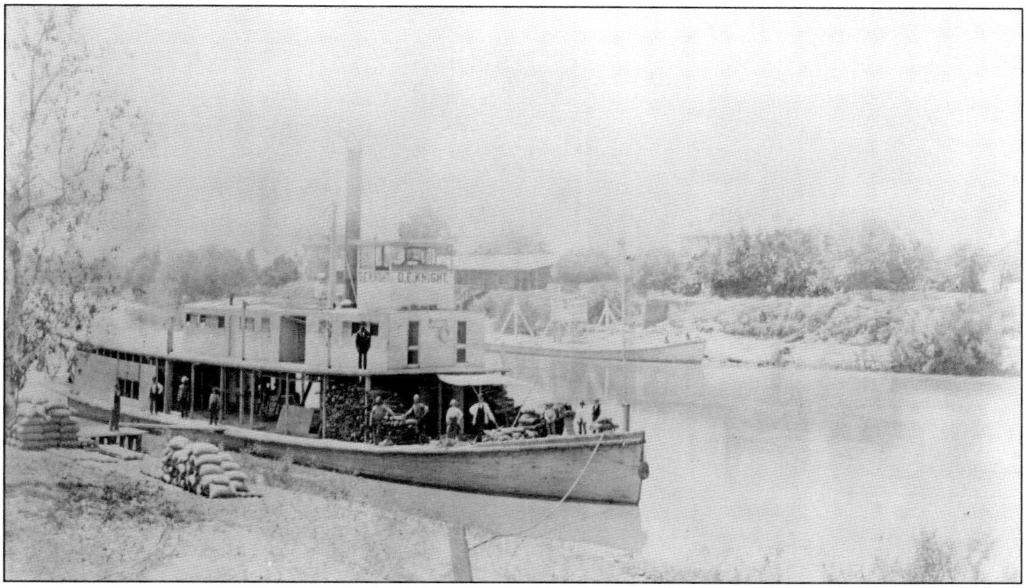


The sternwheeler *D.E. Knight* was built in 1875. This 131.5-foot-long, 199 tonner earned her keep by putting in along the Sacramento, picking up whatever business was at hand. Landings, such as the one seen here, were referred to as brush landings by riverboat men. (Courtesy Western Railway Museum Archives, No. 49519.)

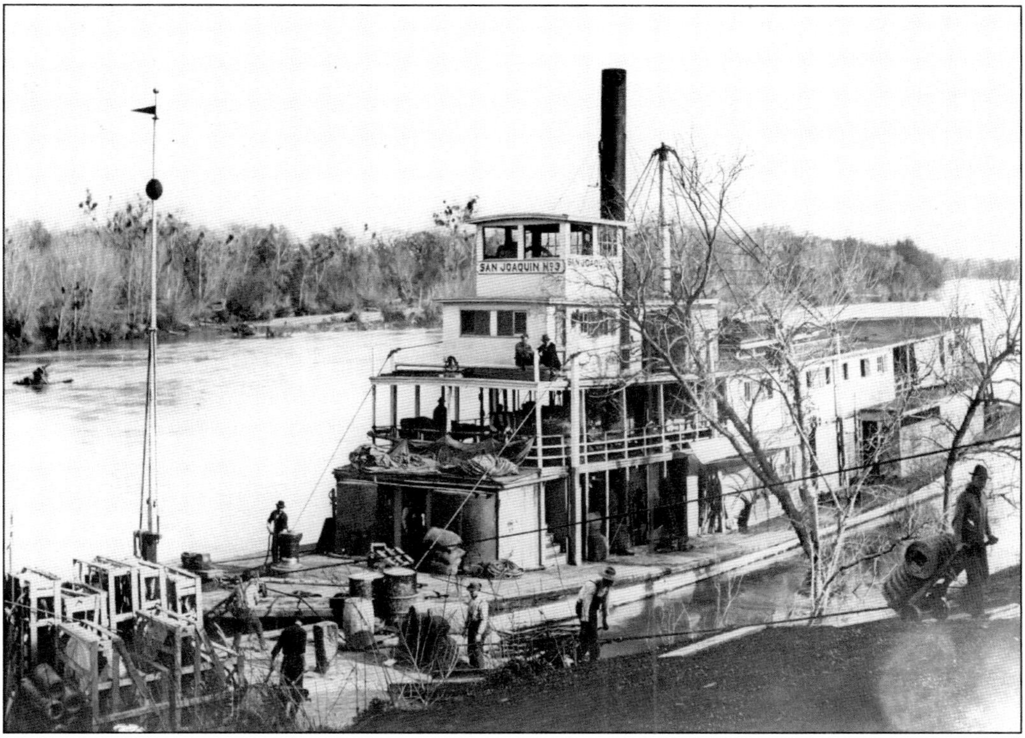


This pleasant scene shows the 148-foot-long *San Joaquin No. 3* off-loading cargo at a brush landing near Corning in Tehama County. The 220.95-ton *San Joaquin No. 3* was built in 1877. At the far left, a snag in the water is a trap for any riverboat pilot, especially at night. (Courtesy Western Railway Museum Archives, No. 49530.)

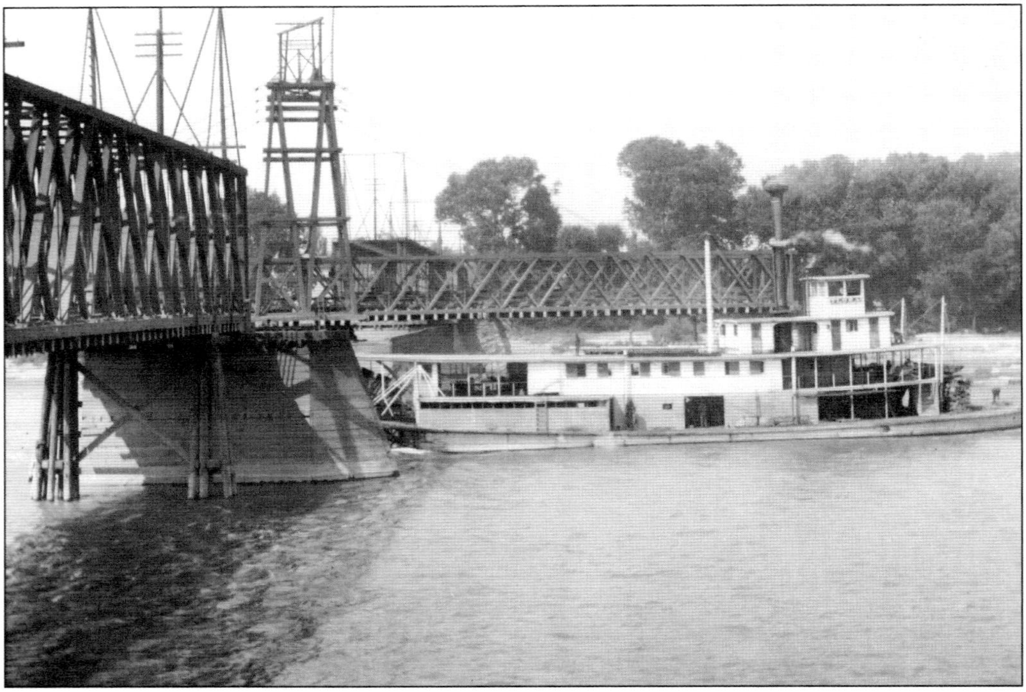

The *Flora II* is starting another trip on the upper Sacramento River. She was tied up at Broderick on the Yolo County side of the river and is passing under the Southern Pacific bridge, originally built by the Central Pacific Railroad. (Courtesy Richard Schlaich Collection.)

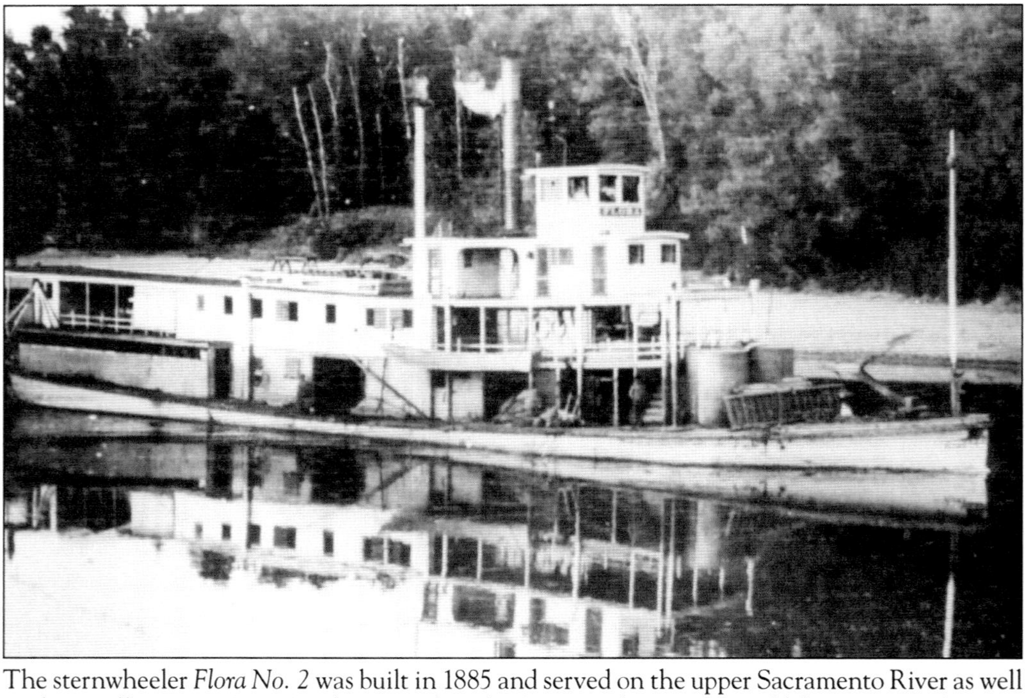

The sternwheeler *Flora No. 2* was built in 1885 and served on the upper Sacramento River as well as the smaller rivers. In 1931, she starred as the *Dixie* in the movie *Huckleberry Finn*. The next year, this 141-foot-long, 141 tonner was lost in the Broderick fire. (Courtesy Stocklmeir Library, California History Center, DeAnza College, Cupertino.)

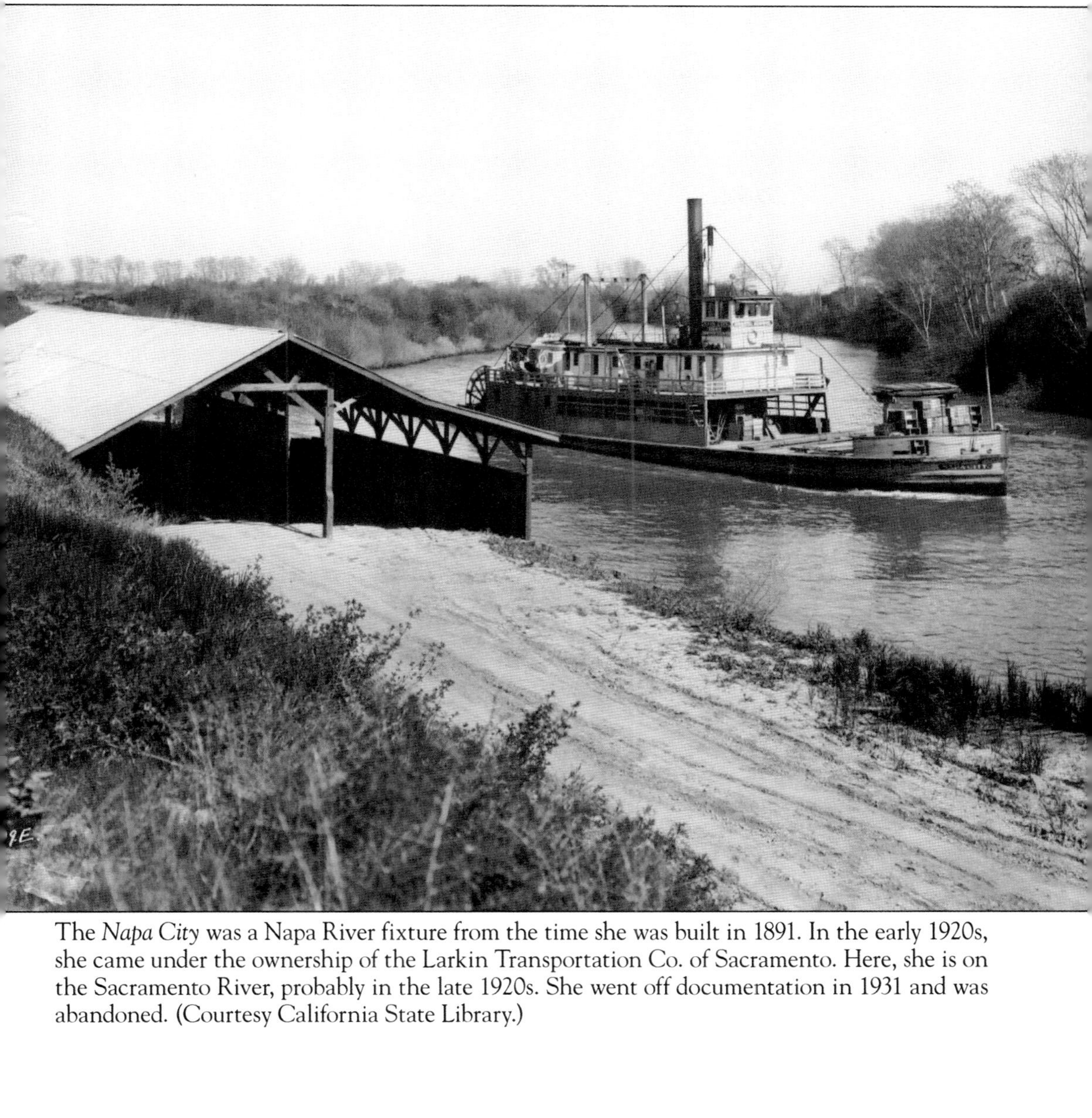

The *Napa City* was a Napa River fixture from the time she was built in 1891. In the early 1920s, she came under the ownership of the Larkin Transportation Co. of Sacramento. Here, she is on the Sacramento River, probably in the late 1920s. She went off documentation in 1931 and was abandoned. (Courtesy California State Library.)

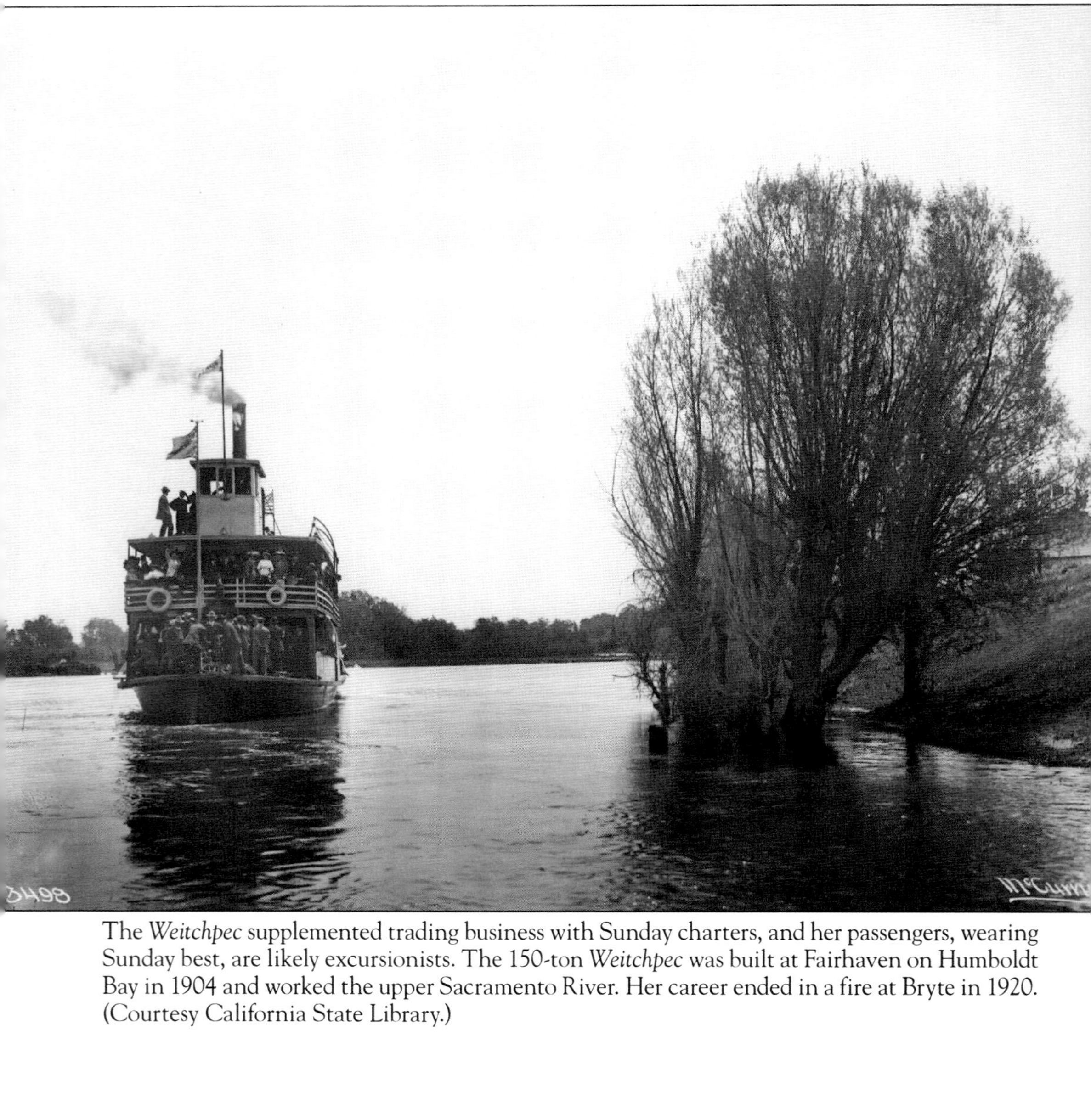

The *Weitchpec* supplemented trading business with Sunday charters, and her passengers, wearing Sunday best, are likely excursionists. The 150-ton *Weitchpec* was built at Fairhaven on Humboldt Bay in 1904 and worked the upper Sacramento River. Her career ended in a fire at Bryte in 1920. (Courtesy California State Library.)

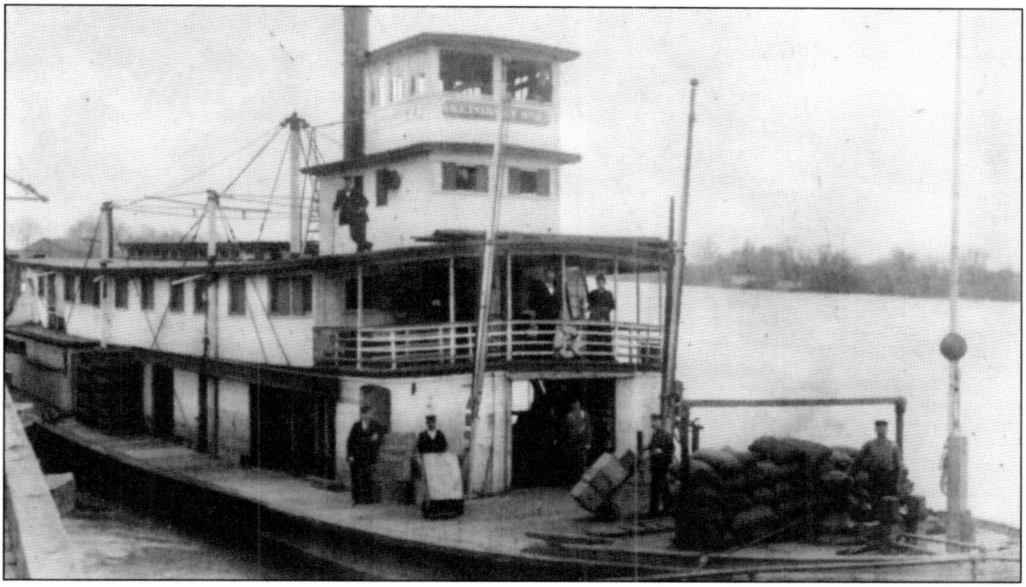

The *Neponset II*, built in 1884, was rated 224 tons, yet she was a mere 125.1 feet long. She was a trader, working upriver from Sacramento, stopping at any available landing for anyone with money or trading goods. She sank in Georgiana Slough on November 21, 1921, becoming the last California riverboat to be snagged. (Courtesy San Francisco Maritime National Historical Park, No. P88-074.1n.)

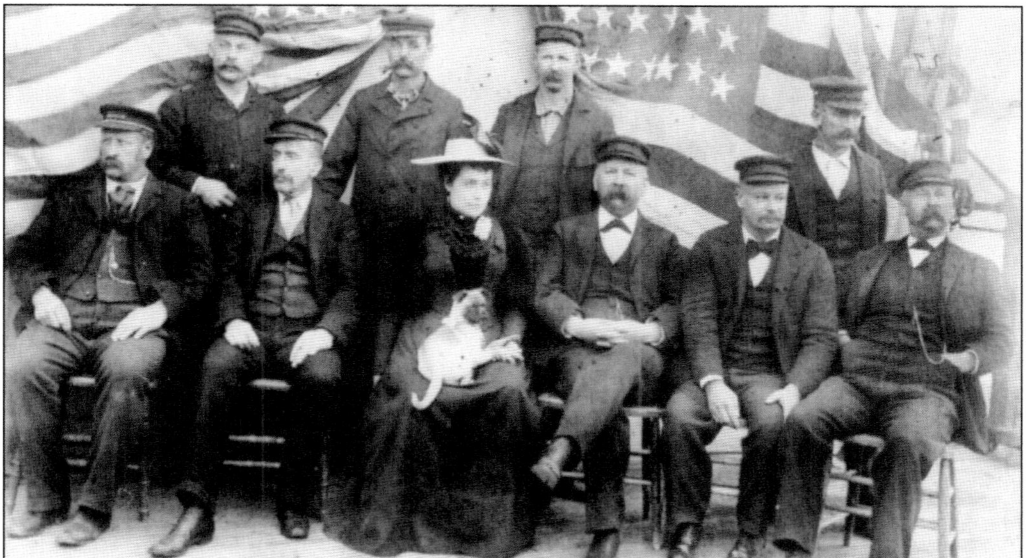

The hirsute crew of the *Neponset II* has assembled, recording for posterity that vests, ties, caps, and high-top shoes were also considered de rigueur. The lady could be the skipper's wife, as owner-captains sometimes brought their wives with them. (Courtesy San Francisco Maritime National Historical Park, No. P88-074.2n.)

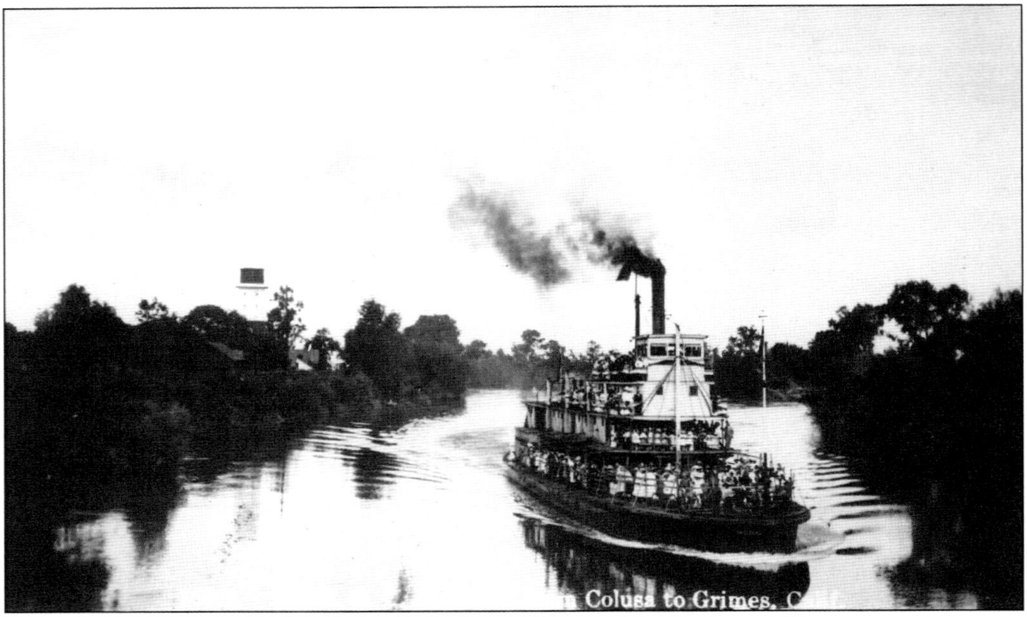


The *Valletta*'s decks are crowded with IOOF members on a 1910 picnic charter from Colusa to Grimes. During the era of the six-day workweek, one can assume that this picture was taken on a Sunday or a holiday. Also, regulations concerning passenger safety would be different today. (Courtesy San Francisco Maritime National Historical Park, No. P84-064n.)

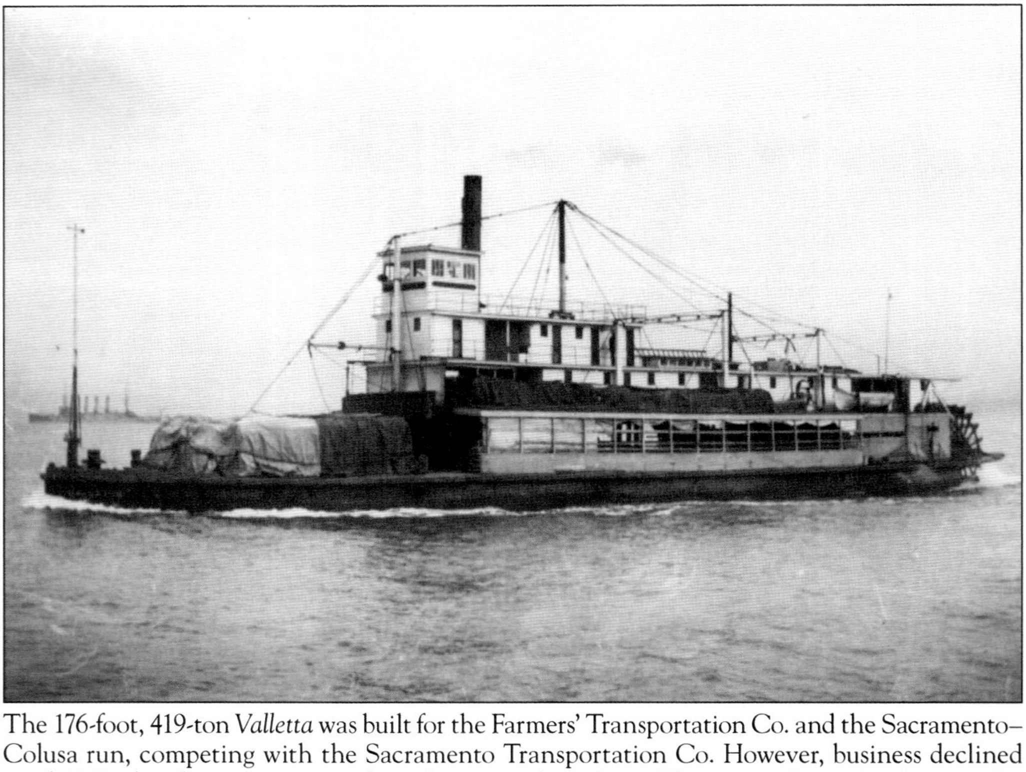

The 176-foot, 419-ton *Valletta* was built for the Farmers' Transportation Co. and the Sacramento–Colusa run, competing with the Sacramento Transportation Co. However, business declined until 1917 when by agreement each outfit removed one boat. They merged in 1920, forming the Sacramento Navigation Co. (Courtesy John Schmale Collection.)

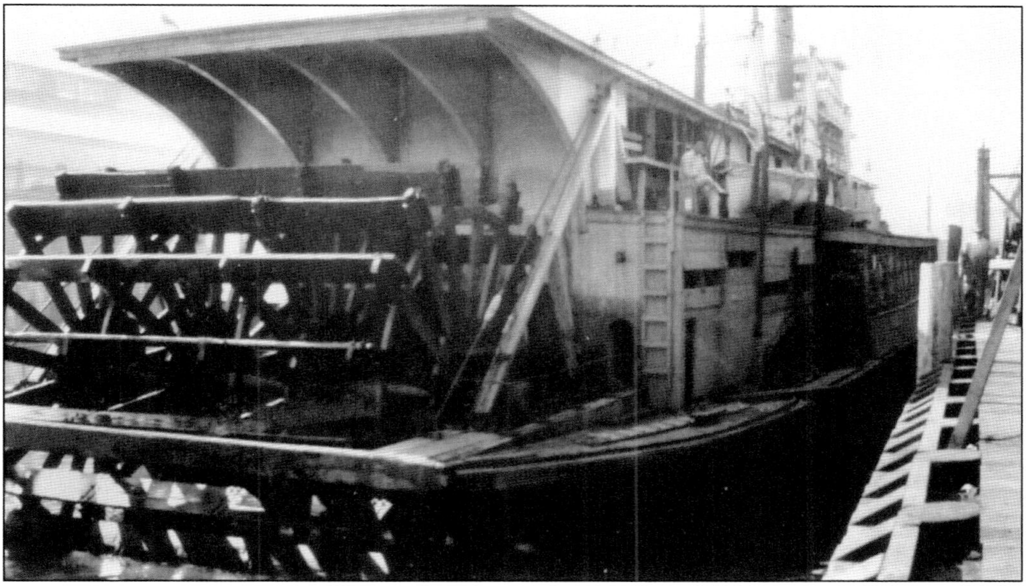

The sternwheeler *Valletta* is tied up at San Francisco, revealing a riverboat built more for freight efficiency than for passengers. The date is October 26, 1914, and the *Valletta* is far from her usual Sacramento–Colusa run, indicating an extent of her travel. (Courtesy San Francisco Maritime National Historical Park, No. P79-081.16p1.)

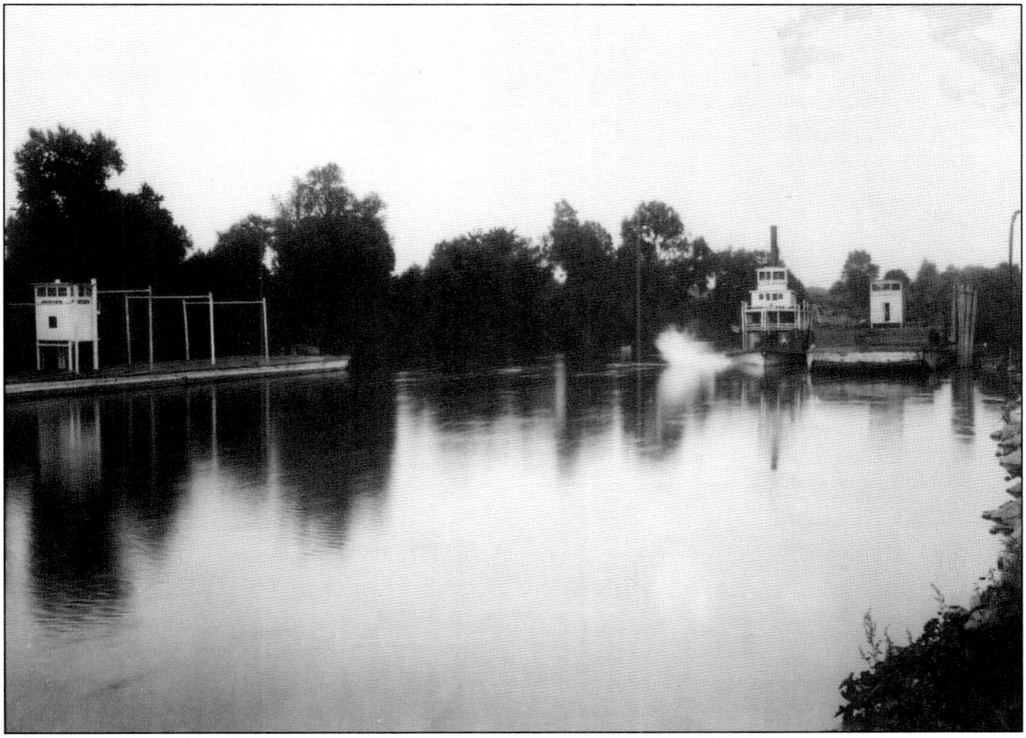

On the Sacramento in Colusa County, the 246-ton *Red Bluff III* passes the barges *Iowa* (left) and *Alabama* (right). Built in 1894 by the California Transportation Co. at Broderick, the *Red Bluff* was 150 feet long with a 3.2-foot draft. She escaped the Broderick fire only to be broken up in 1936. (Courtesy California State Library.)

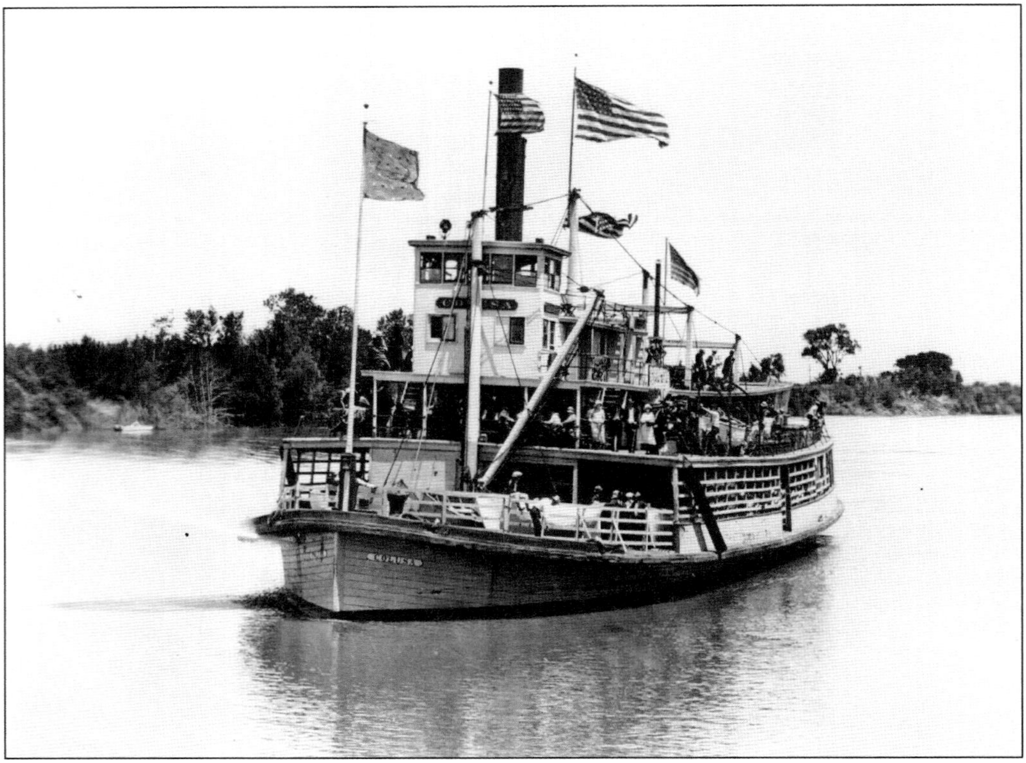

The second *Colusa* was built in 1911 by Schultz and Robertson of Sacramento and served upriver from Sacramento until succumbing to fire at Broderick on August 28, 1932, taking a fair fleet of riverboats, barges, and tugs with her. (Courtesy John Schmale Collection.)

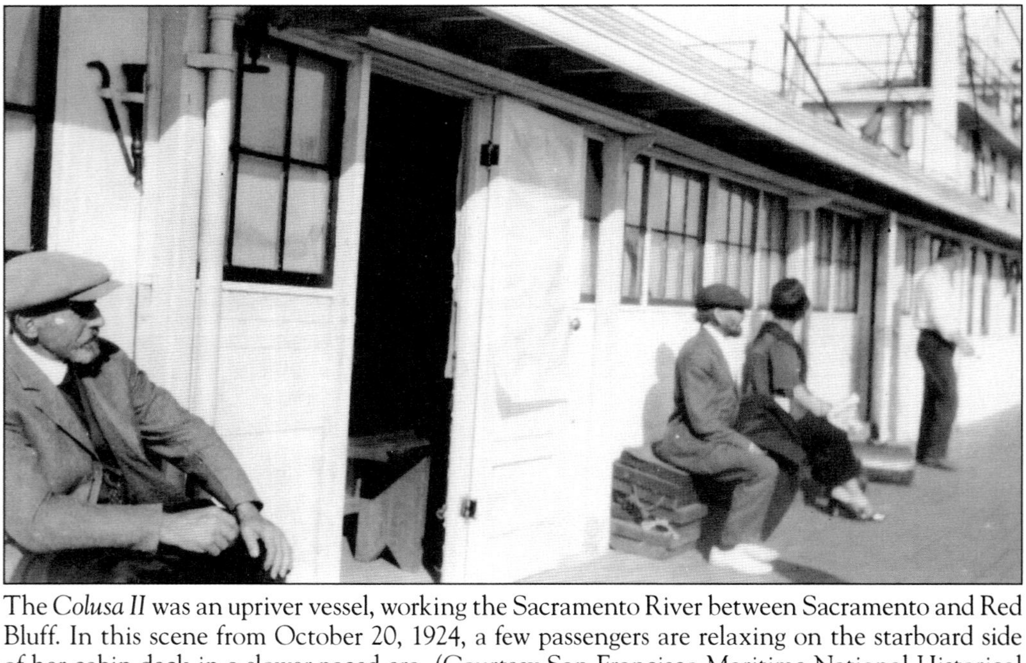

The *Colusa II* was an upriver vessel, working the Sacramento River between Sacramento and Red Bluff. In this scene from October 20, 1924, a few passengers are relaxing on the starboard side of her cabin deck in a slower-paced era. (Courtesy San Francisco Maritime National Historical Park, No. P79-089a.122p1.)

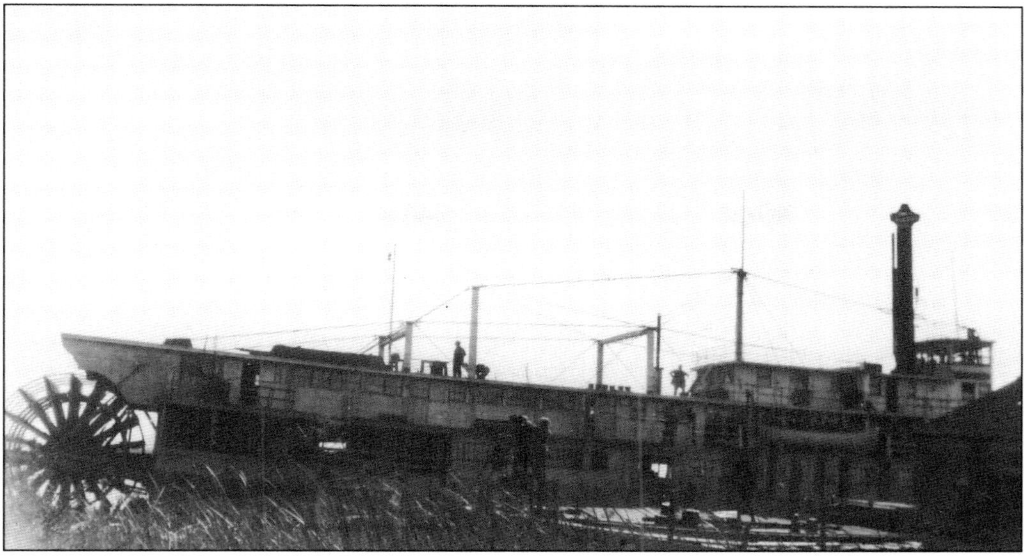

The 1911-built *Colusa II* rated 795 tons to go with her 177.5-foot length. The length of her cabin deck reveals that she carried passengers, but the money was in freight. Later pictures show the bulkheads removed from the aft half of her cabin deck for freight purposes. (Courtesy San Francisco Maritime National Historical Park, No. P79-089a.123p1.)

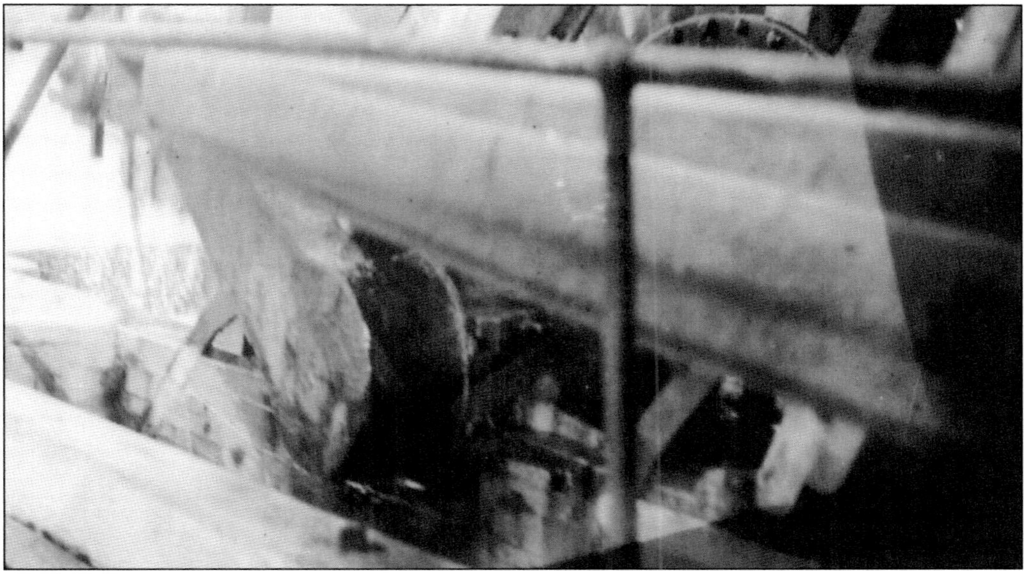

Cranks and shafts connected to the *Colusa II*'s engine turned the axle of her paddle wheel. It seems simple enough, but the engine works made it a bit complicated. Yet, the *Colusa* was a reliable craft until idled by the Great Depression at Broderick, where she burned in 1932. (Courtesy San Francisco Maritime National Historical Park, No. P79-089a.123p1.)

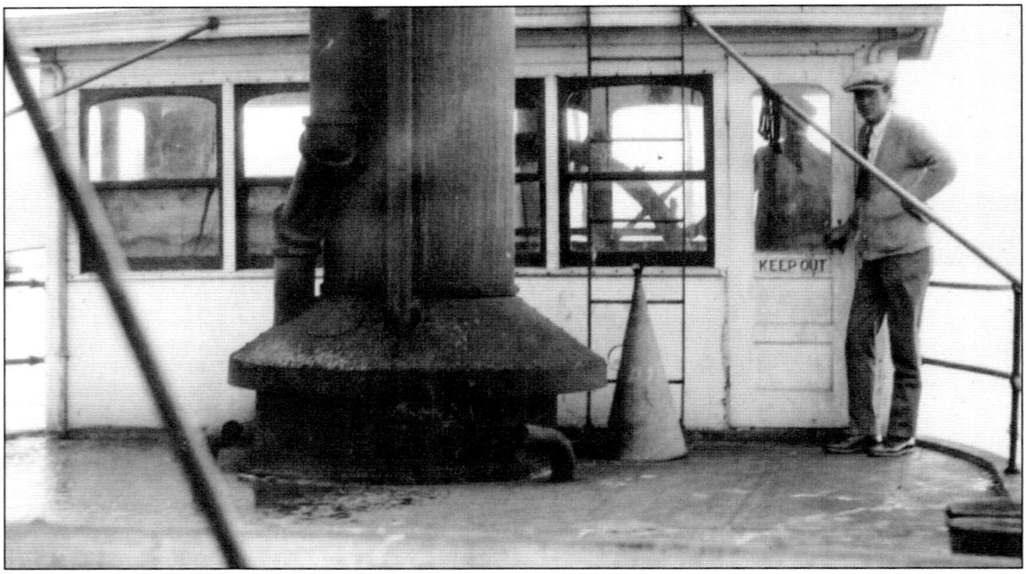


This October 20, 1924, photograph was taken from atop the texas deck of the *Colusa II*, looking inside the wheelhouse. Of importance is the "KEEP OUT" sign. Piloting a riverboat was a serious matter, and pilots were expected to tend to business and not engage in idle conversation. (Courtesy San Francisco Maritime National Historical Park, No. P79-089a.128pl.)

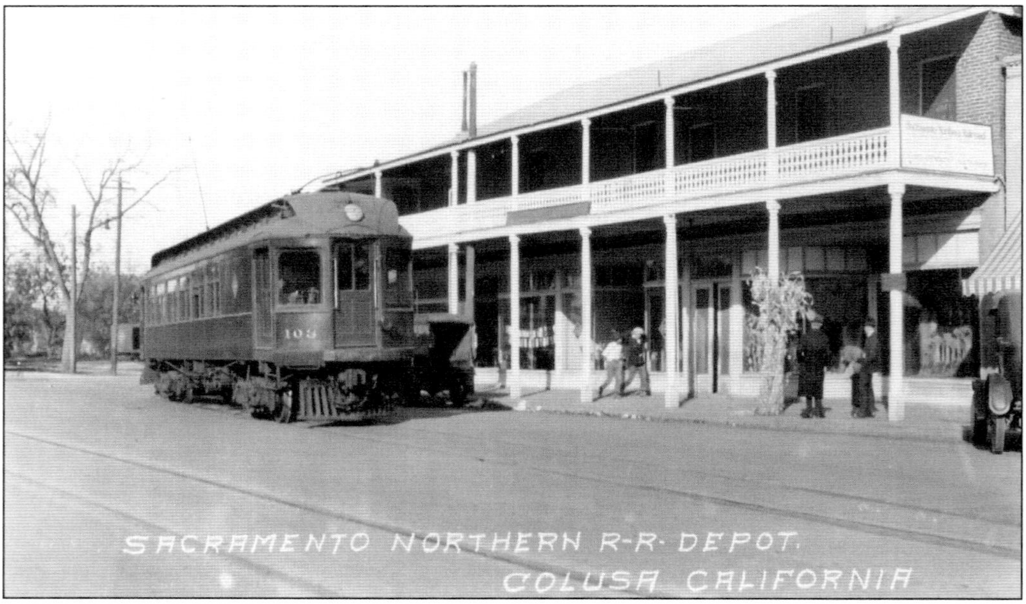


It is hard to believe in this day of the ubiquitous automobile that the small town of Colusa (population 5,892) was once served not only by the upriver steamers between Sacramento and Red Bluff but by the Southern Pacific's steam trains and the Sacramento Northern's electric interurbans as well. (Author's collection.)

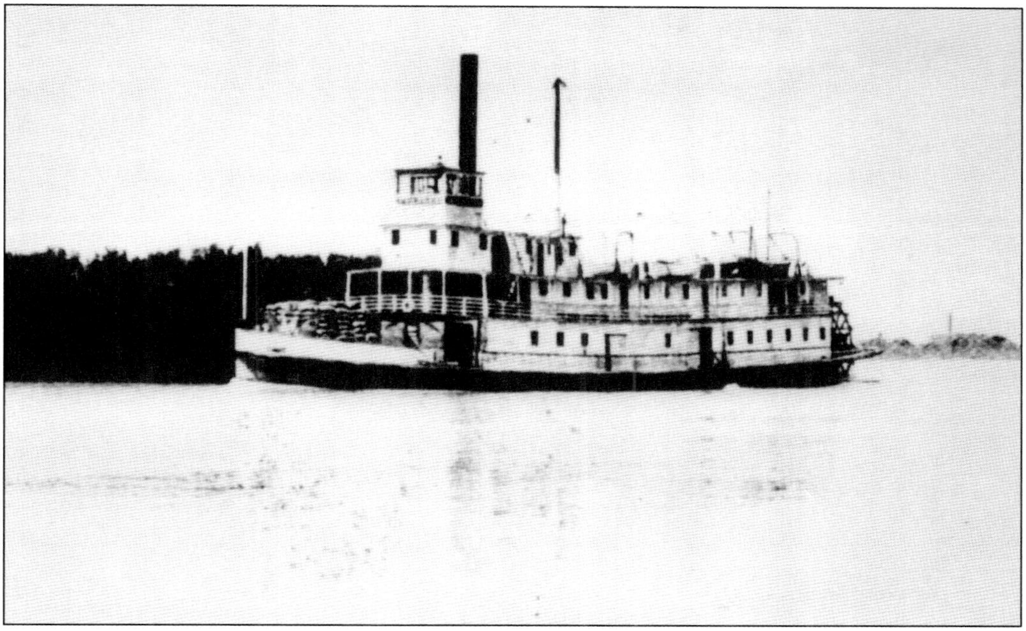

It is unknown why some riverboats with a relatively short life are so well known or photographed while others, such as the 145-foot-long *Aurora* seen here (which rated at 406 tons and lasted from 1885 until abandoned in 1932), are comparatively unknown or rarely photographed. (Courtesy California State Library.)

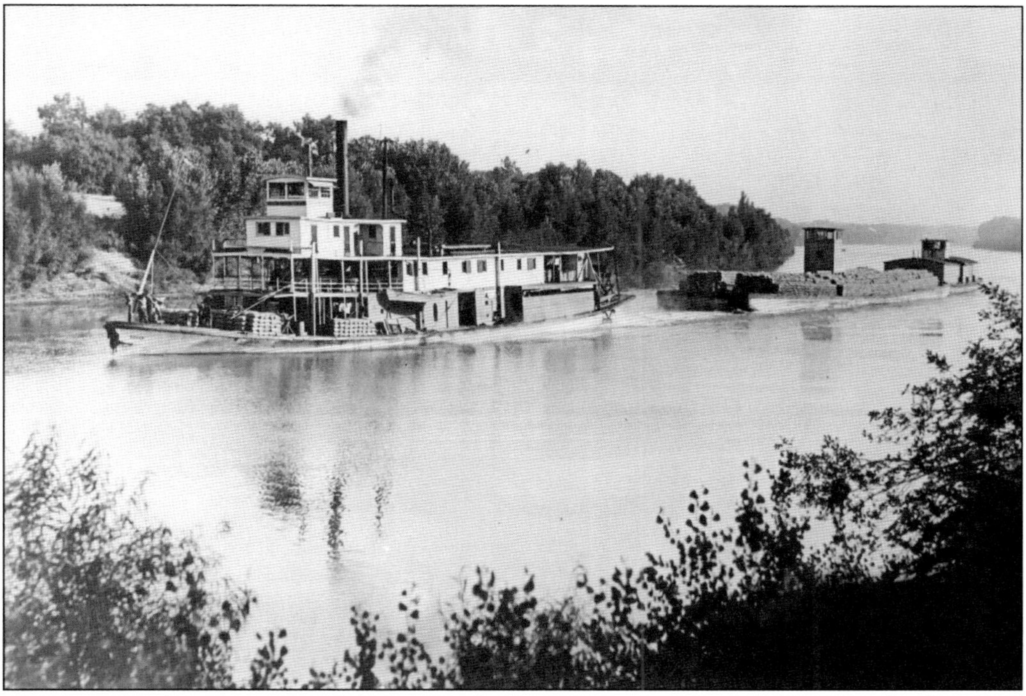

The *Dover II*, shown towing two barges on the Sacramento River c. 1931, was 150 feet long and rated at 244 tons. Built in 1891, she was one of only two riverboats to survive the Broderick fire in 1932—the other being the *Red Bluff*. The *Dover II* was broken up in 1935. (Courtesy Sacramento Public Library.)

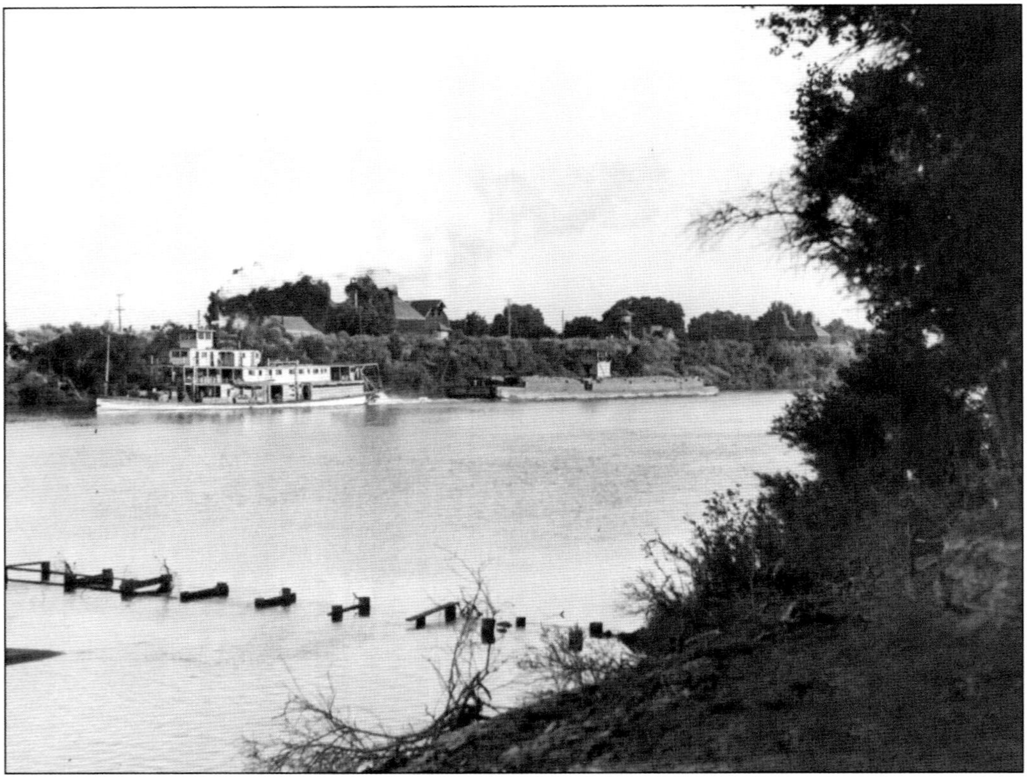

Towing barges with produce from Northern California farms and ranches was profitable. Barges were less labor intensive than riverboats and kept many riverboats in business. Seen above, the *Jacinto* is towing a fully loaded barge on the Sacramento River in the 1930s. (Courtesy Sacramento Public Library.)

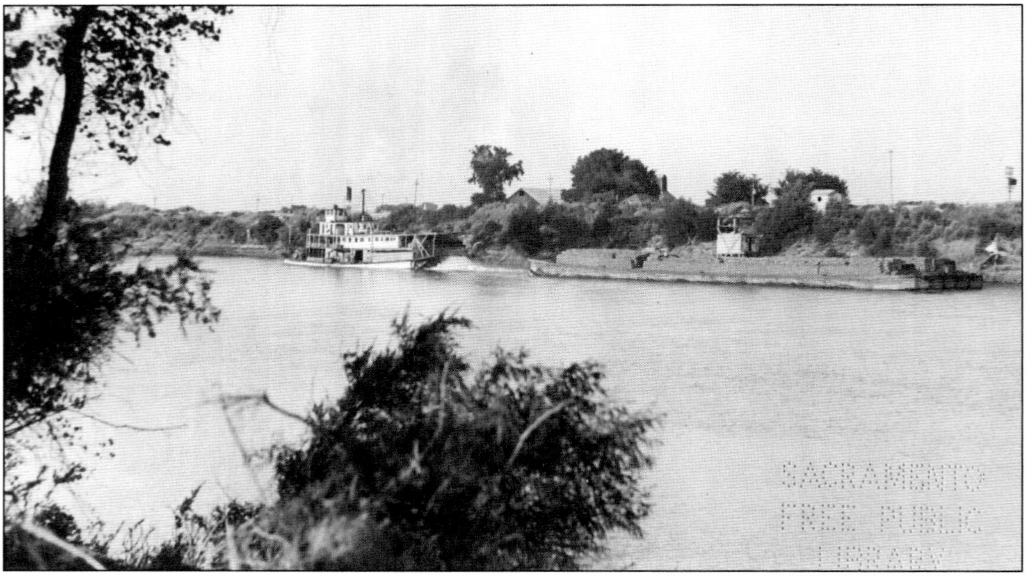

The *Jacinto* was a freighter, offering affordable and reliant transport for Northern California's farms and ranches. The barges' amidships structures were wheelhouses where helmsmen steered the barges, making tows more energy efficient and cost effective. (Courtesy Sacramento Public Library.)

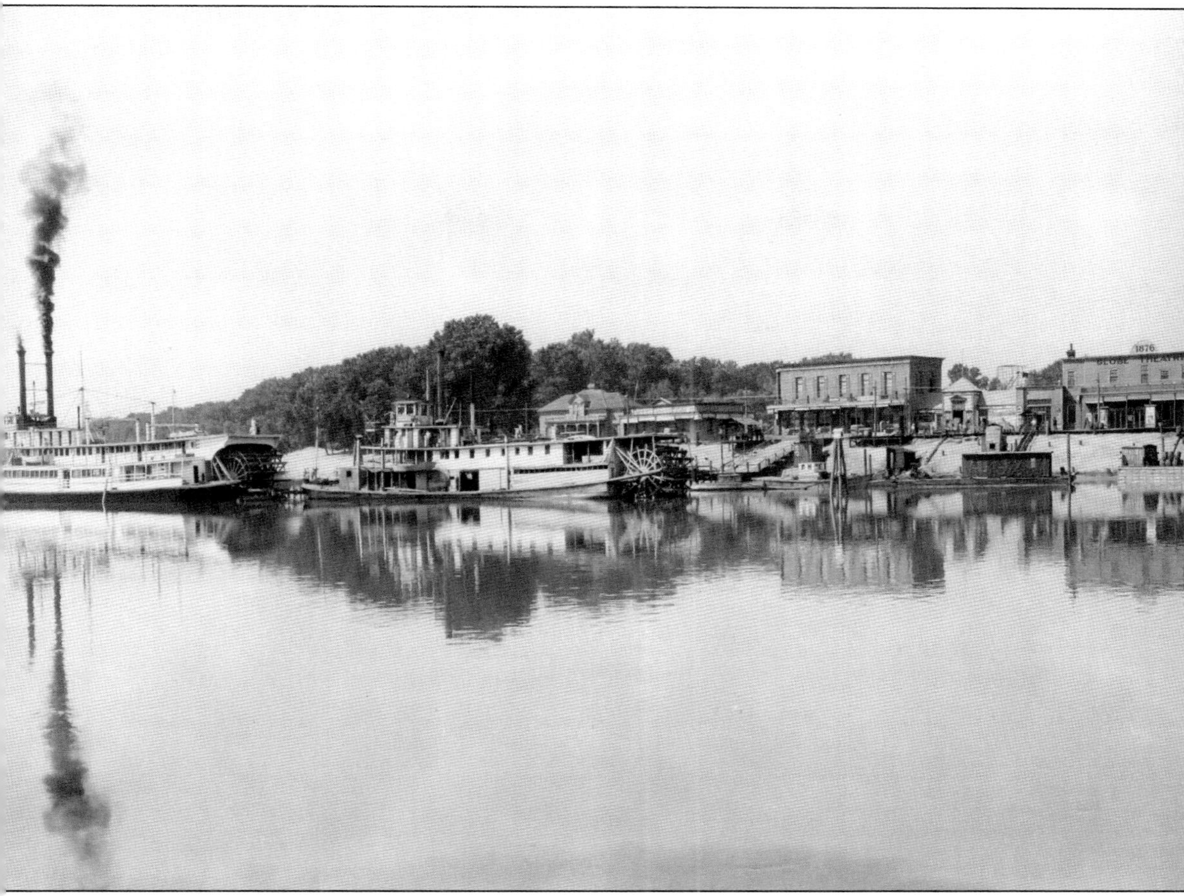

Hollywood studios found the Sacramento River an ideal location for filming movies involving riverboats. Here, two riverboats are on the Sacramento River near where the movie *Steamboat Bill Jr.* was made in 1927. The twin stacks are fake, making the *Port of Stockton* resemble a Mississippi packet. (Courtesy Sacramento Public Library.)

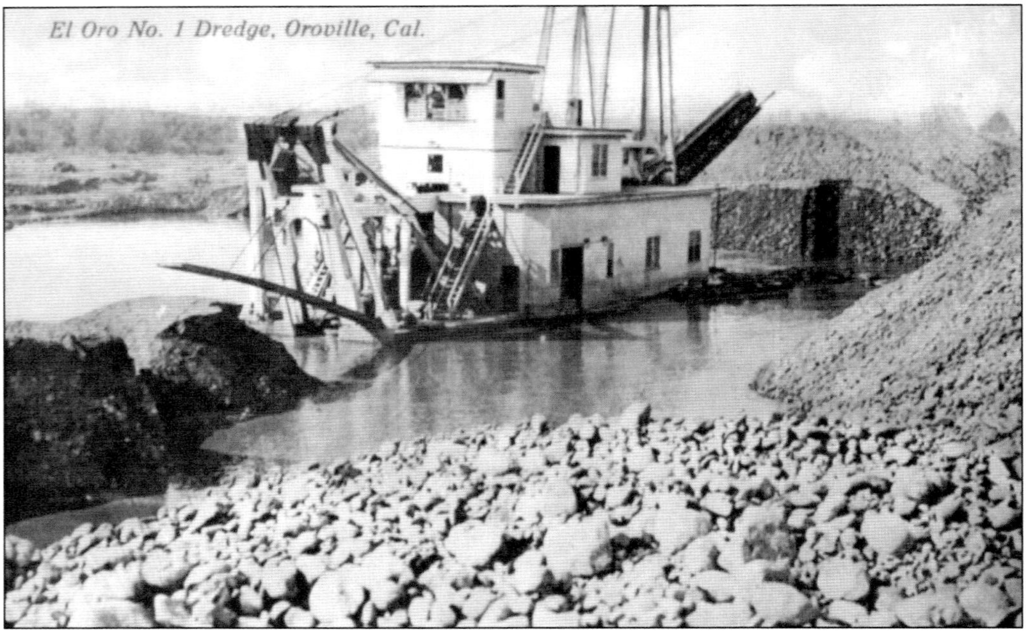


The environmental disaster of hydraulic mining literally dumped hills of silt and gravel into the Sacramento River, clogging lanes and leaving unknown quantities of gold in the river's bottom. The dredge *El Oro No. 1* is trying to open the river while salvaging gold. (Author's collection.)

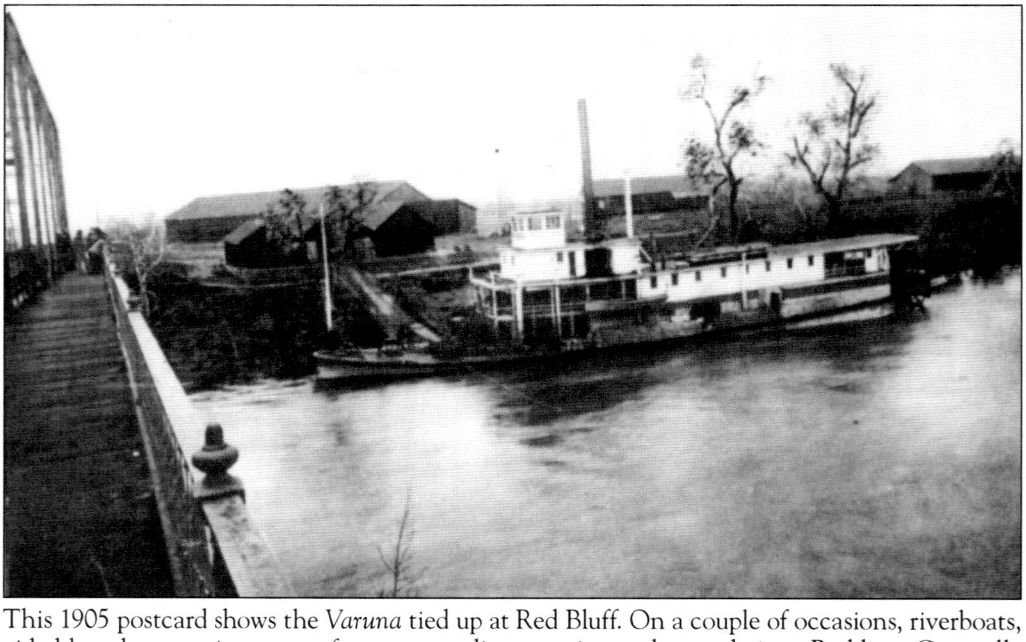

This 1905 postcard shows the *Varuna* tied up at Red Bluff. On a couple of occasions, riverboats, aided by adequate river water from extraordinary spring melts, made it to Redding. Generally speaking, however, Red Bluff, 270 miles from Sacramento and 304 feet above sea level, was the Sacramento River's head of navigation. (Courtesy San Francisco Maritime National Historical Park, No. I1.22,985p.)

# *Four*

# The San Joaquin River

The winter snowpacks in the Sierra Nevada Mountains feeding the San Joaquin and its tributaries were rarely equal to those in the same mountain range some 300 miles farther north as well as in the Cascade Range, which feeds the Sacramento River. Also, San Joaquin water was diverted for irrigating the vast grain fields that produced such prodigious yields, particularly wheat, which made riverboating prospects look good. Because of the diversions for irrigation, water levels dropped too low for either riverboats or barges. For all of that, there were regular runs to Watson's Ferry, 248 miles upriver from Stockton. During the high water period from January to July, riverboats could go past Firebough to Sycamore Point, 272 miles upriver from Stockton and about eight miles north of Fresno, where connections by stage to that city could be found. The *Tulare*, a 111.8 footer built in 1867, made regular trips for a while between San Francisco and Tuolumne City, and in this case, Stockton was merely an intermediate stop. Driven by Gold Rush demands, the *John A. Sutter* became the first known paddle wheel steamer to arrive at Stockton on November 15, 1849, delivering gold-hunting forty-niners. Less than a year before, Stockton had been known as Tuleberg, or Weber's Settlement, named for Capt. Charles M. Weber, a Swiss immigrant who founded the community. By 1850, the Delta was a busy place with boats going to Sacramento, while three boats a week were steaming between San Francisco and Stockton. As with the Sacramento–San Francisco runs, it was not unusual for a riverboat company to schedule four boats a day, two each to and from San Francisco. One boat would leave Stockton with a scheduled arrival time at San Francisco while another had only a scheduled departure, stopping off at every landing where business was to be had and arriving when the work was done. This was also the case for boats running between San Francisco and Stockton.

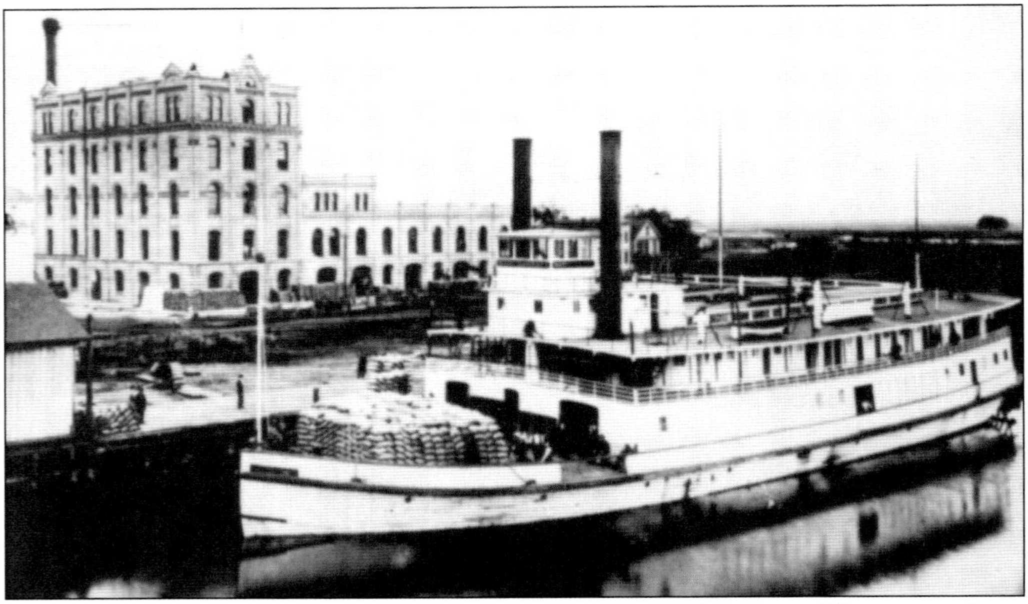

Built in 1878, the *Mary Garratt* was a fixture on the runs out of Stockton. This picture shows her in Stockton near Madison Street and Weber Avenue in the mid-1880s. She was one of the last twin stackers on Northern California's rivers before going off documentation around 1915. (Author's collection.)

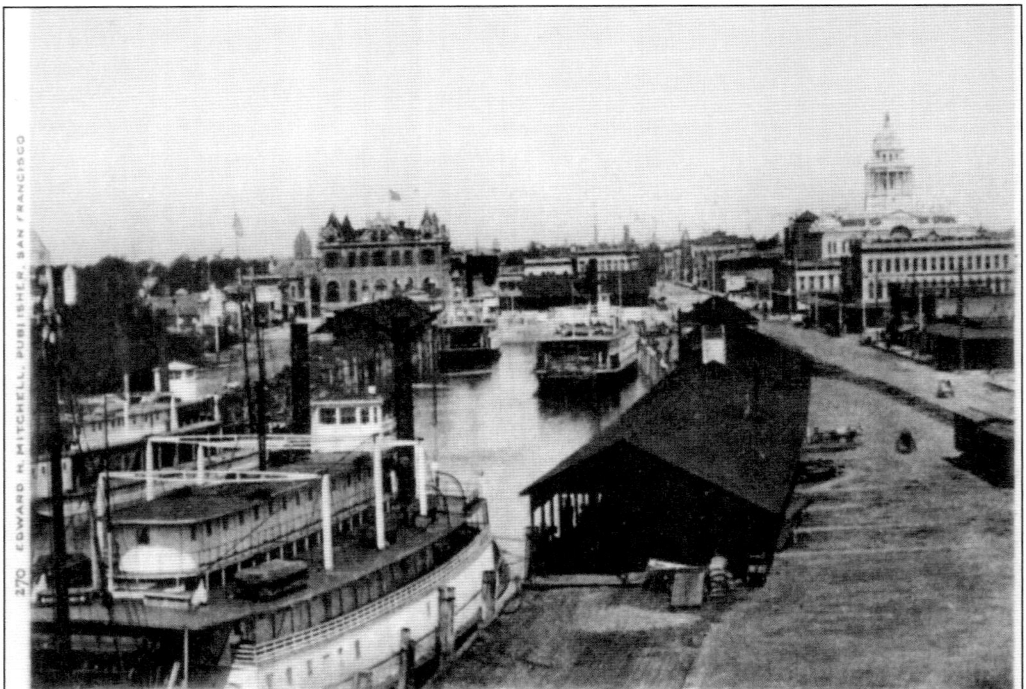


This undated postcard shows the Stockton Channel and a stern starboard view of the 200-foot-long, 786.9-ton *T.C. Walker II,* built in 1885. She was a twin stacker, rare among California riverboats. A November 27, 1888, explosion killed nine, destroying her forward superstructure. Once repaired, she served until abandoned in 1938. (Author's collection.)

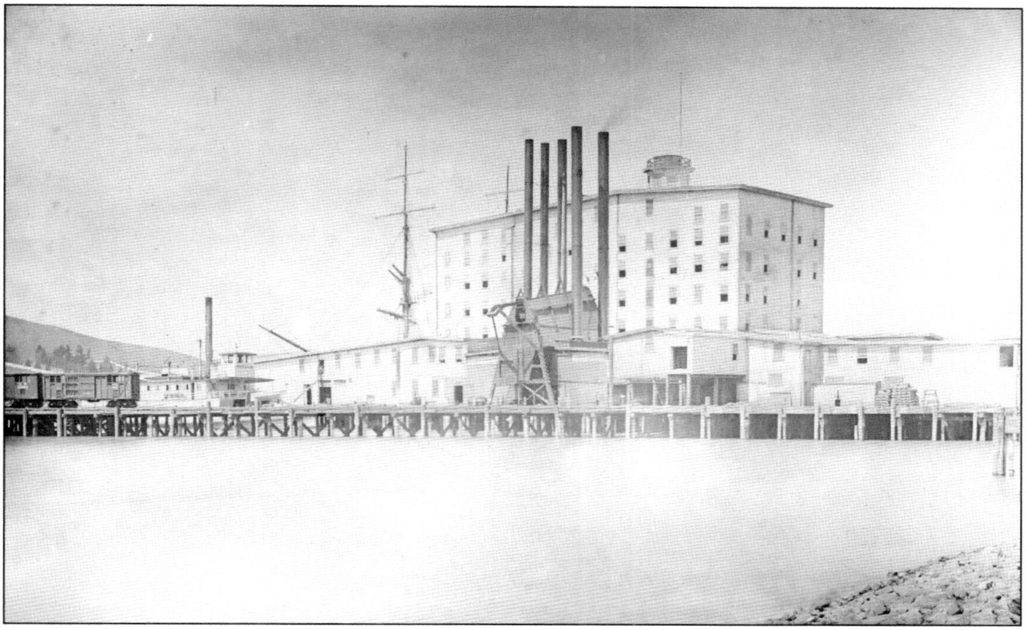

The *Herald* is shown at Stockton where she was built in 1878 by Stephen Davis. At left are two wooden freight cars of the Central Pacific Railroad, dating the picture as pre-1885. The *Herald* later served the Napa River trade before becoming a Southern Pacific riverboat. (Courtesy Western Railway Museum Archives, No. 49458.)

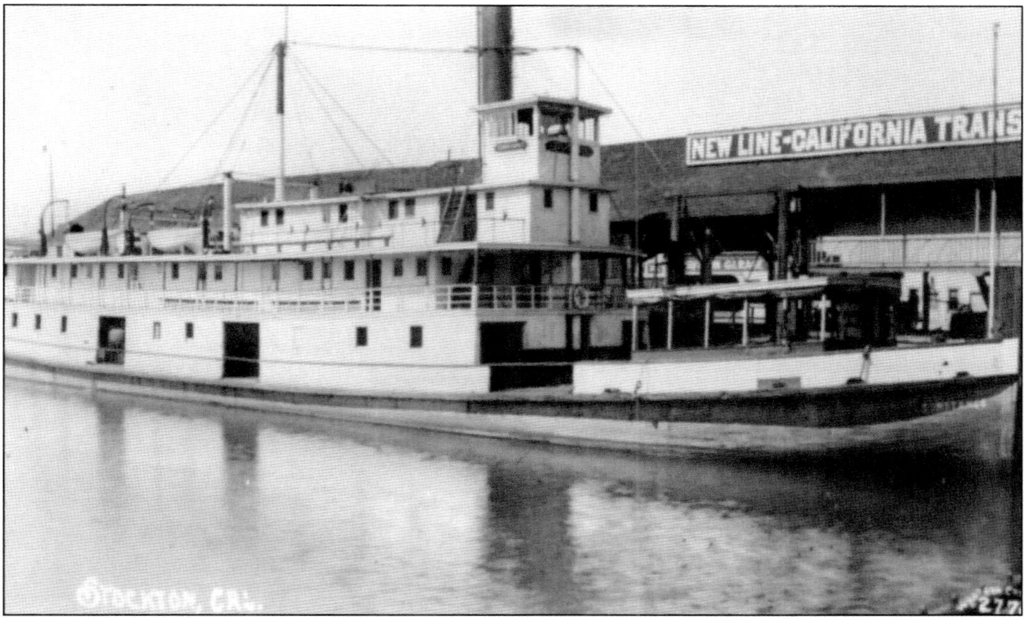


The *Constance* was built in 1874 and abandoned in 1918. She rated 422 gross tons, measured 161.5 by 32 by 5.6 feet, yet had a 29-horsepower engine. John Leale took command in 1876, making three trips per week on the Mokelumne River for the California Transportation Co. She carried passengers but mainly transported freight consisting mostly of potatoes and grain. (Courtesy San Francisco Maritime National Historical Park, No.P82-110.3n.)

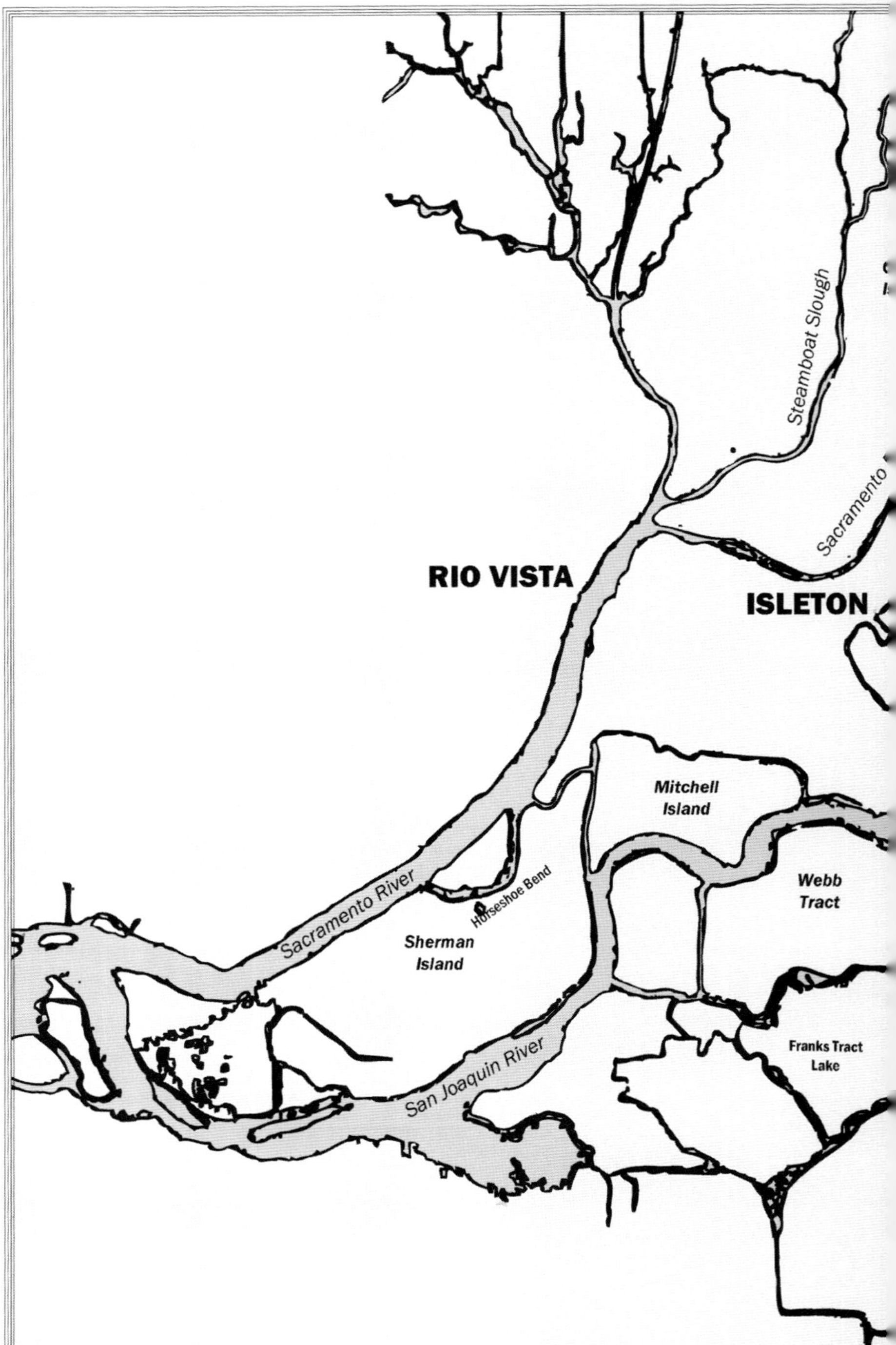


This map shows the twists and turns the San Joaquin River takes through the Delta between Stockton and the Sacramento River. The inset shows the riverboats' fartherest reach on the upper

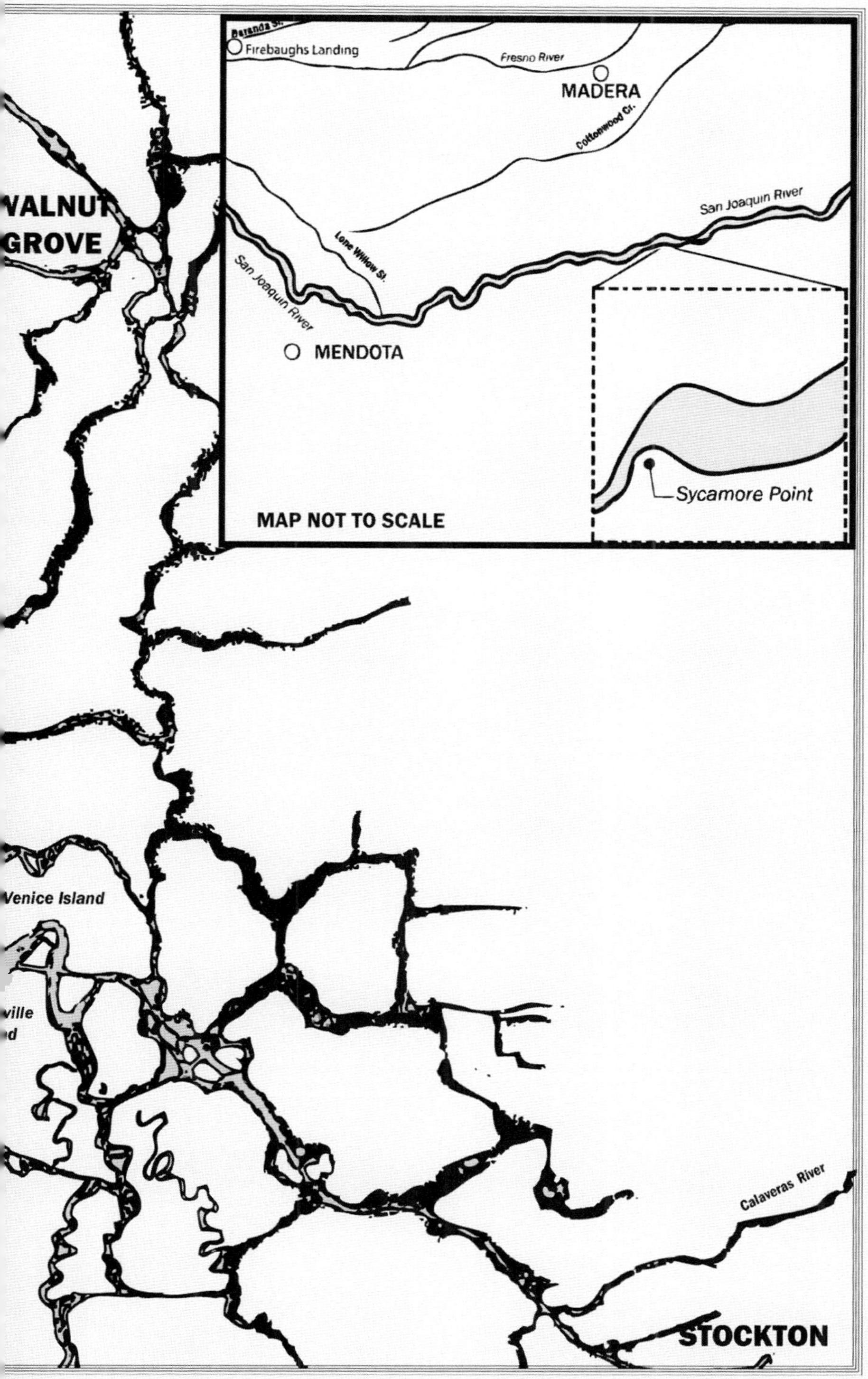


San Joaquin at Sycamore Point, eight miles north of Fresno and 272 miles south of Stockton. (Map by Kevin Shields.).

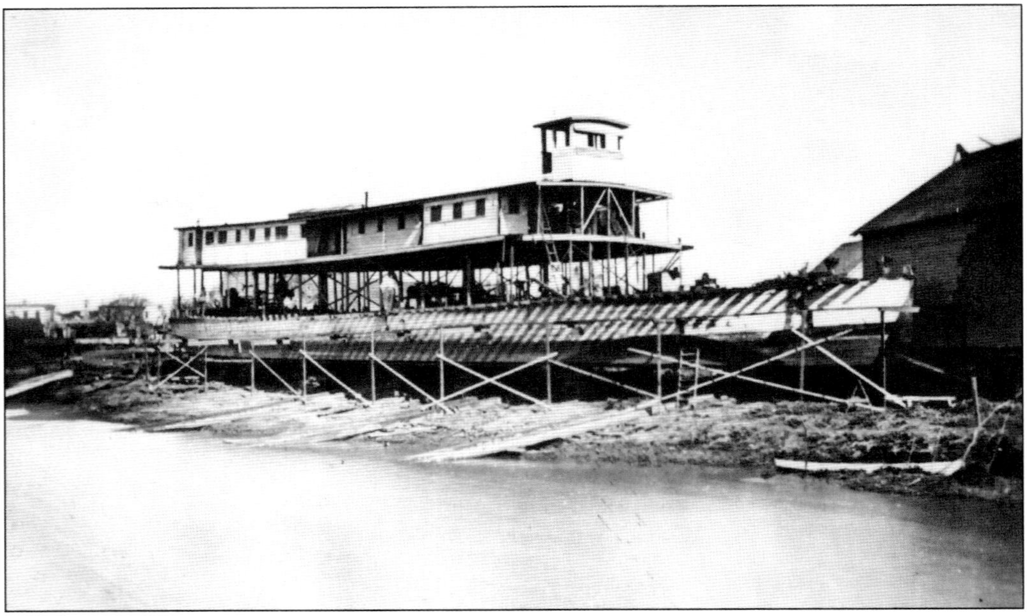

The demand for riverboats capable of navigating Northern California's rivers brought the establishment a number of shipyards. This unidentified Stockton yard was one of at least eight in that one city. Others were at Alameda, Benicia, Broderick, Oakland, Sacramento, San Francisco, Union City, Vallejo, and Yuba City. (Courtesy California State Library.)

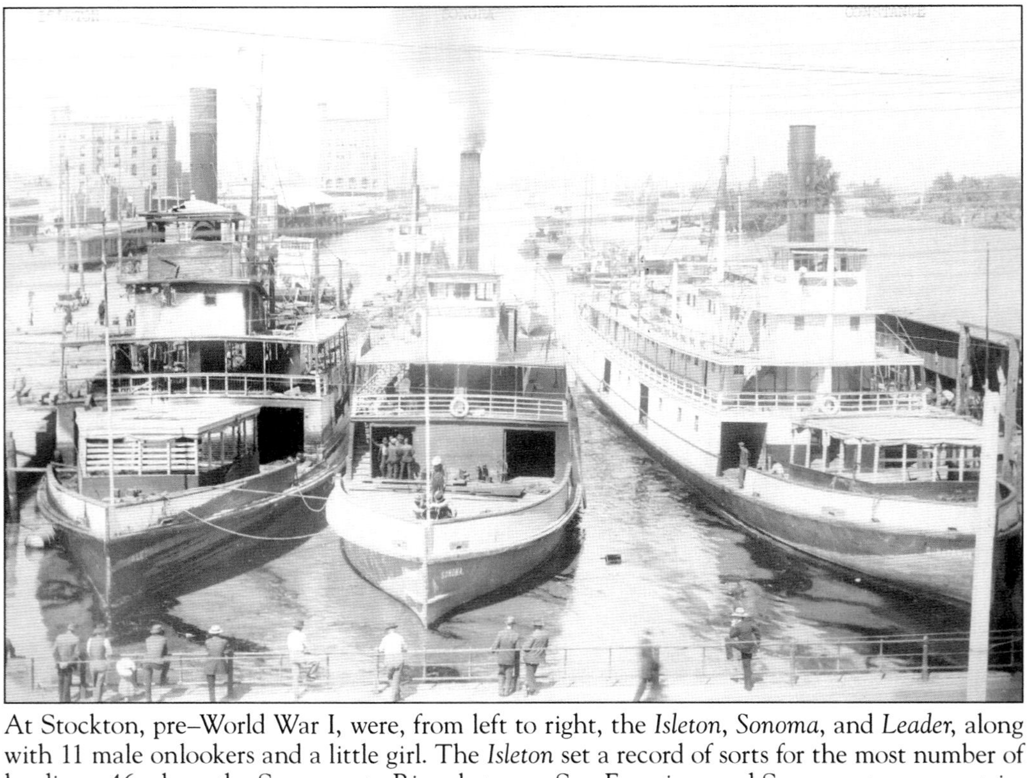

At Stockton, pre–World War I, were, from left to right, the *Isleton*, *Sonoma*, and *Leader*, along with 11 male onlookers and a little girl. The *Isleton* set a record of sorts for the most number of landings, 46, along the Sacramento River between San Francisco and Sacramento on one trip. (Courtesy Western Railway Museum Archives, No. 49520.)

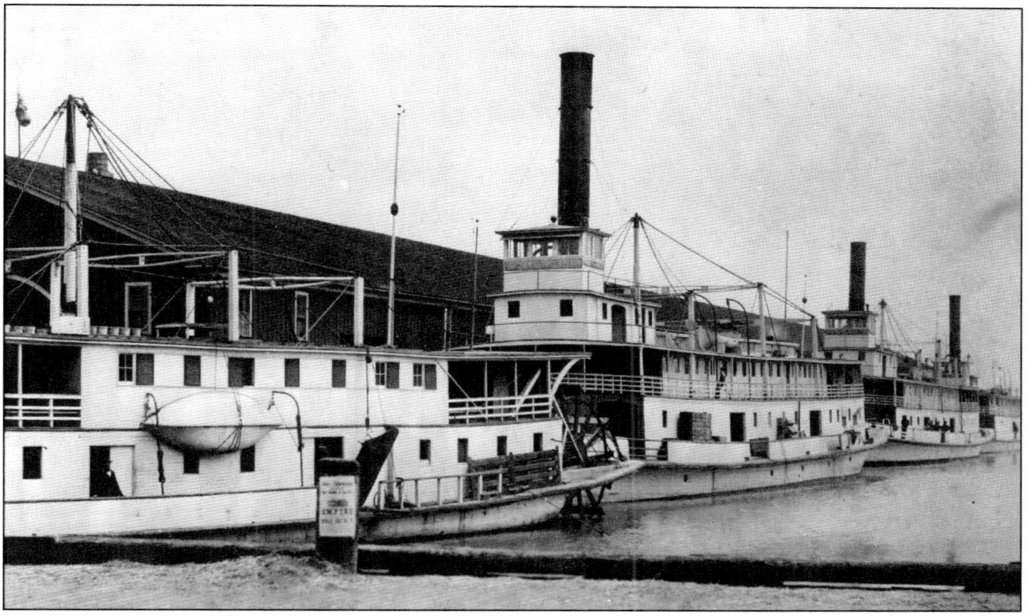

The four riverboats shown here include the *Pride of the River* and *Onward* (second and third from left, respectively). Both vessels were built by George E. Damon of Oakland, the *Onward* in 1877. The *Onward*, which went off documentation by 1909, used the 1866 engine salvaged from the Colorado River steamer *Mohave* that was dismantled in 1874. (Courtesy Western Railway Museum Archives, No. 49507.)

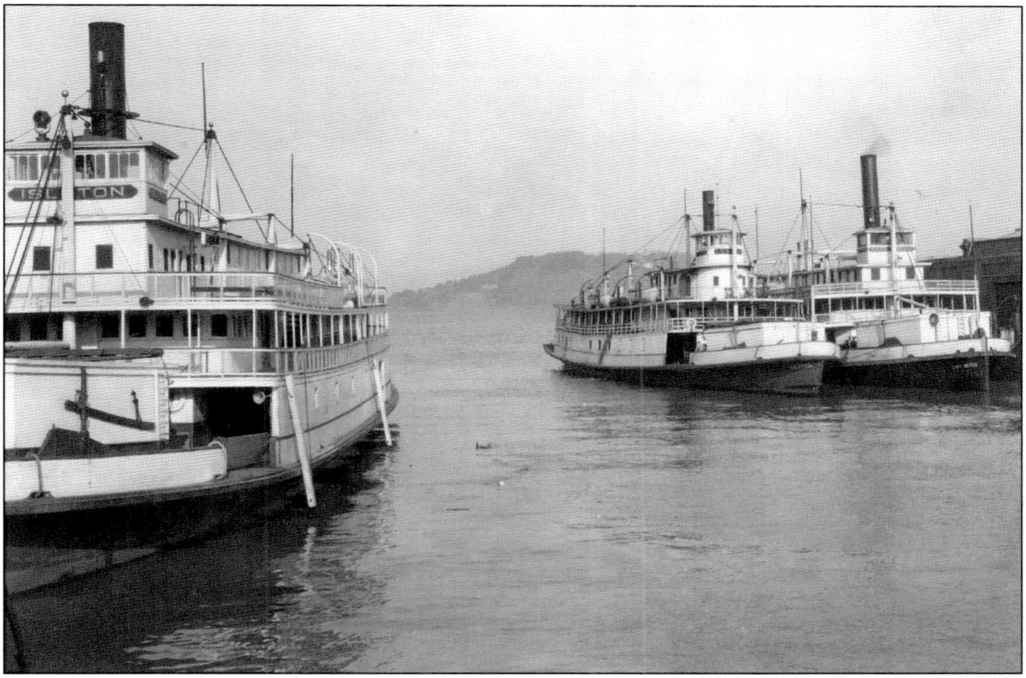

Shown here are, from left to right, the *Isleton*, *Leader*, and *Captain Weber*. Although the *Leader* was chartered by the Petaluma & Santa Rosa Railroad between San Francisco and Petaluma in earlier times, the three veterans were regular callers, for the most part, on the Sacramento and San Joaquin Rivers. (Courtesy Western Railway Museum Archives, No. 49505.)

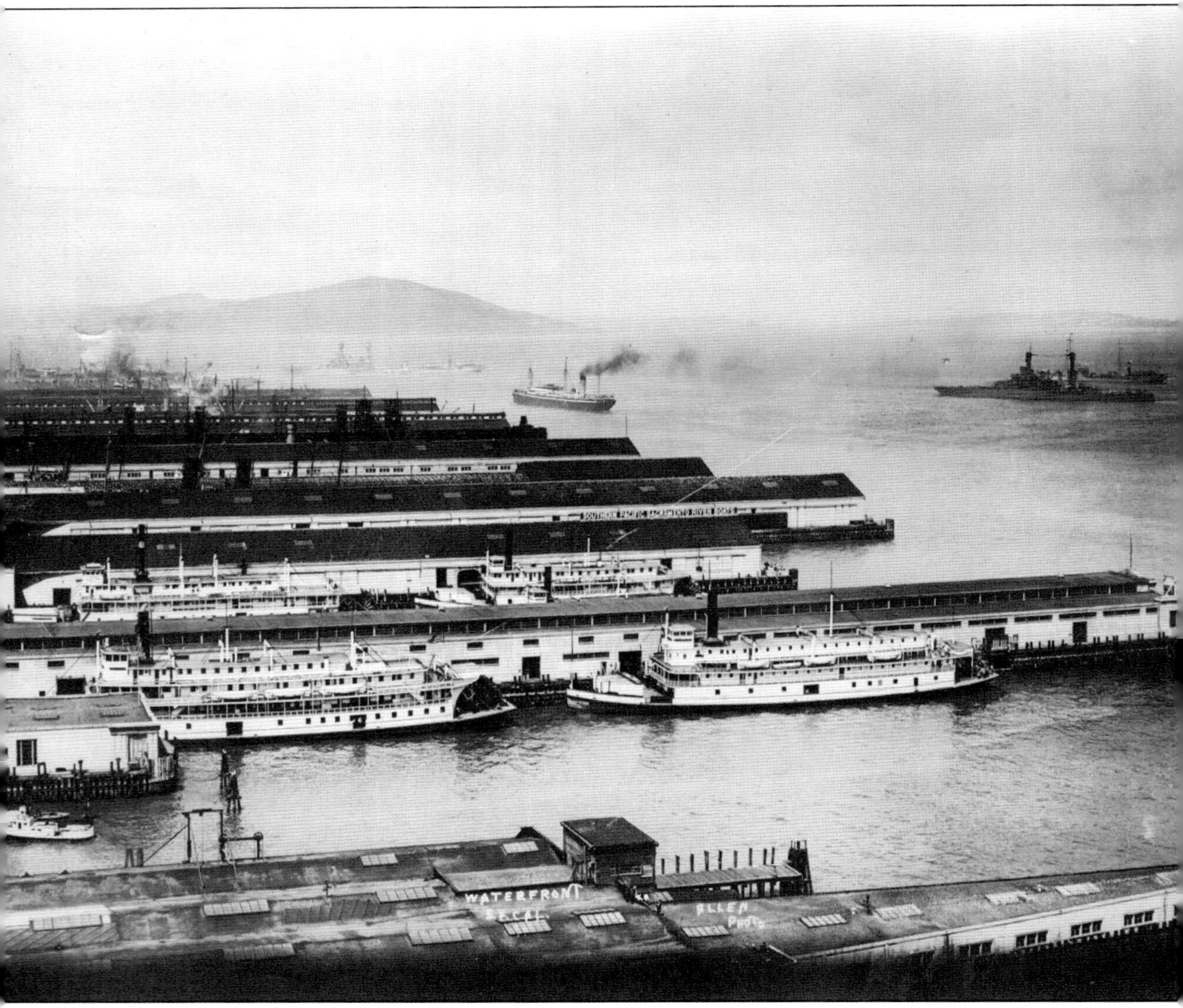


This late 1920s photograph of the riverboat docks north of San Francisco's Ferry Building shows, in the foreground, the *Fort Sutter* (left) and the *J. D. Peters* (right). The *Leader* (mostly hidden) is at Pier 3 opposite the Southern Pacific riverboats *Apache* and *Modoc*. (Author's collection.)

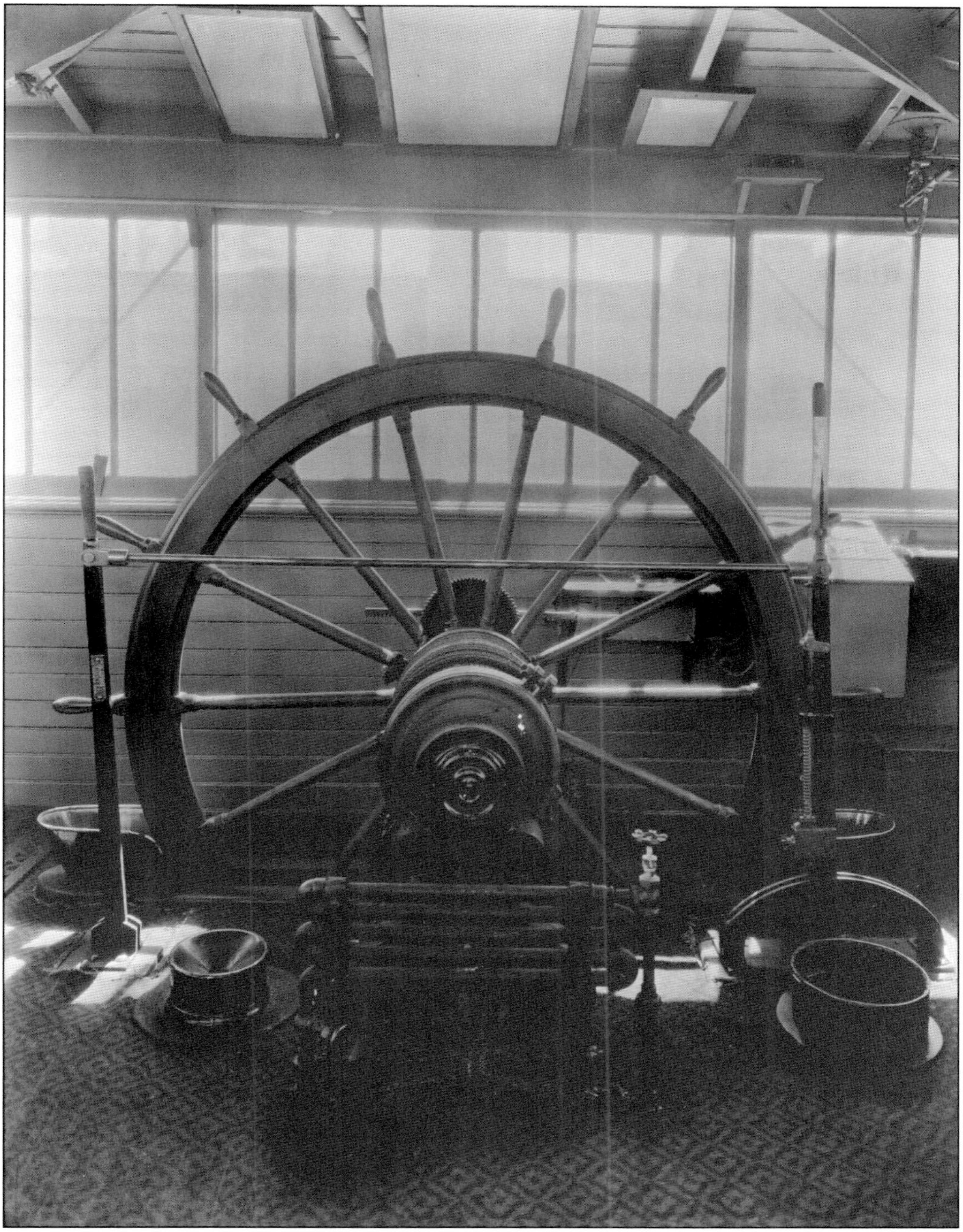

This is the interior of a riverboat pilothouse, perhaps the *Modoc* or *Apache*. The steering wheel reaches below the deck, with the wheel's center about 30 inches above the deck, giving helmsmen needed leverage. In rough weather or tides, two men were usually required to steer. Smoking was generally forbidden in pilothouses, although a bit of chaw was permissible, hence the spittoons. (Courtesy Western Railway Museum Archives.)

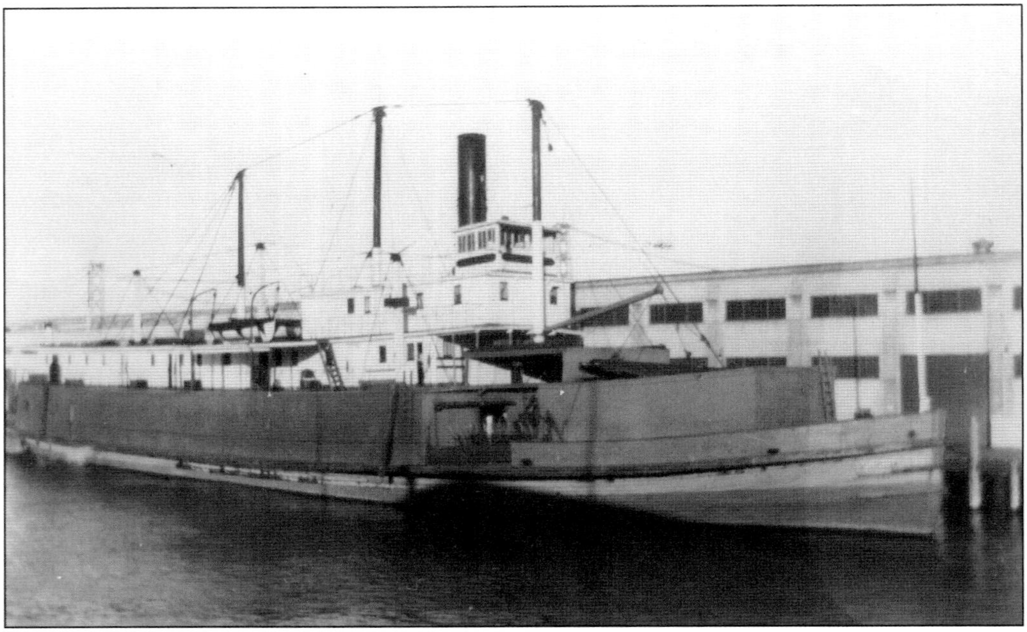

The 612-ton, 174.5-foot-long sternwheeler *Dauntless* is at San Francisco, as seen in this c. 1938 photograph. She was built in 1892 for the Union Transportation Co. The *Dauntless* and *Captain Weber* were California's only two dry riverboats. The Union Transportation Co.'s president's wife was a Woman's Christian Temperance Union (WCTU) leader and held views on the demon rum. (Courtesy John Schmale Collection.)

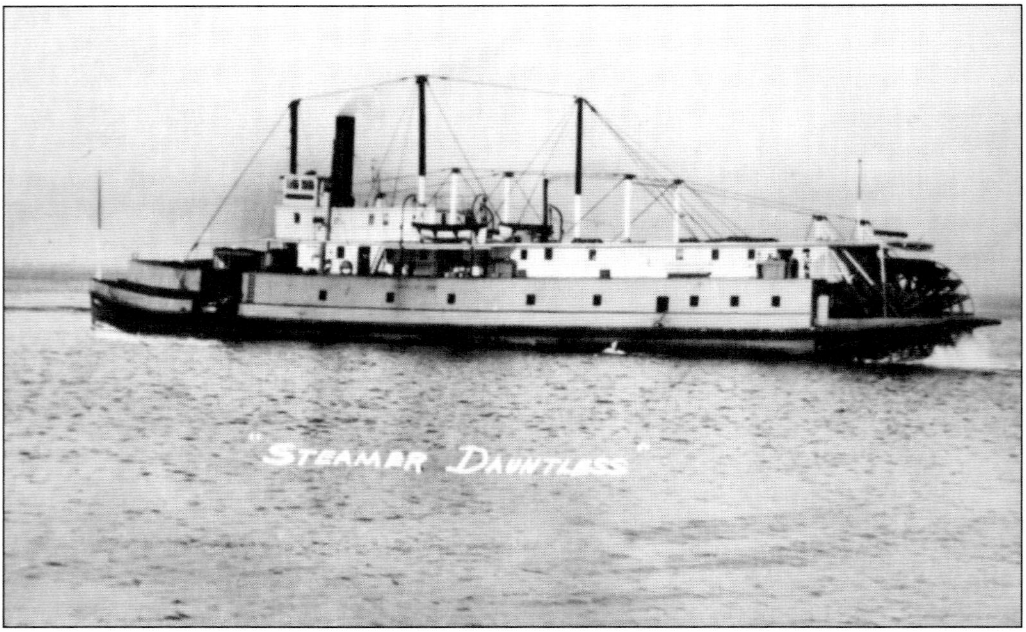


Under a full head of steam, the Union Transportation Co.'s *Dauntless* is completing a 127-mile trip from Stockton, steaming on the San Joaquin River through the Sacramento–San Joaquin River Delta, then on to Suisun Bay through the Carquinez Strait, across San Pablo Bay, and into port on San Francisco Bay. (Capt. Charles Rasmussen photograph; courtesy San Francisco Maritime National Historical Park, No. P82-100.08p1.)

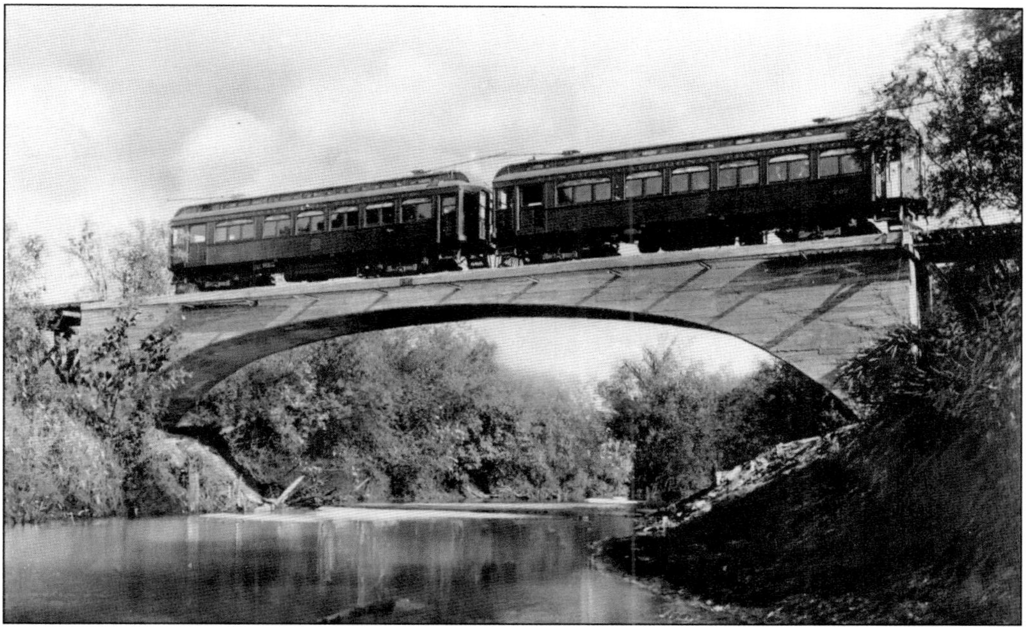

The Central California Traction Co. was a competitor to the riverboats on the Stockton–Sacramento run, as well as a feeder to both riverboats and main line railroads. The CCT ran both electric interurbans, shown here, as well as full-freight services between Stockton, Lodi, and Sacramento. (Author's collection.)

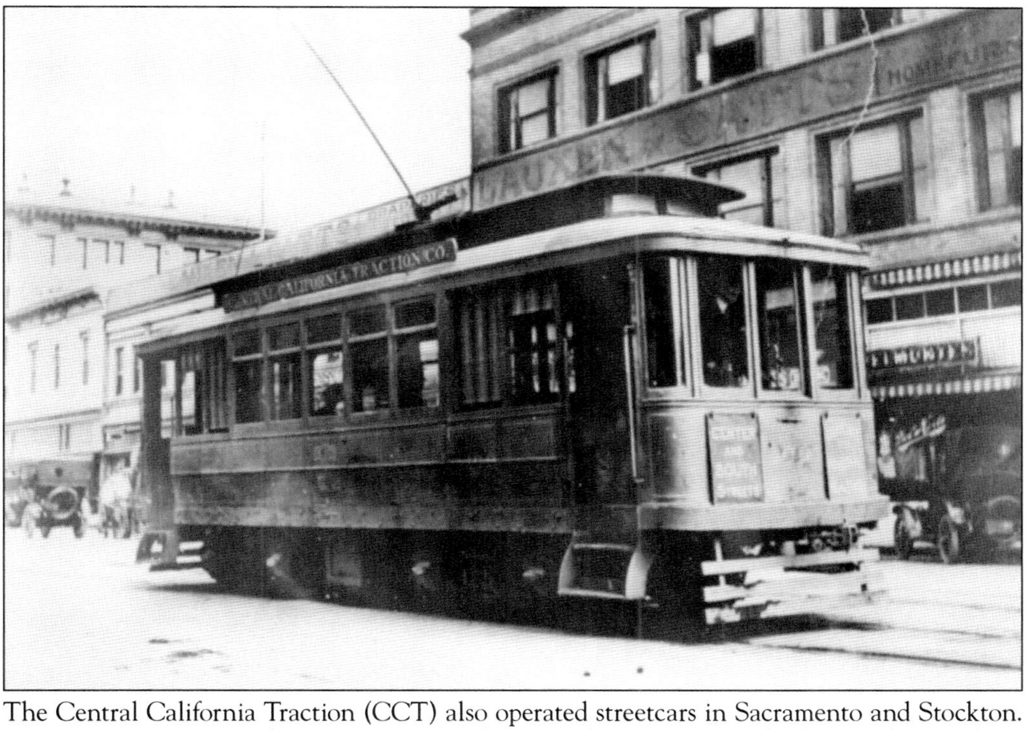

The Central California Traction (CCT) also operated streetcars in Sacramento and Stockton. CCT No. 108 is pictured in service on Stockton's Weber Avenue on the line to the Stockton Channel in 1915. Weber Avenue was named for Charles M. Weber, Stockton's founder and namesake of the riverboat *Captain Weber*. (Author's collection.)

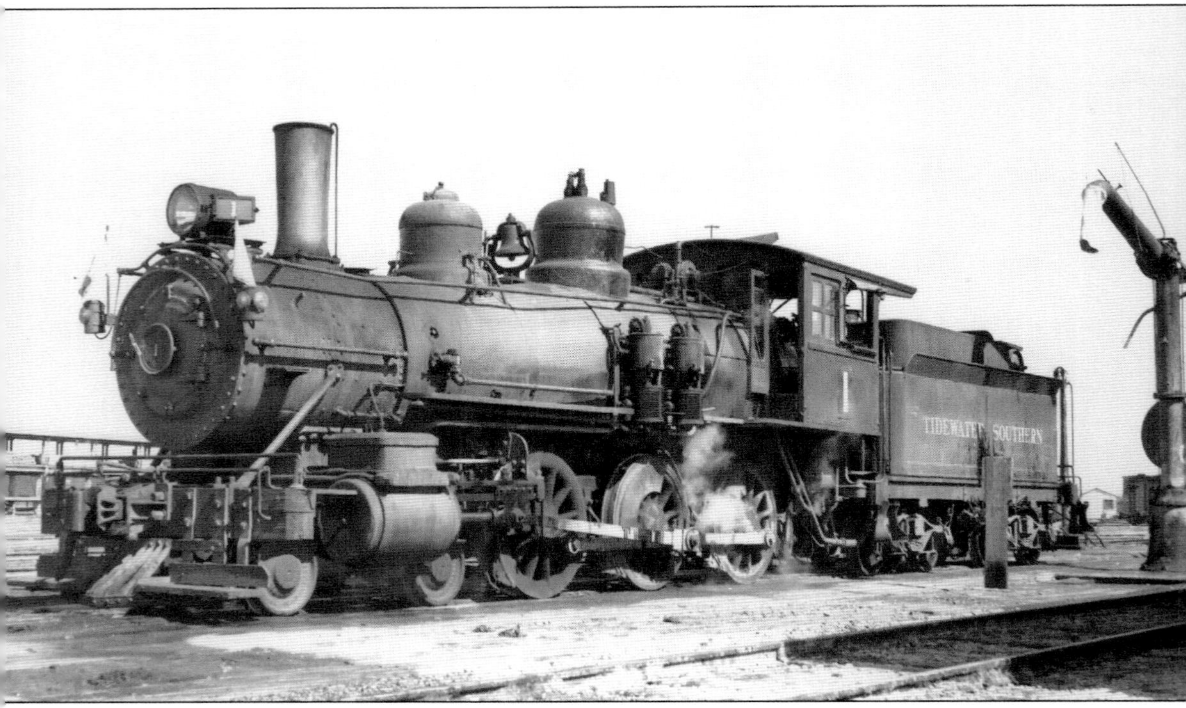

The Tidewater Southern Railway (TS) was another short line serving Stockton, connecting to Manteca, Modesto, Hatch, and Turlock using both steam and electric locomotives. This picture of TS's One Spot was taken at Stockton in 1946, long after the San Joaquin River steamers were gone. (Author's collection.)

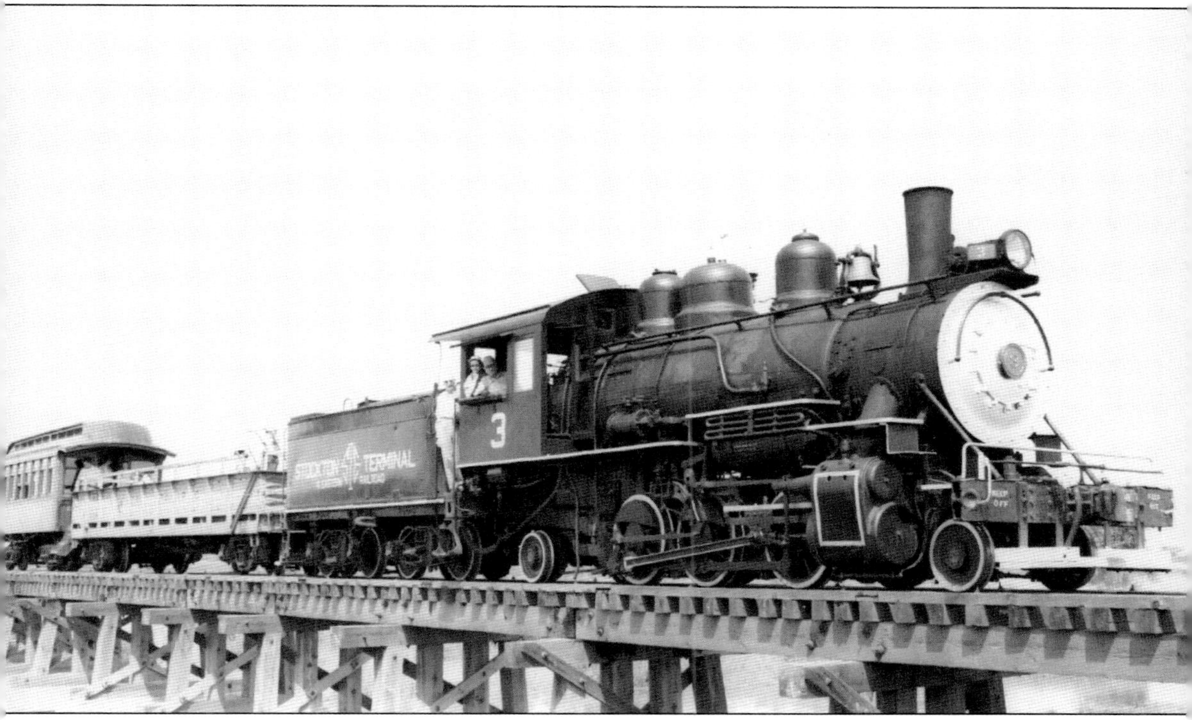


The Stockton, Terminal & Eastern Railroad (ST&E) acted as a feeder, bringing freight to the Stockton Channel for shipment via riverboat to San Francisco or Sacramento. Short lines such as the ST&E often went where the main line railroads did not, helping to create an effective transportation network. (Author's collection.)

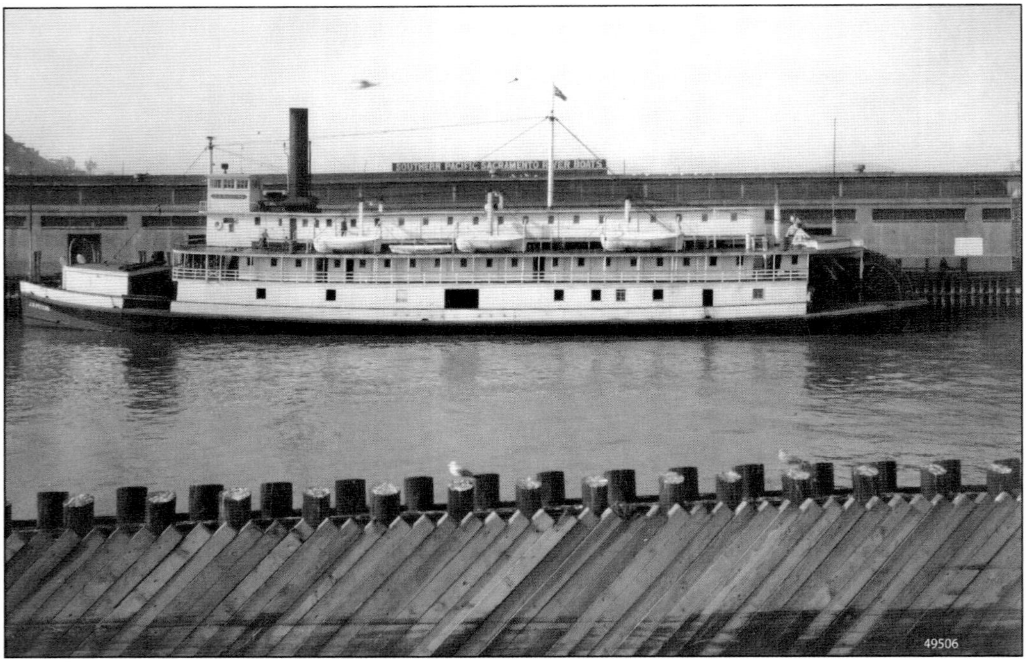


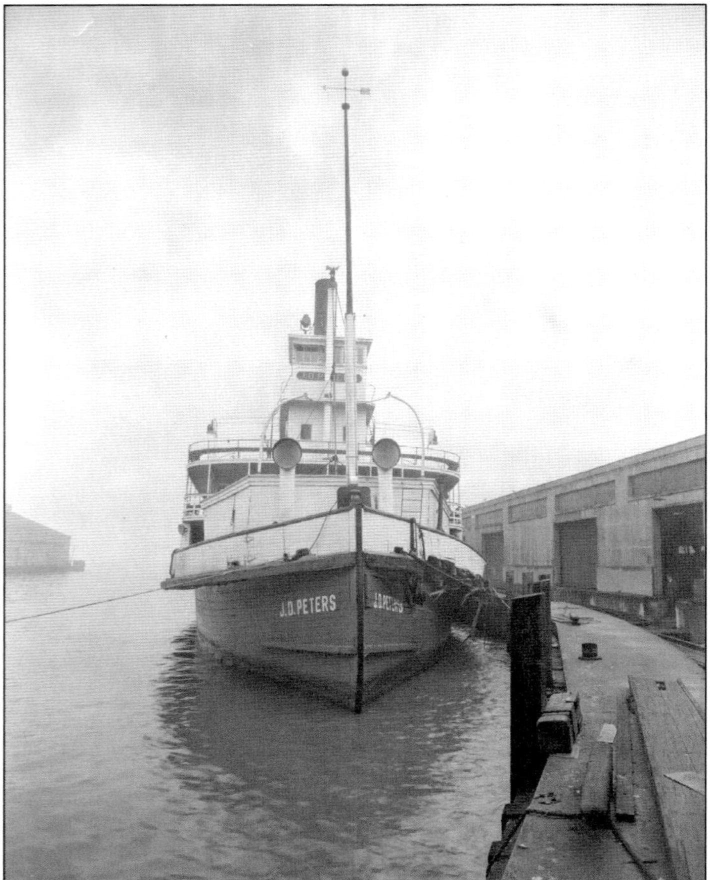


This fine port-side view of the *J. D. Peters* shows just how photogenic a California riverboat can be. She is tied up in San Francisco opposite the old Southern Pacific dock. For years, she paired with the *T. C. Walker* on the California Navigation & Improvement Co.'s Stockton runs. (Courtesy Western Railway Museum Archives, No. 49506.)

The *J. D. Peters*, in from Stockton, is at her familiar berth in San Francisco. As these riverboats left the saltwater of San Francisco Bay, their hulls were cleaned of barnacles and other marine life in the freshwater of the rivers. (Courtesy Western Railway Museum Archives, No. 49523.)

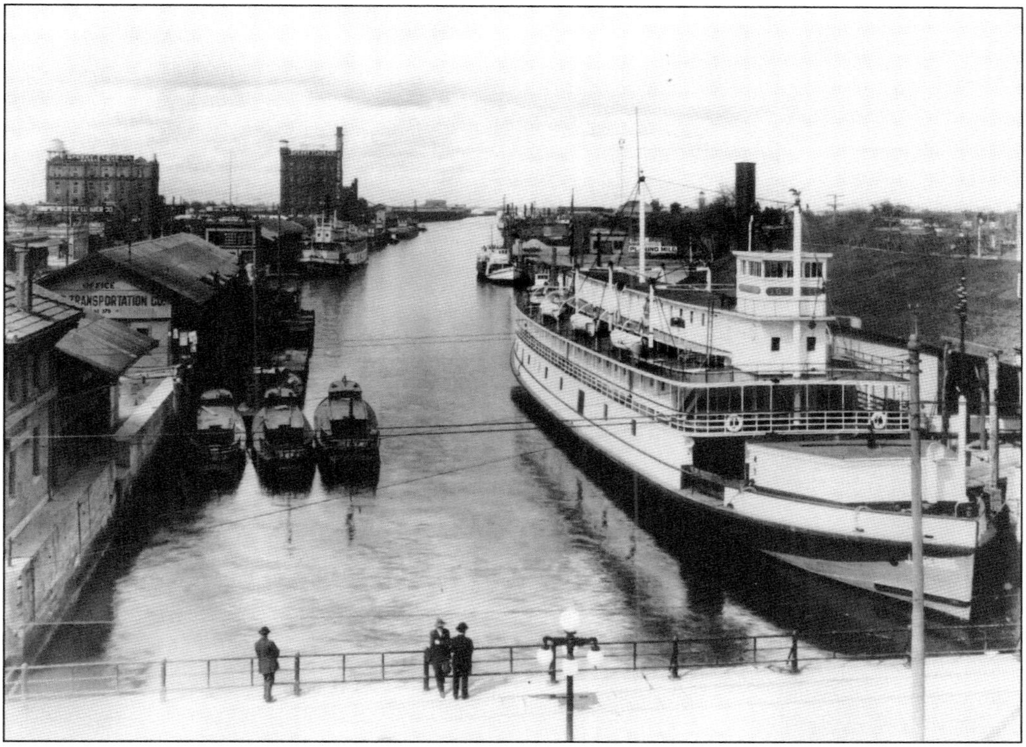

This undated Stockton Channel photograph shows the bow starboard of the *J. D. Peters*, built in 1889. At 880.7 tons and 206.5 feet in length, she was the third California riverboat that featured a surface condenser for reusing steam. The *J. D. Peters* made the last Stockton–San Francisco run on Christmas Day in 1932. (Courtesy San Francisco Maritime National Historical Park, No. P84-081.08p1.)

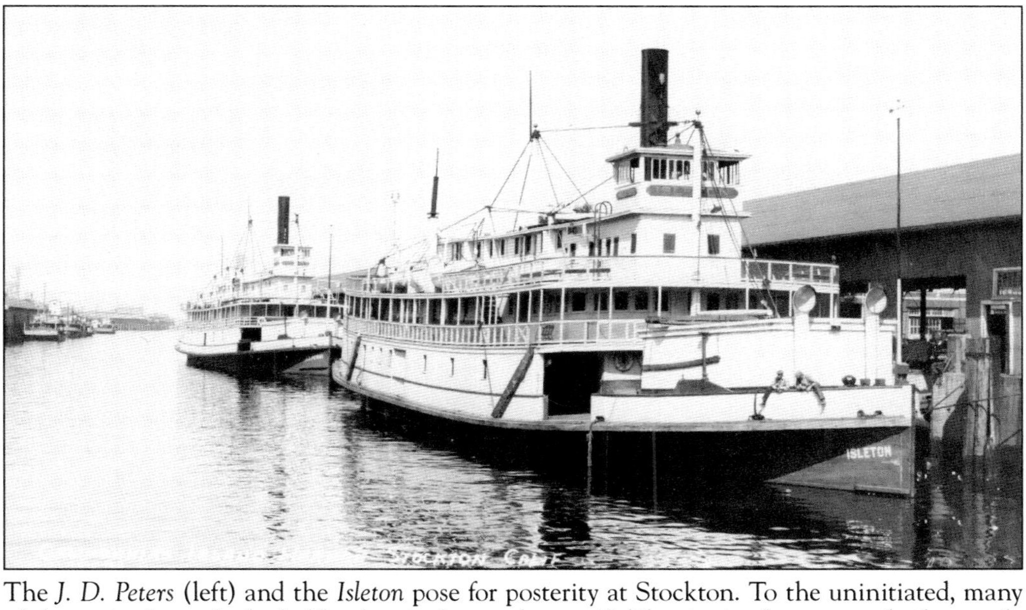


The *J. D. Peters* (left) and the *Isleton* pose for posterity at Stockton. To the uninitiated, many of these riverboats looked alike, but in fact, only two California riverboats were built exactly alike—the *Delta King* and *Delta Queen*. (Courtesy Western Railway Museum Archives.)

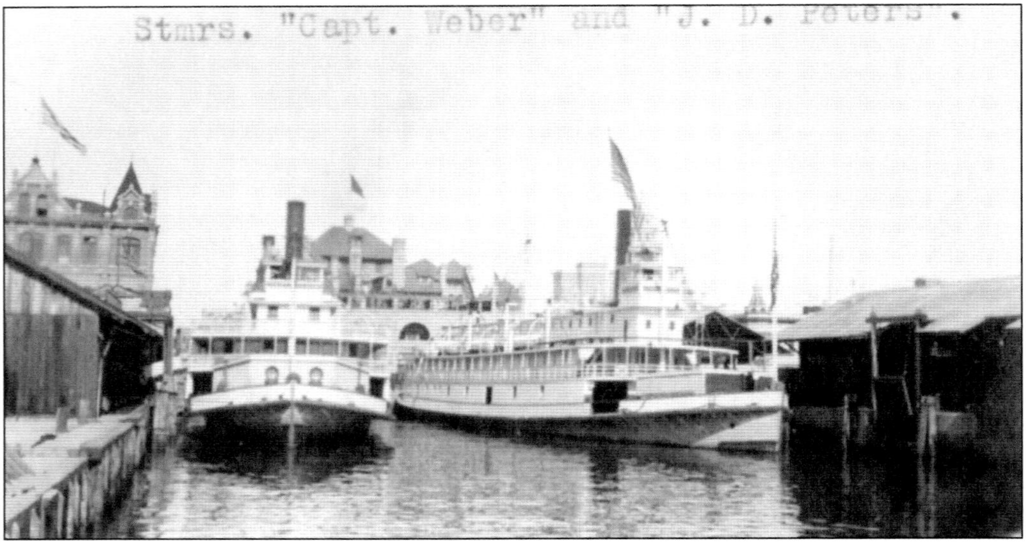


Tied up in the Stockton Channel are the *Captain Weber* (left) and the *J.D. Peters*. Without dispute, they were a handsome pair. It is unfortunate that their demise (*Captain Weber* by fire and *J.D. Peters* by abandonment) came too early for preservationists to save them for posterity. (Courtesy Western Railway Museum Archives.)

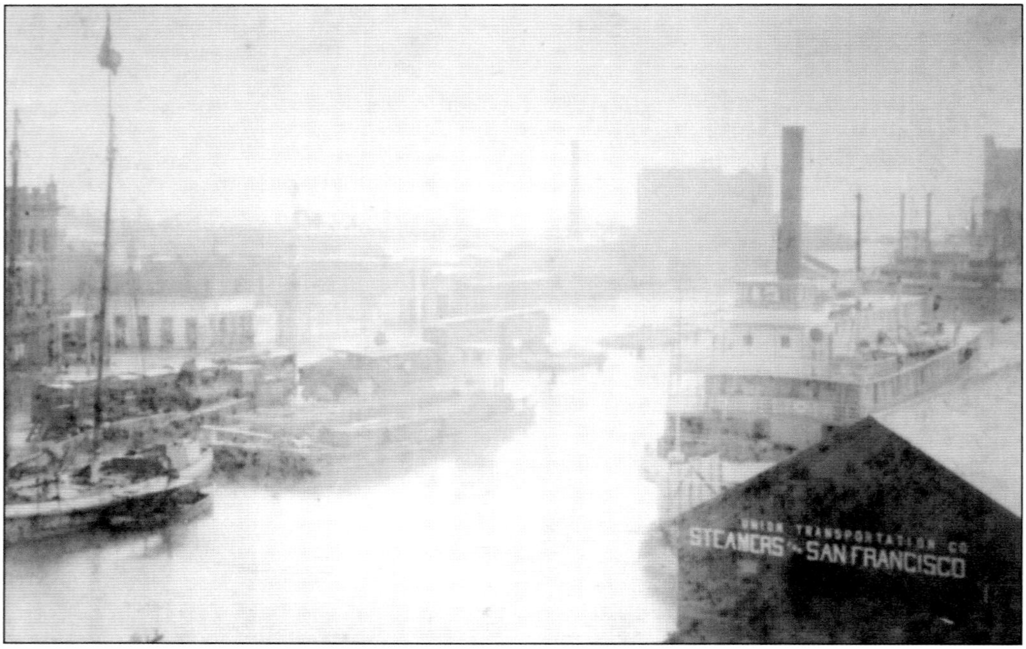


The *Captain Weber* is at the Union Transportation Co. dock in Stockton. The *Captain Weber* was built in 1892. She appeared in two movies: *Steamboat Round the Bend* (1935) and *Dixie* (1943), in which she became the last riverboat from Tidewater to Sacramento. When the filming of *Dixie* was finished, she burned on May 22, 1943. (Courtesy California State Library.)

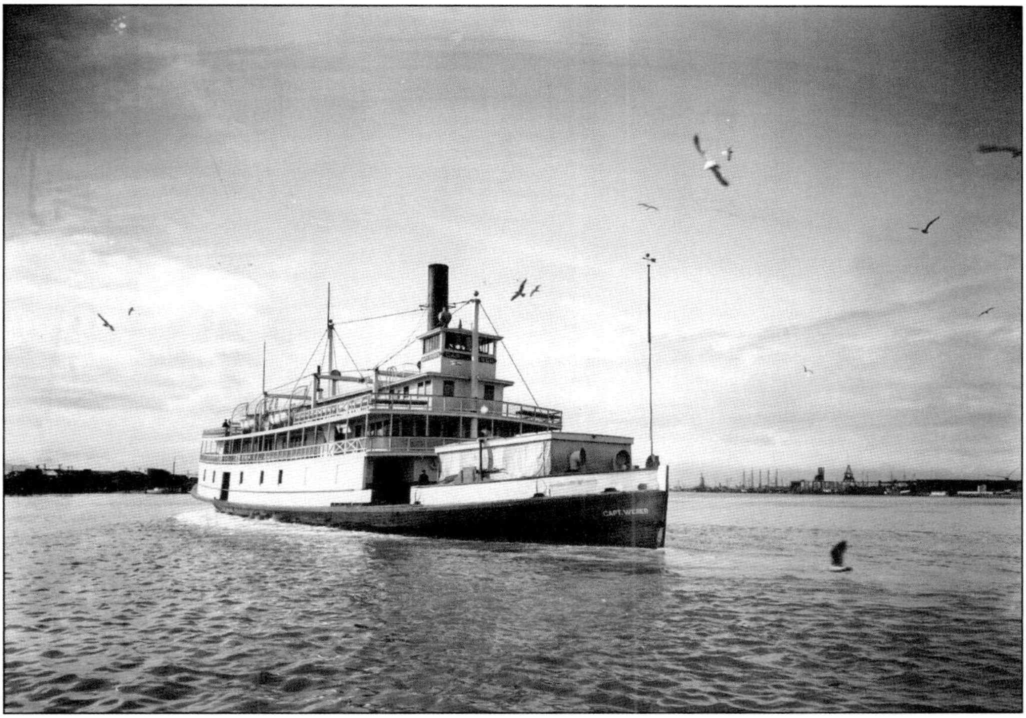

The California Transportation Co.'s *Captain Weber* steams across San Francisco Bay. Only five visible crewmembers appear to grace her deck. (Courtesy Western Railway Museum Archives.)

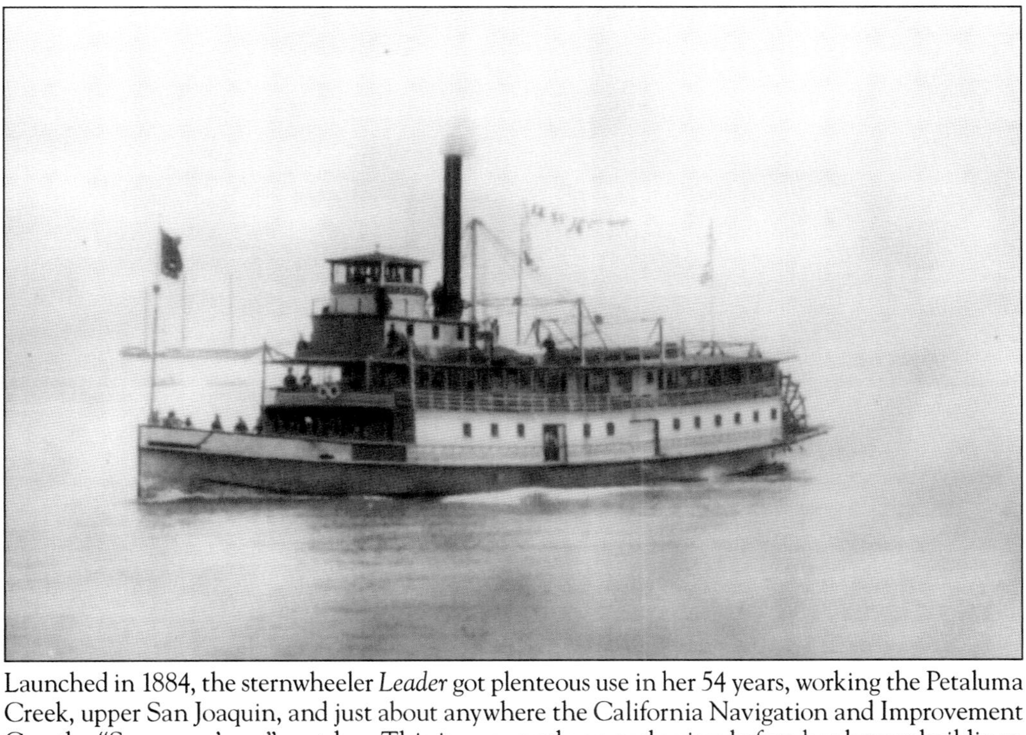

Launched in 1884, the sternwheeler *Leader* got plenteous use in her 54 years, working the Petaluma Creek, upper San Joaquin, and just about anywhere the California Navigation and Improvement Co., the "See-en-an'-eye," sent her. This is apparently an early view before her later rebuildings. (Courtesy Stocklmeir Library, California History Center, DeAnza College, Cupertino.)

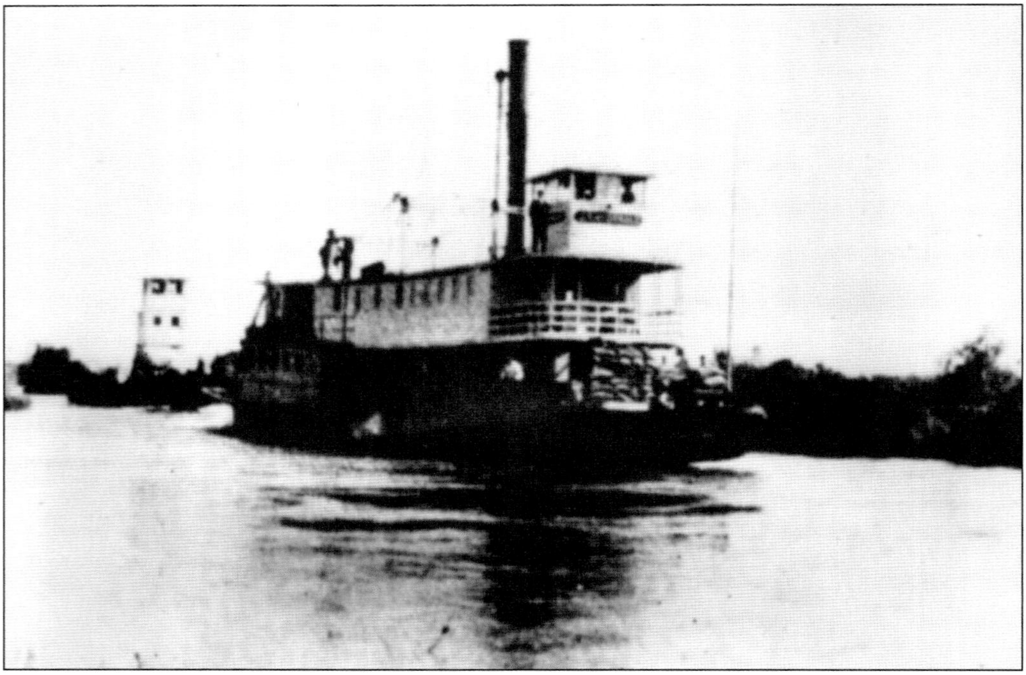

The *J. R. McDonald* carried a monkey rudder, a rarity among California riverboats. Unlike conventional rudders placed forward of the sternwheel, the monkey rudder was placed abaft of the sternwheel, which only reached the vessel's waterline, using the force of water in the sternwheel's wake for steering. (Courtesy California State Library.)

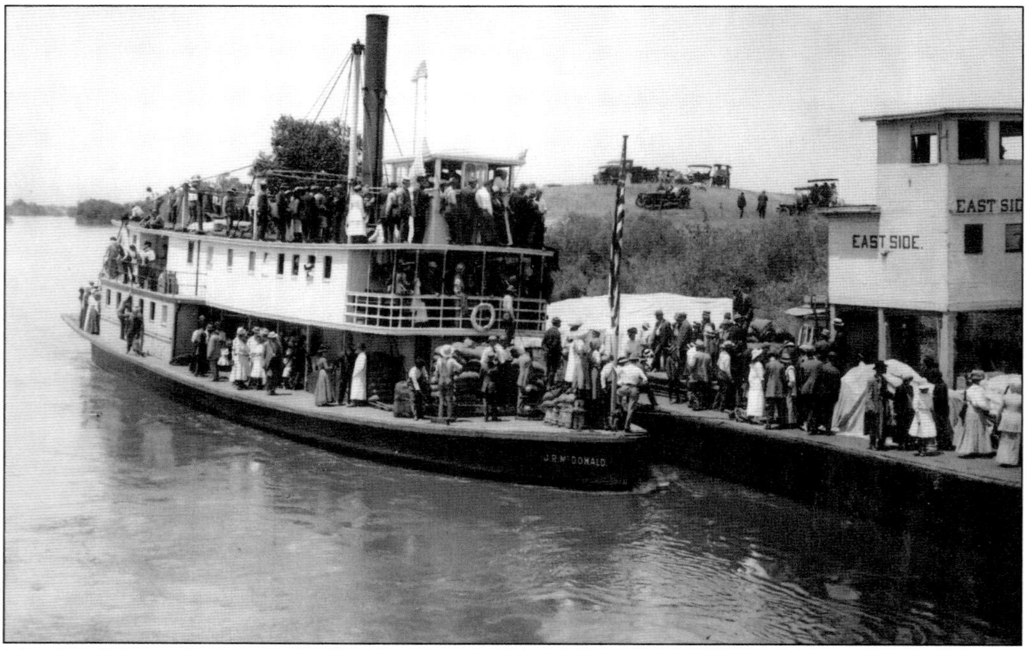


The 137.56-ton *J. R. McDonald* ties up alongside the barge *East Side* on the San Joaquin River at Sycamore Point near Fresno. It is March 1911, and this is reportedly the last riverboat trip that far upriver. Compare the expanse of the San Joaquin then with its diminished circumstance today. (Courtesy San Francisco Maritime National Historical Park, No. P82-019a1917pl.)

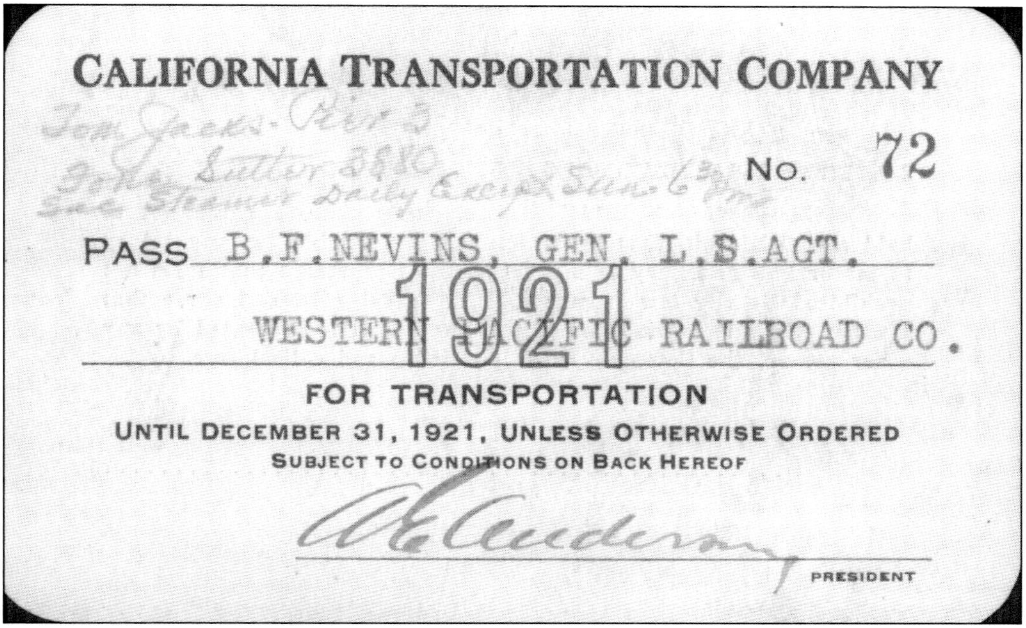


Riverboat companies issued passes for free transportation for various reasons, such as reciprocity with other companies and goodwill toward freight customers and employees. This one was issued to a Western Pacific Railroad agent in 1921 by the California Transportation Co. of Stockton. (Courtesy Western Railway Museum Archives.)

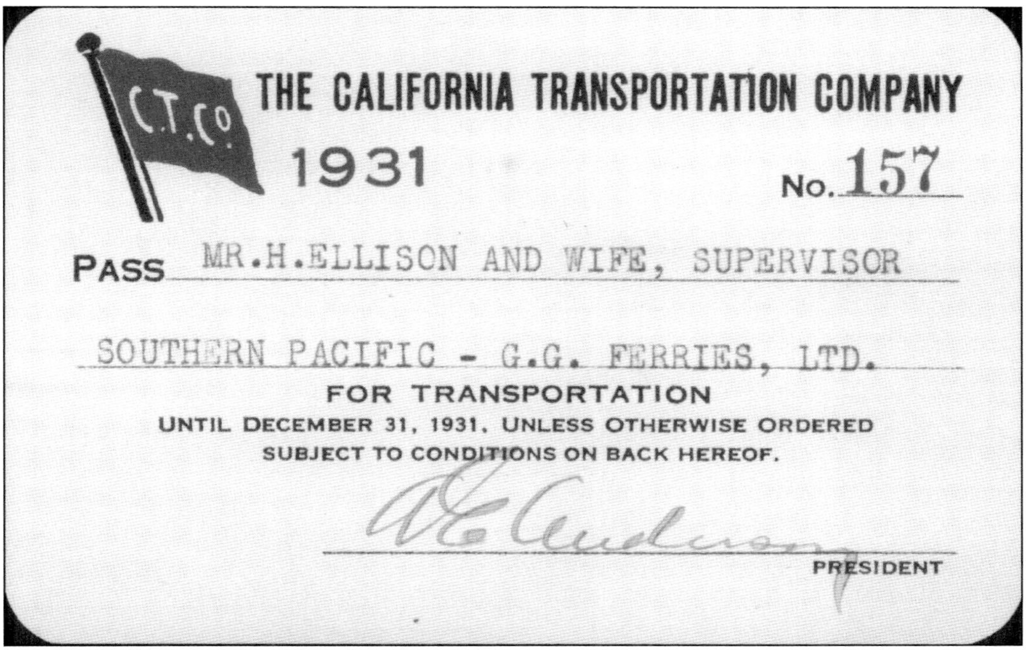


This is a typical transportation pass issued by the California Transportation Co. to a supervisor for the Southern Pacific–owned automobile ferryboat company, Southern Pacific-Golden Gate Ferries, Ltd., in 1931. (Courtesy Western Railway Museum Archives.)

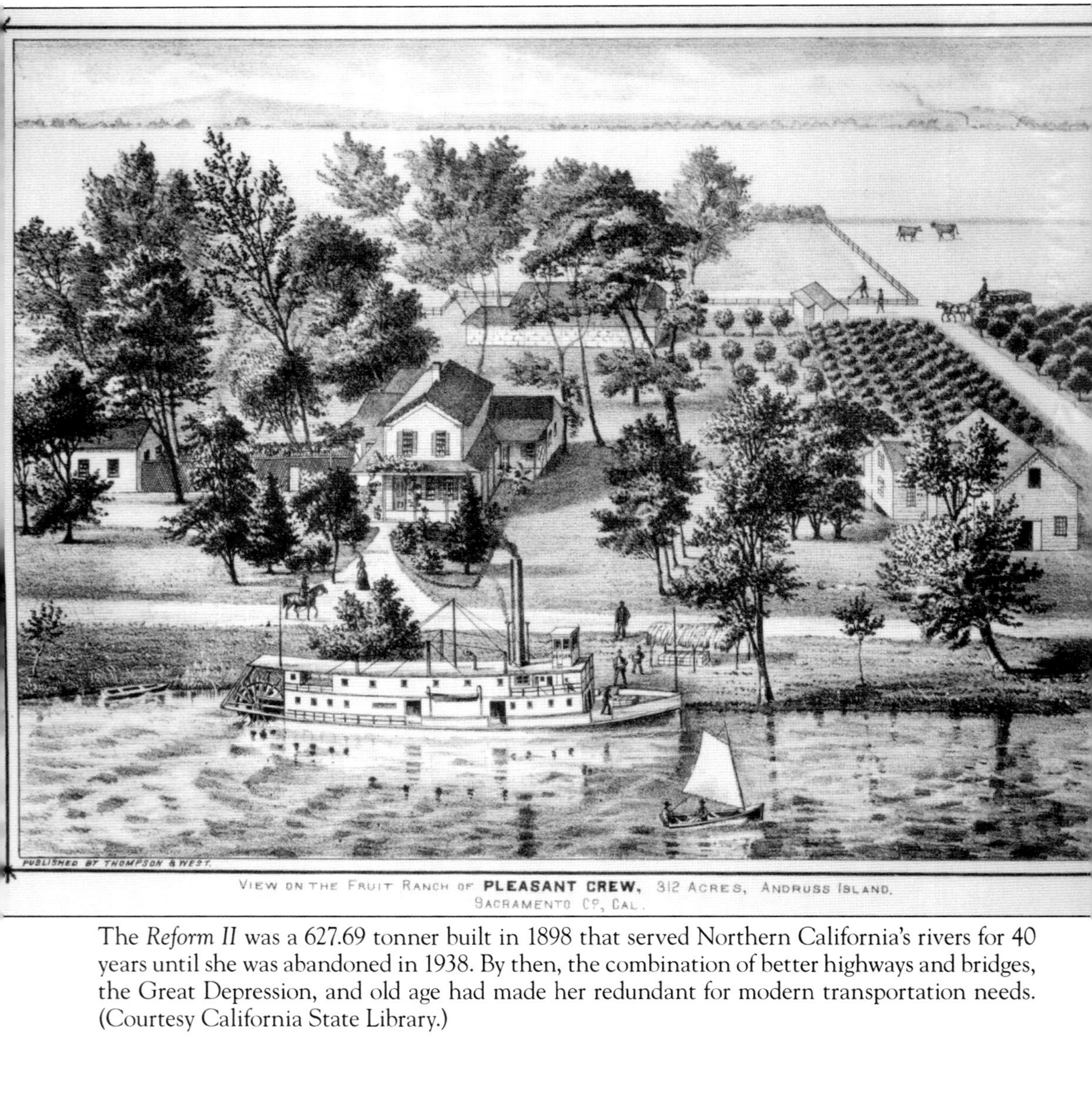


The *Reform II* was a 627.69 tonner built in 1898 that served Northern California's rivers for 40 years until she was abandoned in 1938. By then, the combination of better highways and bridges, the Great Depression, and old age had made her redundant for modern transportation needs. (Courtesy California State Library.)

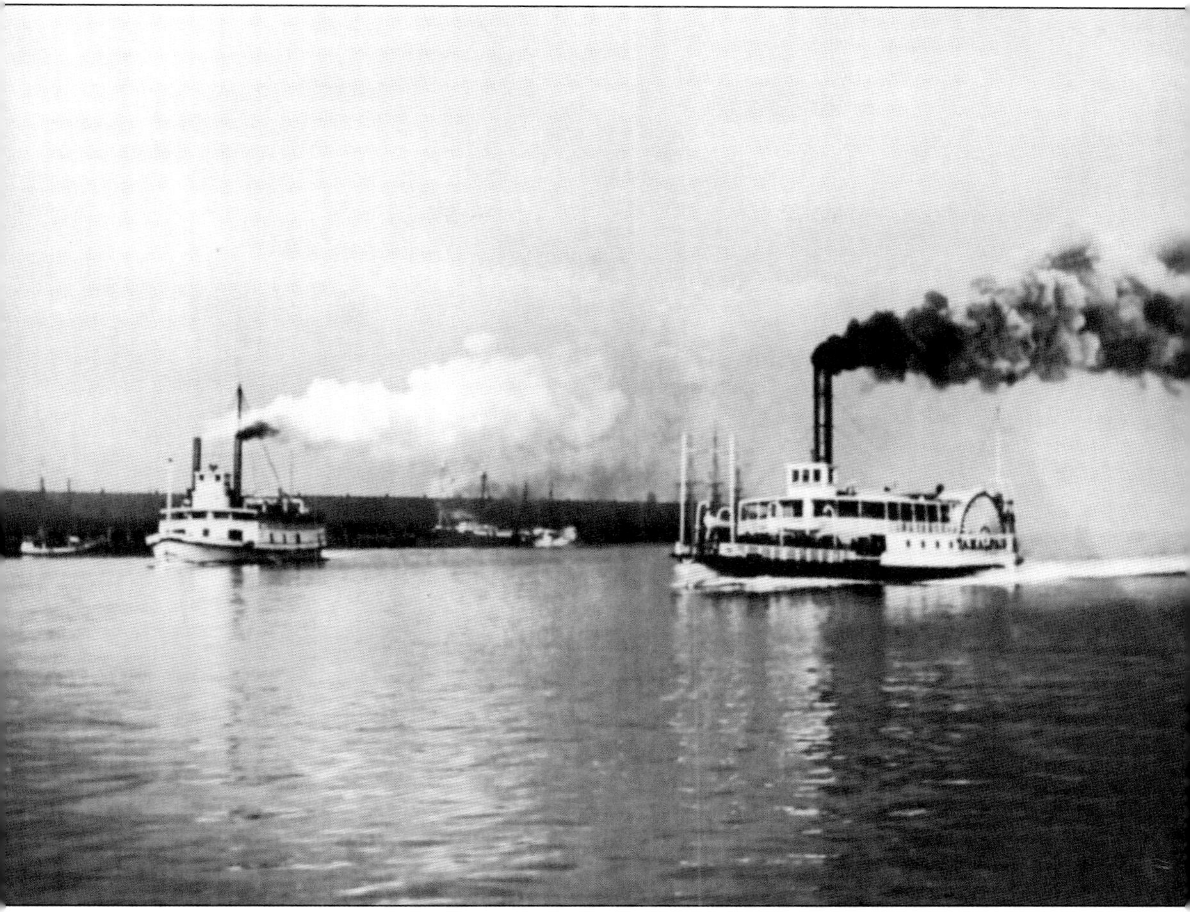

In this 1888 image, the *Mary Garratt* (left) has departed San Francisco and is turning around for another trip through the Delta en route to Stockton, while the ferryboat *Tamalpais* is heading into port. (Courtesy Northwestern Pacific Railroad Historical Society Archives.)

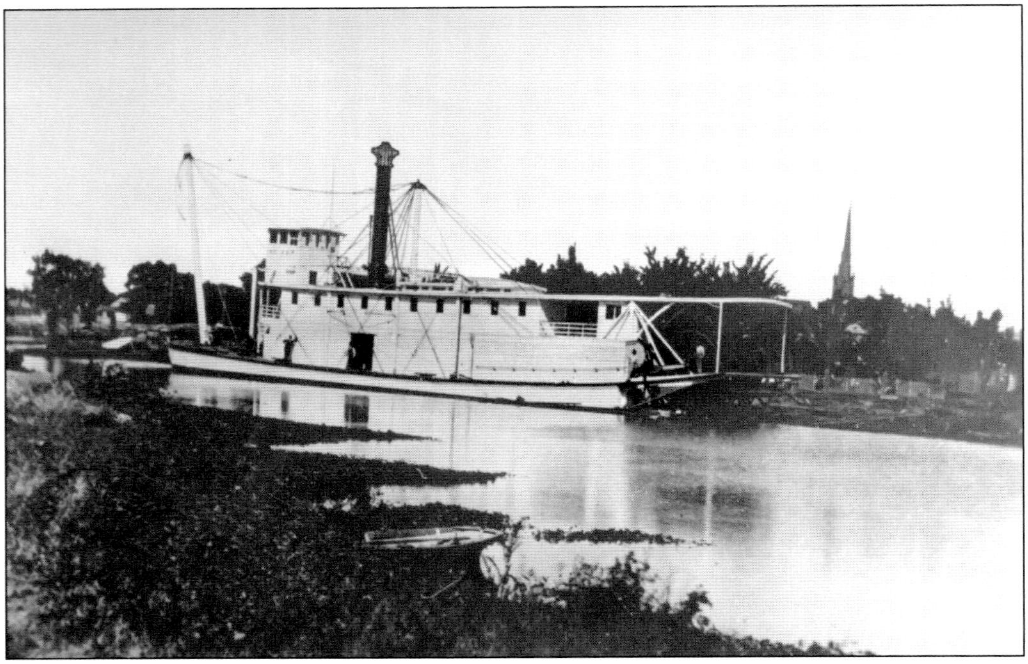

The snagboat *Seizer* was built in 1881 by the California Navigation & Improvement Co. of Stockton, where this photograph was taken. The *Seizer* was 157 feet long, and her boom was what was called a "stiff leg" type. She was scrapped in 1921, ending a 40-year career. (Courtesy Richard Schlaich Collection.)

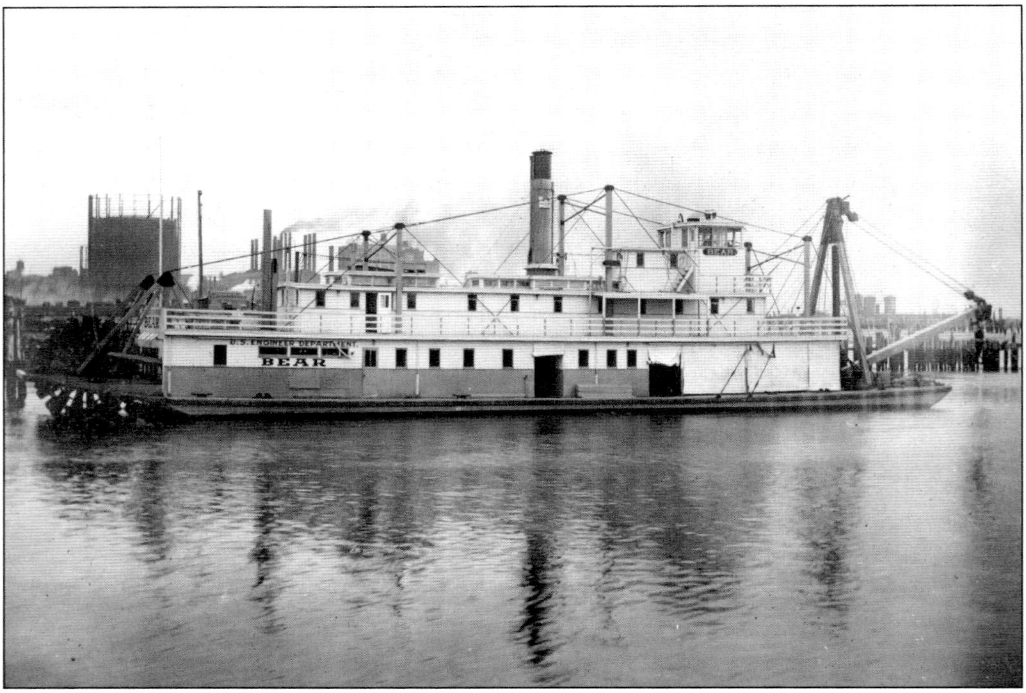


The 157.8-foot-long, 242-ton Army Corps of Engineers' snagboat *Bear* was built during 1920 and 1921—the same year the *Neponset II* became the last California riverboat to be snagged. The *Bear* was scrapped in 1926. (Courtesy Richard Schlaich Collection.)

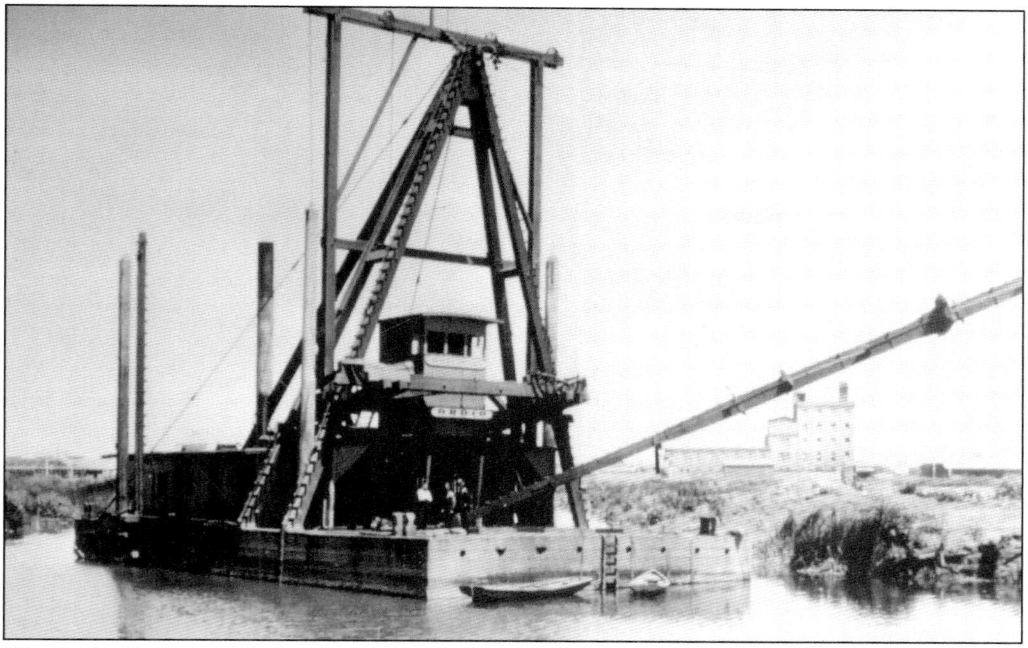

The dredge *Brittannia*'s hull was built by John Grant, and her equipment came from Stockton Iron Works in 1850. The *Brittannia* may have been the longest serving dredge on California's rivers, lasting until 1905. In this picture, she is in Mormon Slough. (Courtesy Richard Schlaich Collection.)

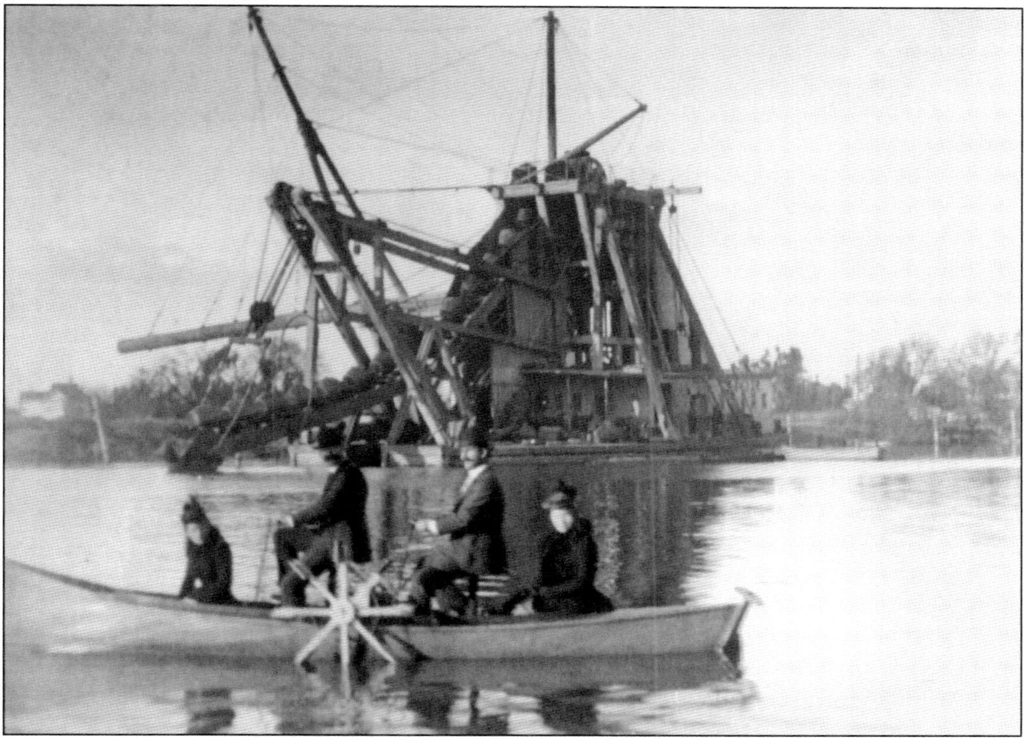

The steam-powered dredge *Thor* was built in Stockton in the early 1890s and was used for island reclamation work in the Delta in 1894. This photograph is dated 1892 or 1893, but *Thor*'s legacy is alive today in the Delta's rich farmlands. (Courtesy Richard Schlaich Collection.)

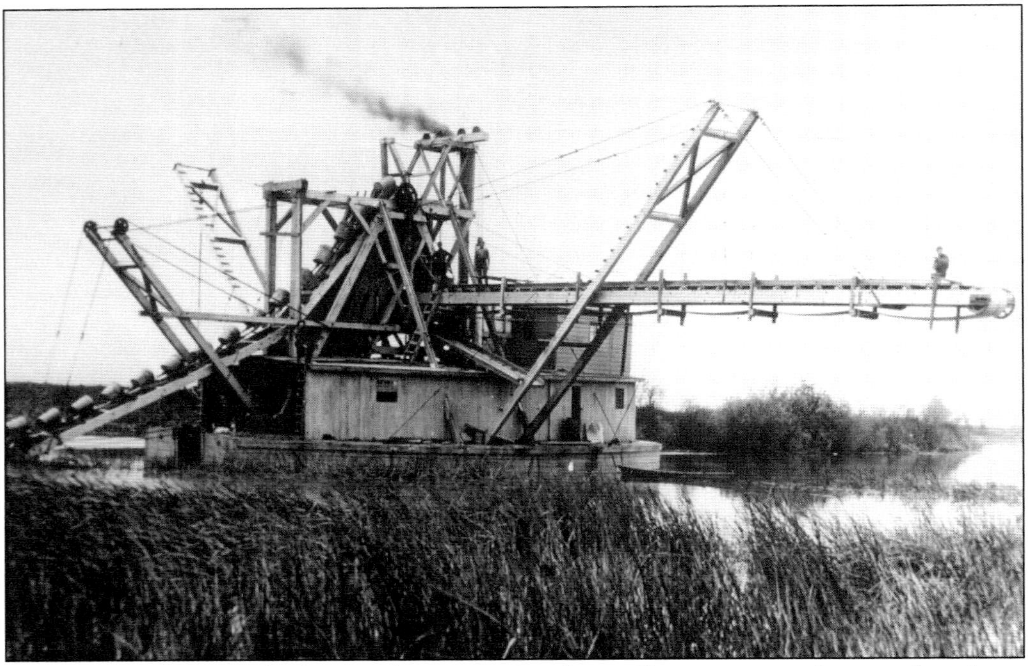

This picture shows a dredger working near Stockton. Her name is unknown, but she is using an experimental system called a bucket line where mud is dredged, then carried to the riverbank and dumped. This picture is very rare since the experiment failed. (Courtesy Richard Schlaich Collection.)

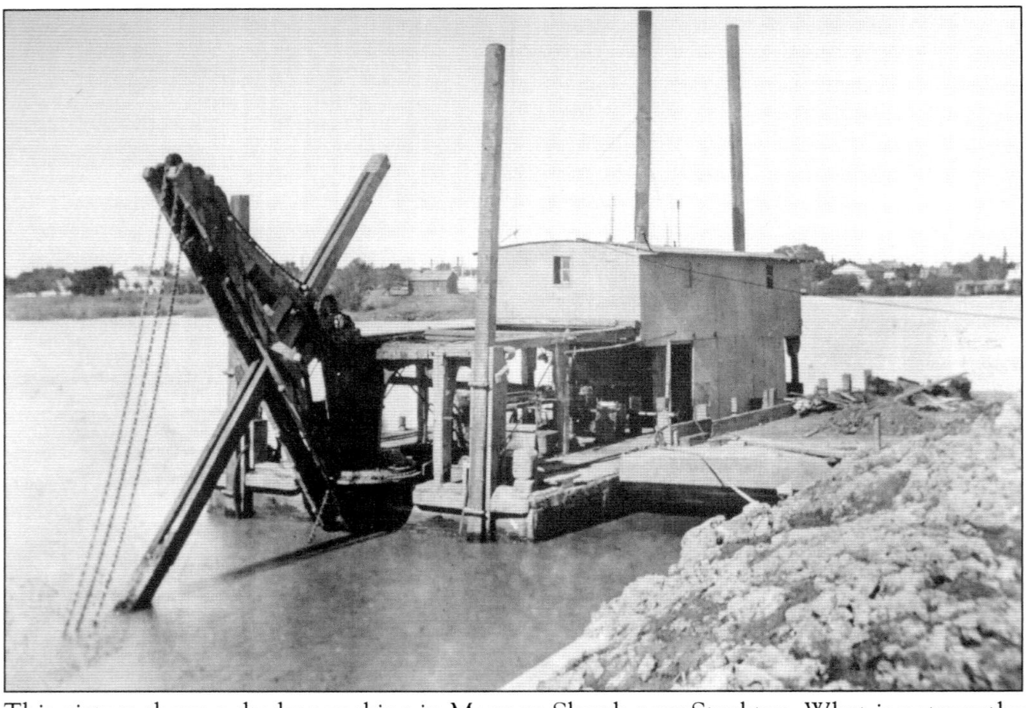

This picture shows a dredger working in Mormon Slough near Stockton. What is noteworthy is that this was the same type of dredger used in the Panama Canal. (Courtesy Richard Schlaich Collection.)

# *Five*

# North Bay Creeks and Rivers

North of San Pablo Bay, Napa and Sonoma Counties are part of the North Bay. The Mare Island Strait, into which the Napa River empties, is in Solano County. It is almost impossible to list all the Napa River steamers, but it is known that about 37 made the run after the *Commodore Jones* did it in 1849. Traffic increased until the coming of the railroads, after which only the *St. Helena*, *Napa City*, and *Zinfandel* were left. By the early 1920s, they were gone. Sonoma Creek was the least important of the North Bay runs. The riverboats went only as far as Hallow's or Poppe's Landing (about one mile south of today's Schellville firehouse on Millerick Road), then called St. Louis, where passengers and freight were off-loaded to continue to Sonoma by land. This was the only North Bay riverboat run not killed off by railroads or publicly funded roads. There just was not enough business in the first place. Evidence of only three Sonoma Creek riverboats has so far surfaced. There was the *Georgiana*, *Princess* in 1862, and *Sonoma*, built in 1874 by local people in Sonoma. The first riverboat that successfully navigated the Petaluma Creek was the *Red Jacket* under Capt. David Van Pelt, the first of an estimated 48 riverboats on the Petaluma Creek. The best-known Petaluma Creek riverboat operator was the Petaluma & Santa Rosa Railroad (PS&R), which ran riverboats in conjunction with their electric interurbans and freight trains. In the end, the rail/water combination outlasted all competitors, making the *Petaluma II* the West's last paddle wheel steamer. The P&SR's *Gold* caught fire on November 8, 1920, and quickly spread, destroying the dock and the warehouse. Assistant engineer Jeff Todd and messboy Trago Santos, age 14, were forced to jump into the water for safety, but Santos could not swim and drowned, becoming the last American death recorded due to steamboat fire.

CALIFORNIA

STEAM NAVIGATION CO.

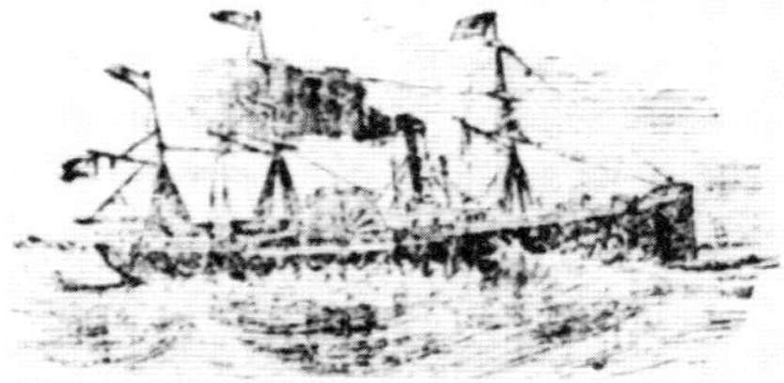

OCEAN AND BAY STEAMERS.

**Tri-Monthly Line for Portland and Victoria.**

Leave about the 9th, 19th, and 29th—the Steamer of the 19th going first to Victoria and then to Portland, and those of the 9th and 29th first to Portland and then to Victoria.

**Steamer PACIFIC........................ Capt. A. M. Burns**
**" BROTHER JONATHAN.........Capt. S. J. De Wolf**

**Tri-Monthly to the Southern Coast and Ports,**

Viz: San Luis Obispo, Santa Barbara, San Pedro, San Diego, touching at Catalina Island, Wilmington.

**Steamer SENATOR..................................Capt. J. S. Butters**

**San Francisco to Napa,**

Touching at Mare Island and Vallejo. Time, Winter Season, Tri-Weekly—Tuesday, Thursday, and Saturday, at 11 A. M. Leaves from Broadway Wharf, returning alternate days, arriving at 1 P. M. Summer Season, Daily Line, Sundays excepted—leaves at 9 A. M.; returning, arrives at 6 P. M.

**Steamer AMELIA.................................. Capt. P. F. Doling**

**San Francisco to Suisun,**

Touching at Benicia. Leaves Tri-Weekly, Monday, Thursday, and Saturday, at 10 A. M., from Pacific Wharf. Returns on alternate days, arriving at 2 P. M.

**Steamer PRINCESS..........................Capt. A. D. Carpenter**

**San Francisco to Petaluma and San Rafael.**

Leave Vallejo and Davis Street Wharf Daily.

**Steamer PETALUMA.....................................Capt. Seaman**
**" CLINTON..........................................Capt. ———**

This advertisement for the California Steam Navigation Co. is interesting in that it advertises oceangoing, riverboating, and ferryboating, all with steam-powered vessels. The *Petaluma* is not to be confused with later riverboats of the same name. (Courtesy Western Railway Museum Archives.)

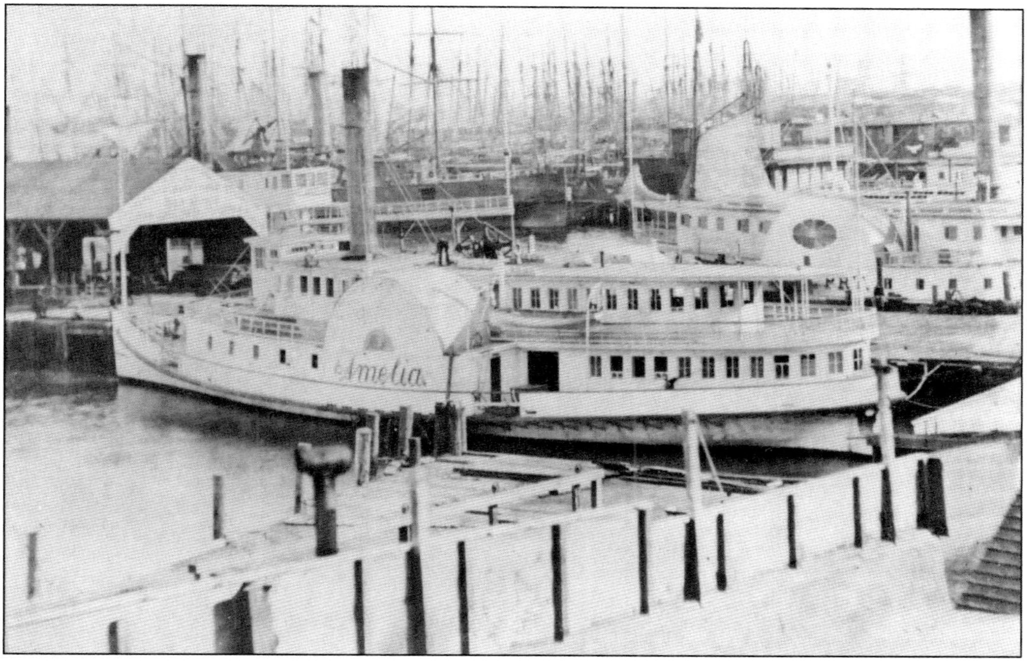

The *Amelia* was built in 1863. Her actual river service was mostly up the Mare Island Strait into Napa River as far as Suscol, meeting Napa Valley Railroad trains, then returning to San Francisco. Around 1875, she began ferryboating for the Central Pacific Railroad until sold in 1882. (Courtesy Western Railway Museum Archives, No. 49502.)

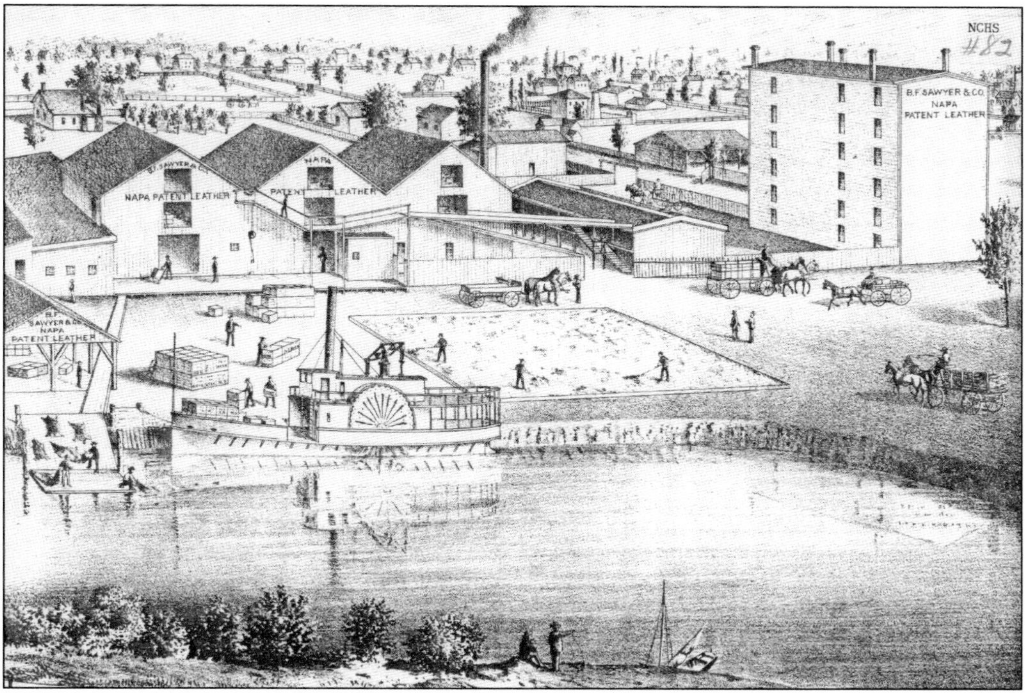


This early-day artist's conception of the Napa riverfront shows the riverboat *Express No. 1*, owned by J.G. White, tied up at the Sawyer Tannery. The *Express*, built in 1851 for the Napa trade, was a mere 105 tons. She went off documentation by 1868. (Courtesy Napa Valley Historical Society.)

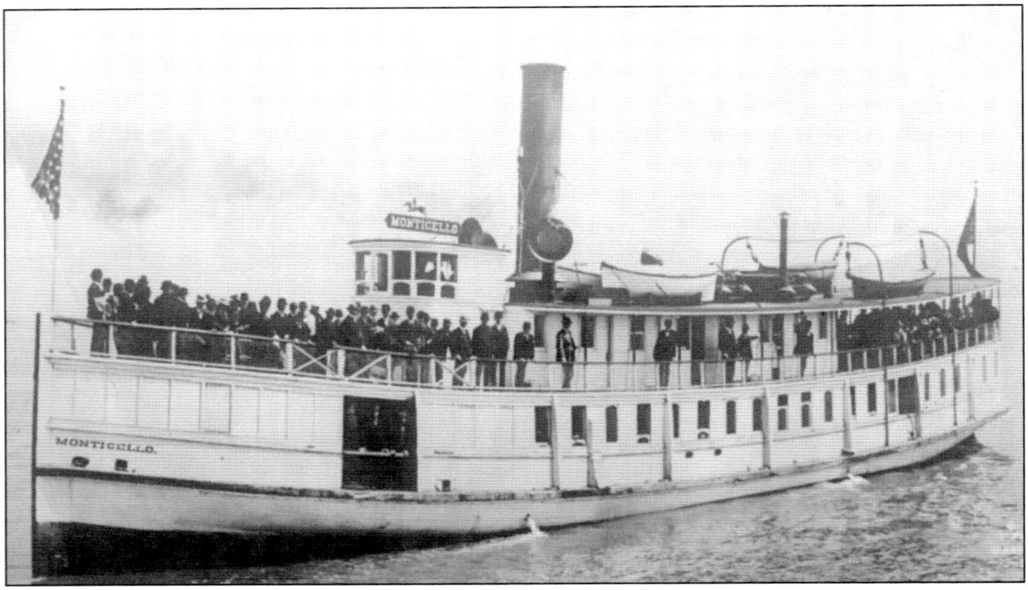


The *Monticello*, built in Ballard, Washington, in 1892, was a rare case of a ferryboat putting a riverboat out of business. On August 10, 1895, the *Monticello* began competing with the Aden brothers' *Sunol*. *Monticello*'s triple expansion engine and screw drive were no match for the *Sunol*'s paddle wheel, as speed counted. (Courtesy Vallejo Naval and Historical Museum.)

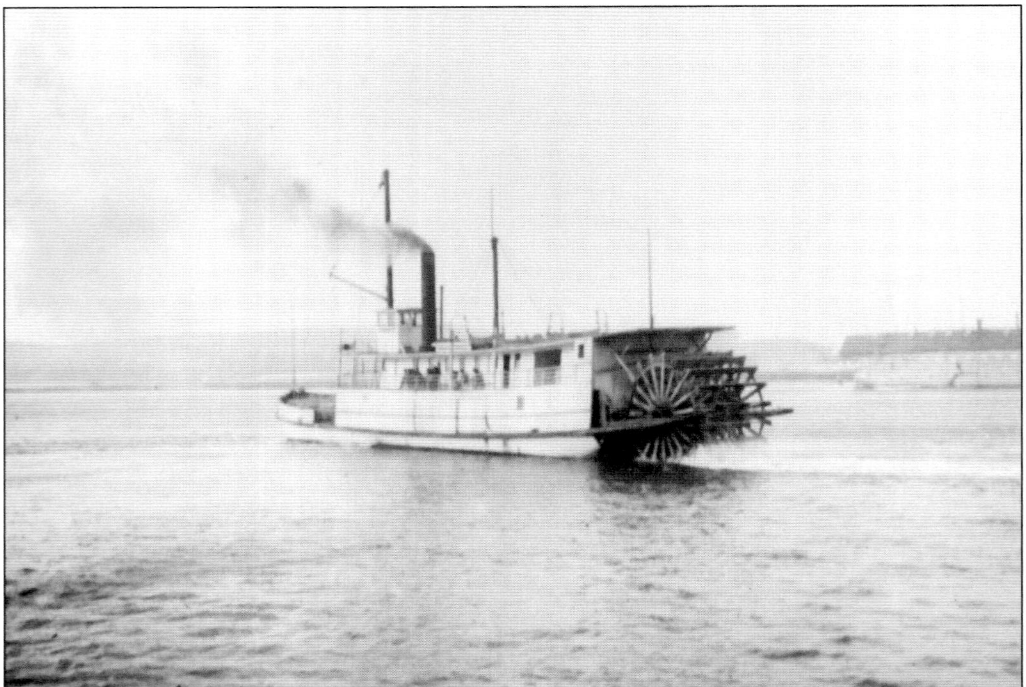

This picture shows the *Sunol* on Mare Island Strait passing the US Naval Shipyard at the right. The *Sunol* could be down from Suscol on the Napa River and has surely stopped off in Vallejo. The appearance of passengers on her cabin deck dates this from before 1905. (Courtesy Western Railway Museum Archives, No. 50345.)

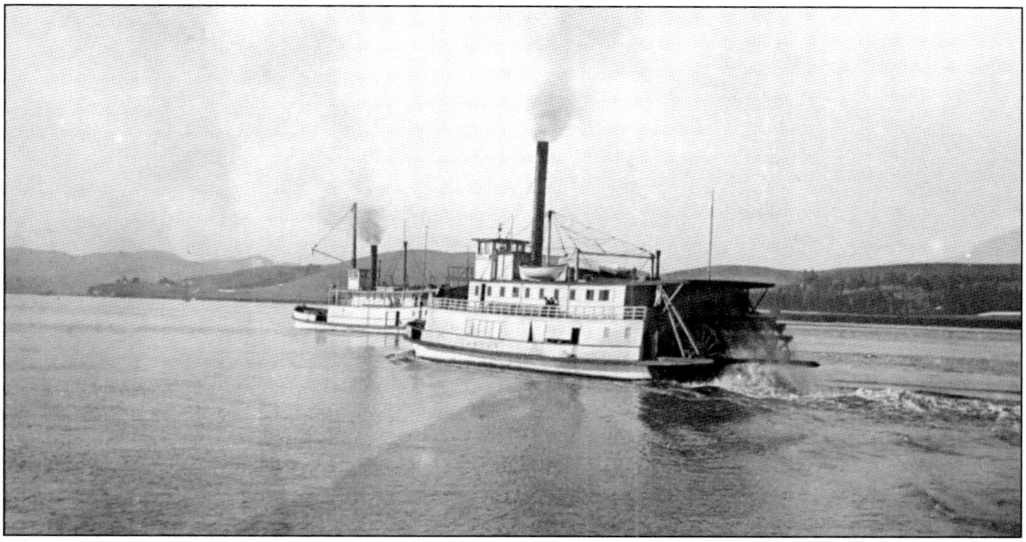

The 147.83-ton *Herald* is about to overtake a smaller *Sunol* on Mare Island Strait. The *Sunol* operated between Vallejo and San Francisco while the *Herald* was a Napa fixture in her pre–Southern Pacific days. The *Sunol* was notoriously slow, so it is unlikely that they are racing in this image. (Courtesy Western Railway Museum Archives, No, 49457.)

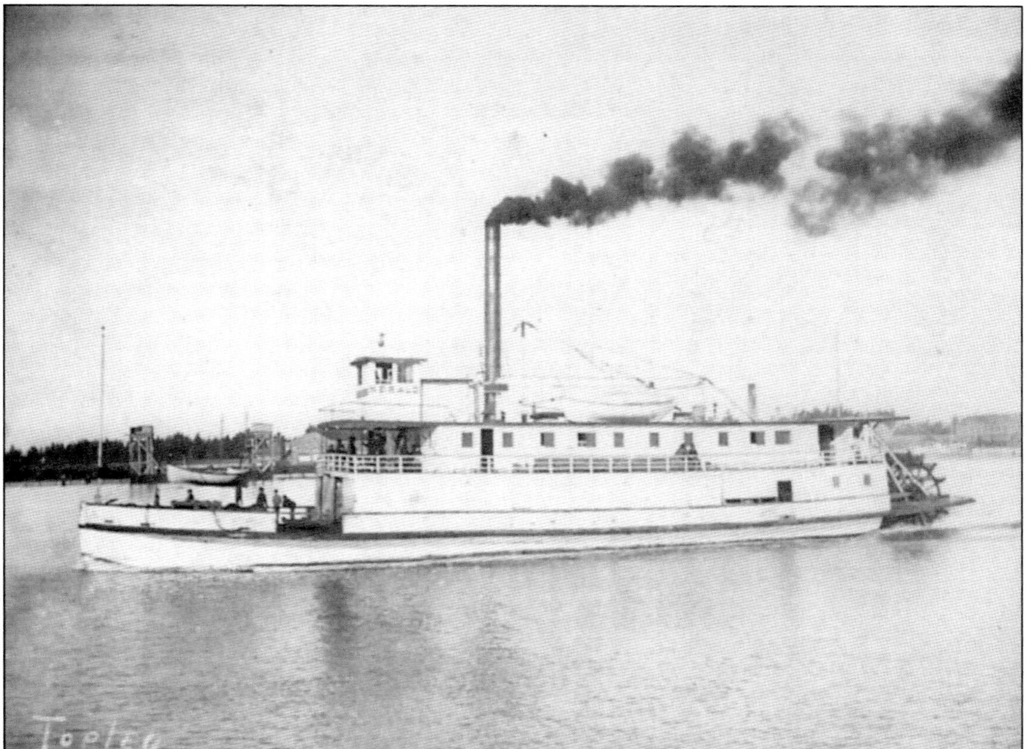

The 127.5-feet-long, 147.8-ton *Herald* was built in 1878. Early on, she worked the Napa River and the Petaluma Creek. As a Southern Pacific boat after 1900, she worked the San Francisco–Sacramento, Stockton, and Sacramento–Marysville runs before retirement in 1912. (Courtesy Vallejo Naval and Historical Museum.)

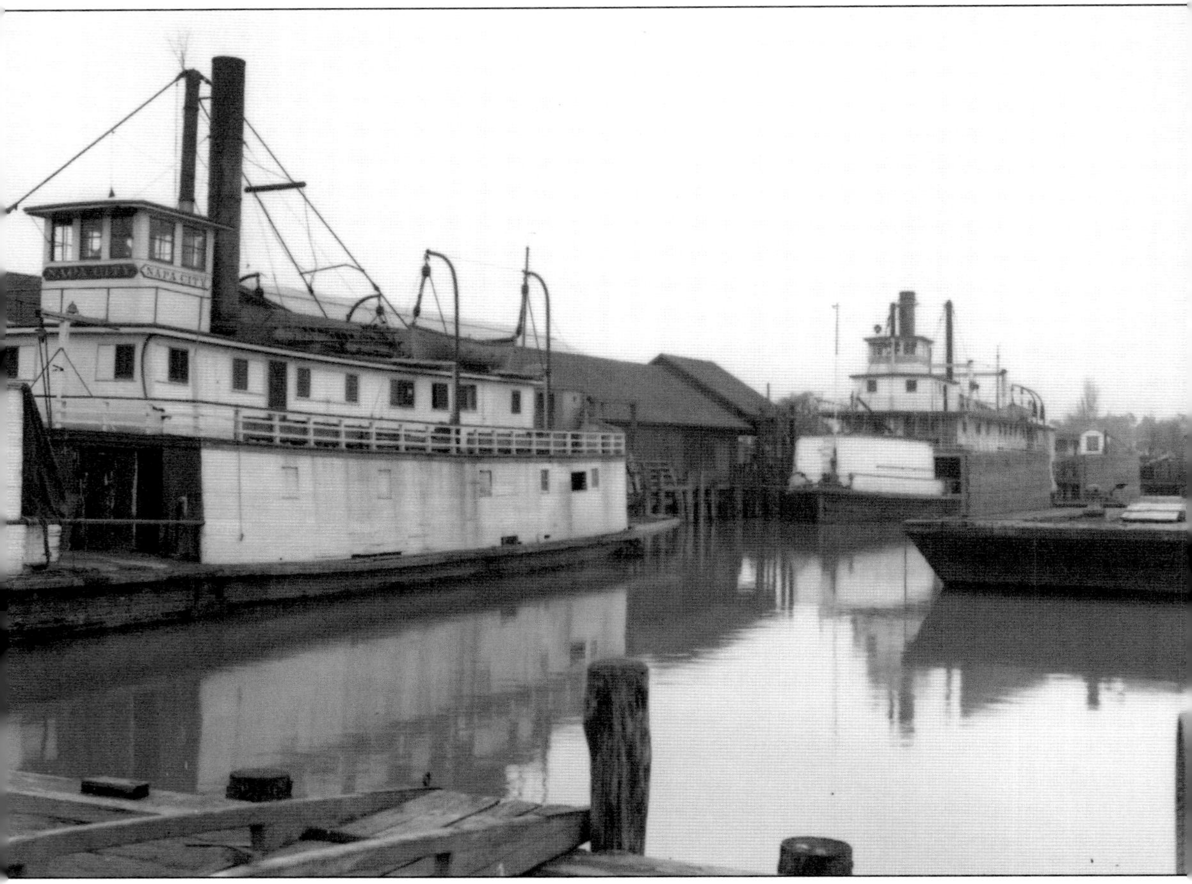


The *Napa City* (left) was a major player in the Napa River trade until railroad competition put an end to it by 1920. The other riverboat docked at Napa is unidentified. This is a rare picture since there was hardly enough business for more than one boat at any given time. (Courtesy Western Railway Museum Archives, No. 50347.)

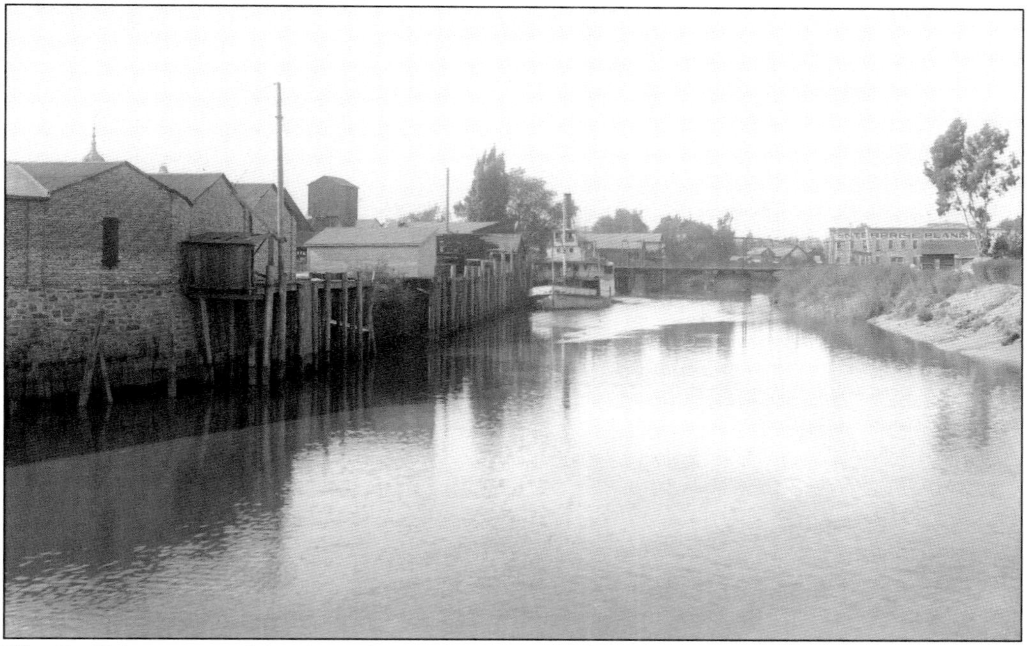

The *St. Helena,* named for the volcanic mountain at the head of the Napa Valley, was built in 1902. She rated 344 tons, measured 135 by 30.5 by 6.8 feet, and had a 14-man crew. As railroad competition killed Napa River steamboating, she went off documentation during 1924. (Courtesy Napa Valley Historical Society.)

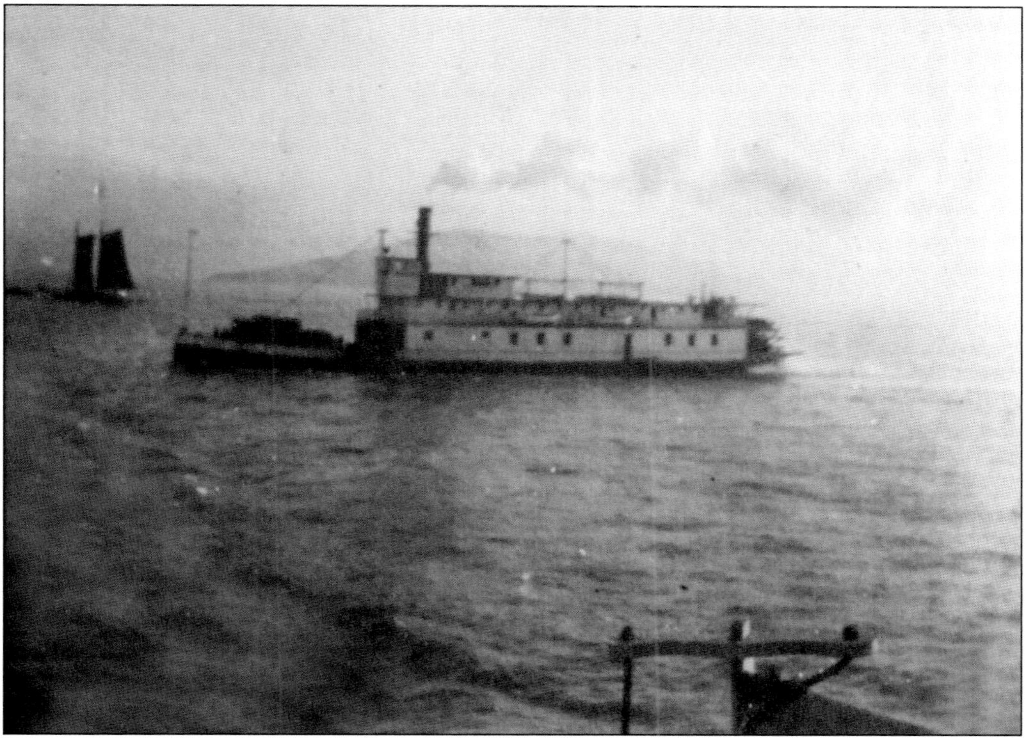

This photograph is believed to be the 1902-built *St. Helena* steaming across San Francisco Bay on her way to Napa via the Mare Island Strait and the Napa River. (Author's collection.)

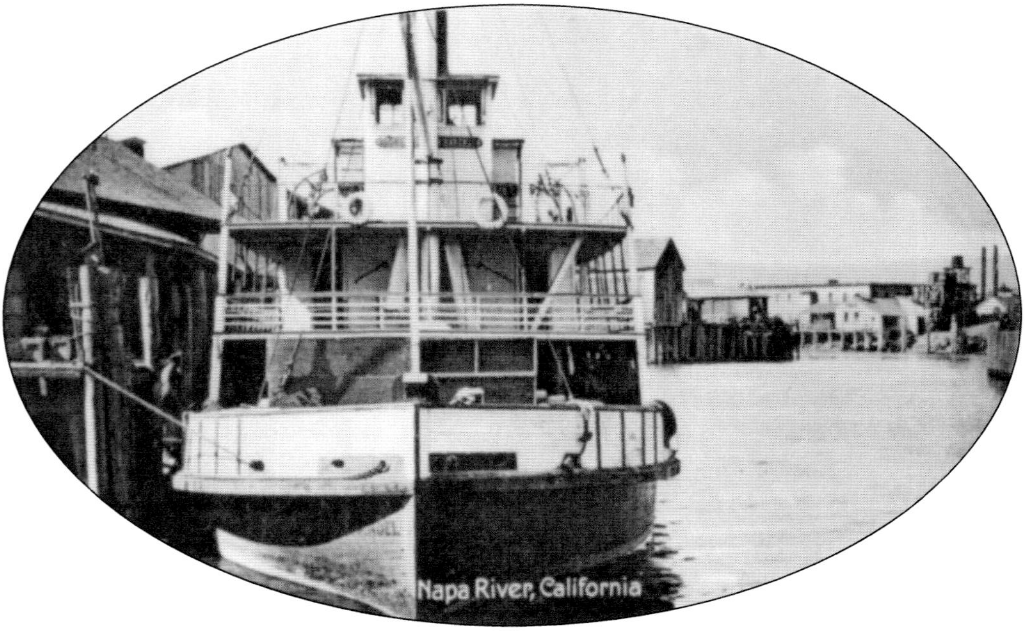


The 329-ton *Zinfandel*, built in 1889 in San Francisco for the Napa River trade, measured 125 by 29.5 by 7 feet and was the longest lasting steamer on that river. Her last service was on the Sacramento River before floundering in Miner Slough in 1922. (Courtesy Napa Valley Historical Society.)

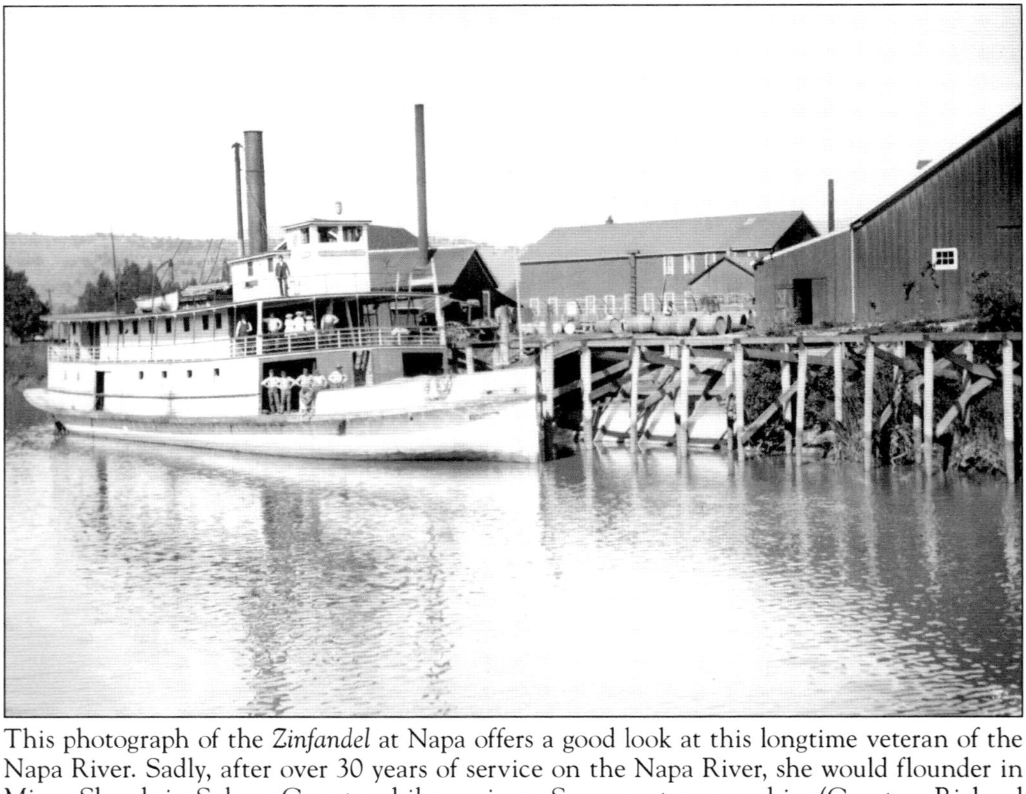

This photograph of the *Zinfandel* at Napa offers a good look at this longtime veteran of the Napa River. Sadly, after over 30 years of service on the Napa River, she would flounder in Miner Slough in Solano County while serving a Sacramento ownership. (Courtesy Richard Schlaich Collection.)

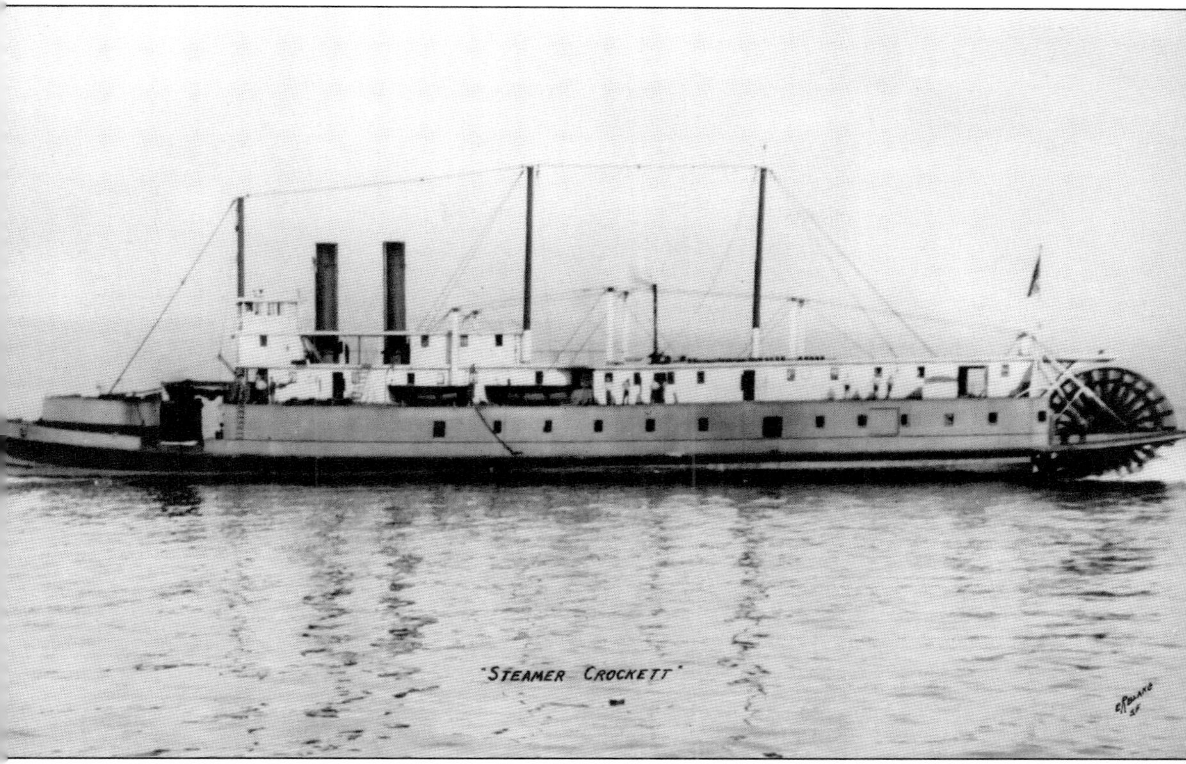


The 1898-built *H. J. Corcoran* was a 209.5-feet-long, 682 tonner and in her day—along with *Captain Weber*—was one of California's two fastest riverboats. During a dense fog in 1913, she rammed and sunk the *Seminole*. The C&H Sugar Co. bought her in 1914, then rebuilt and renamed her the *Crockett*, as seen here. (Courtesy San Francisco Maritime National Historical Park, No. P82-100.9.)

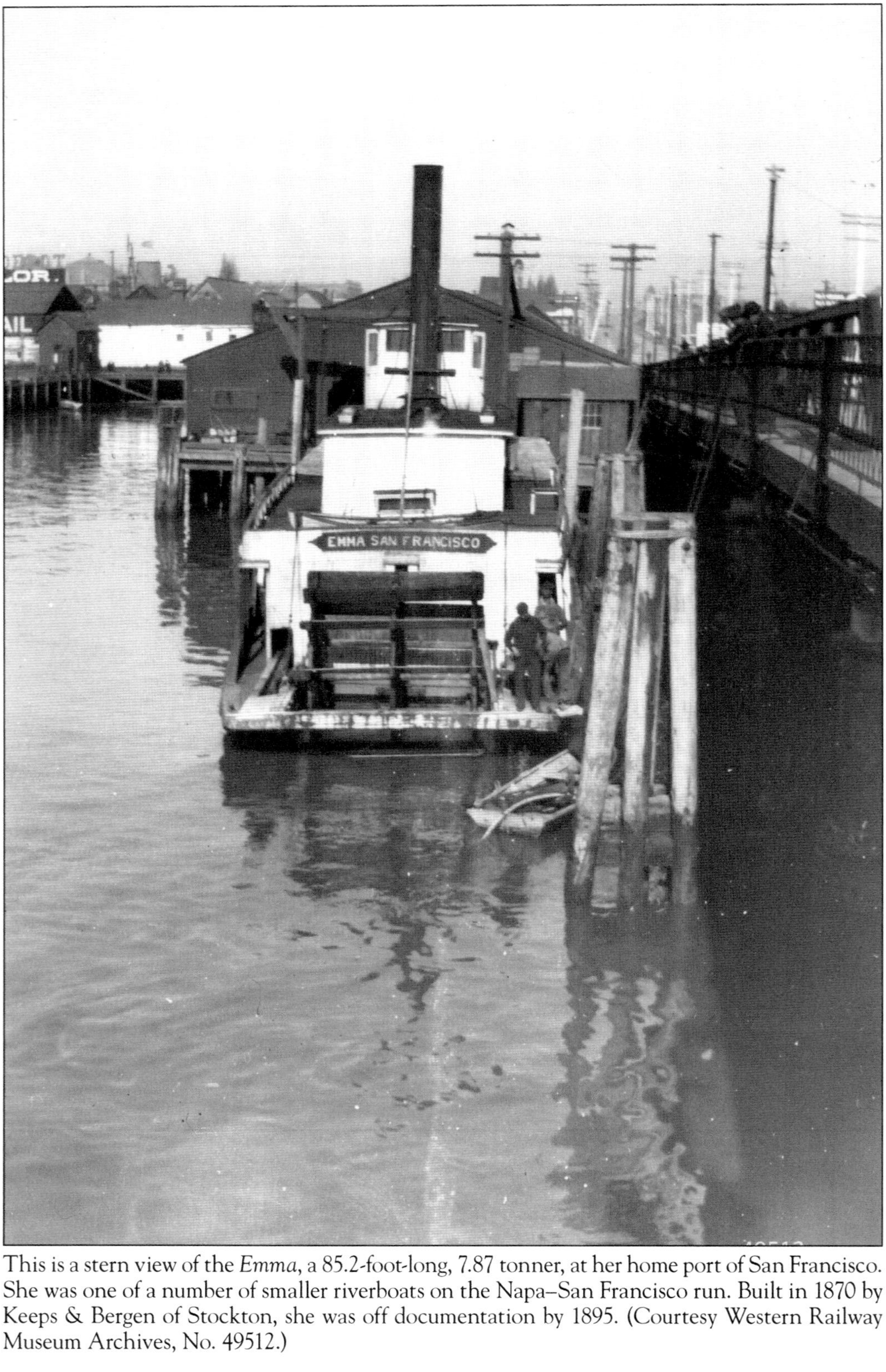


This is a stern view of the *Emma*, a 85.2-foot-long, 7.87 tonner, at her home port of San Francisco. She was one of a number of smaller riverboats on the Napa–San Francisco run. Built in 1870 by Keeps & Bergen of Stockton, she was off documentation by 1895. (Courtesy Western Railway Museum Archives, No. 49512.)

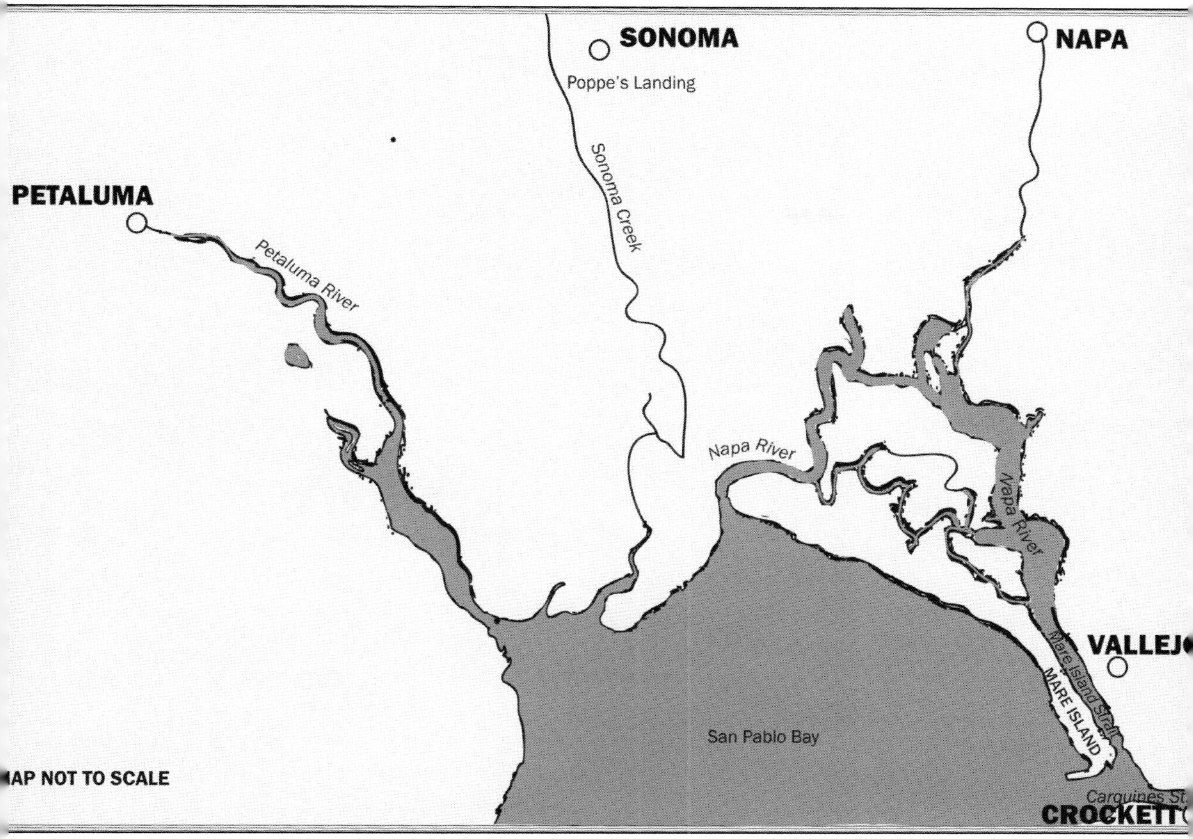


The Petaluma Creek (now called the Petaluma River), Sonoma Creek, and the Napa River with Mare Island Strait provided water routes for North Bay's riverboats. Upon reaching San Pablo Bay, these vessels, and those in from Sacramento, Rio Vista, and Stockton via the Carquinez Strait and Crockett, continued southerly into San Francisco Bay. (Map by Kevin Shields.)

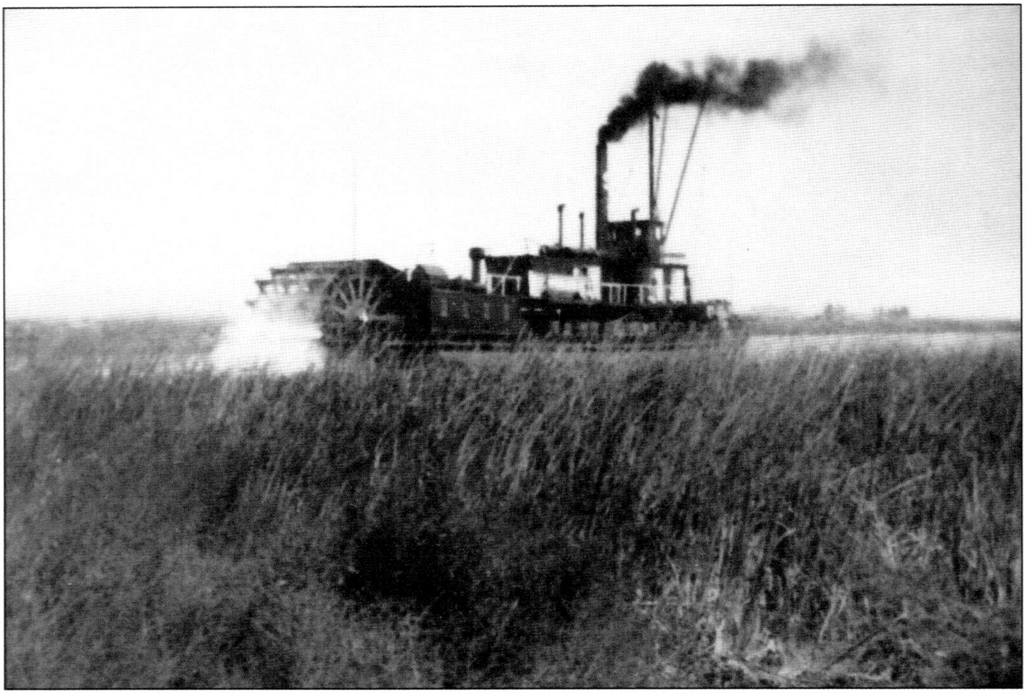

This 1874 or 1875 photograph of the 107-foot-long *Sonoma* shows her steaming downstream toward San Pablo Bay and on to San Francisco. This is the only known picture to date of the *Sonoma* on the Sonoma Creek, and perhaps, the only picture of her original configuration. (Courtesy Sonoma Valley Historical Society.)

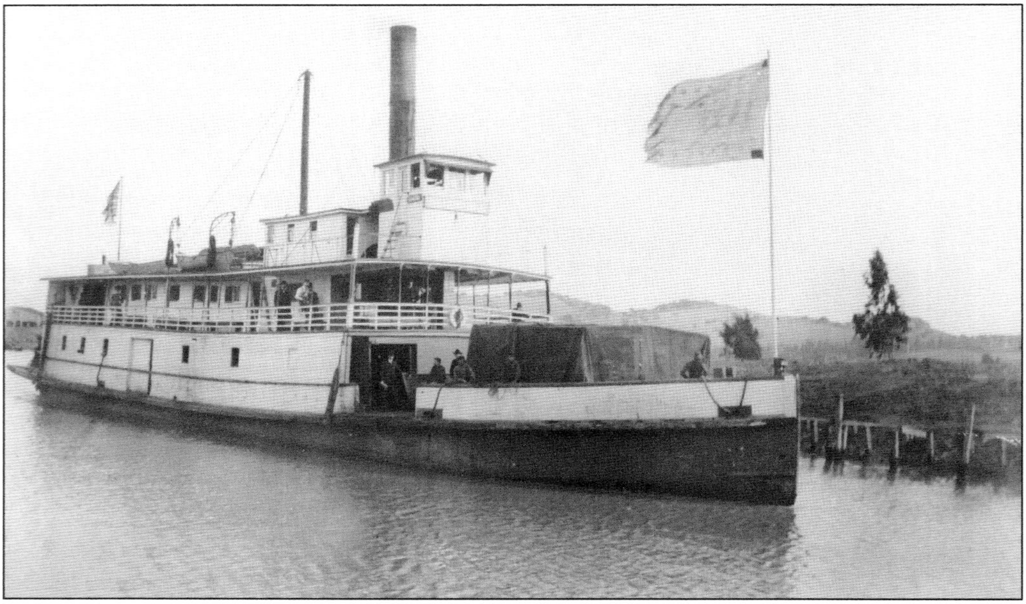

Launched on September 30, 1874, for the Sonoma Creek, the *Sonoma* succeeded the *Princess*. Insufficient business to pay for the investment sent her to the Petaluma Creek, where this image likely was captured. Around 1879, the California Transportation Co. of Stockton bought her and rebuilt her to 135 feet long, raising her to 250 tons. Abandoned in 1915, she went off documentation in 1923. (Courtesy San Francisco Maritime National Historical Park, No. B1.781p1.)

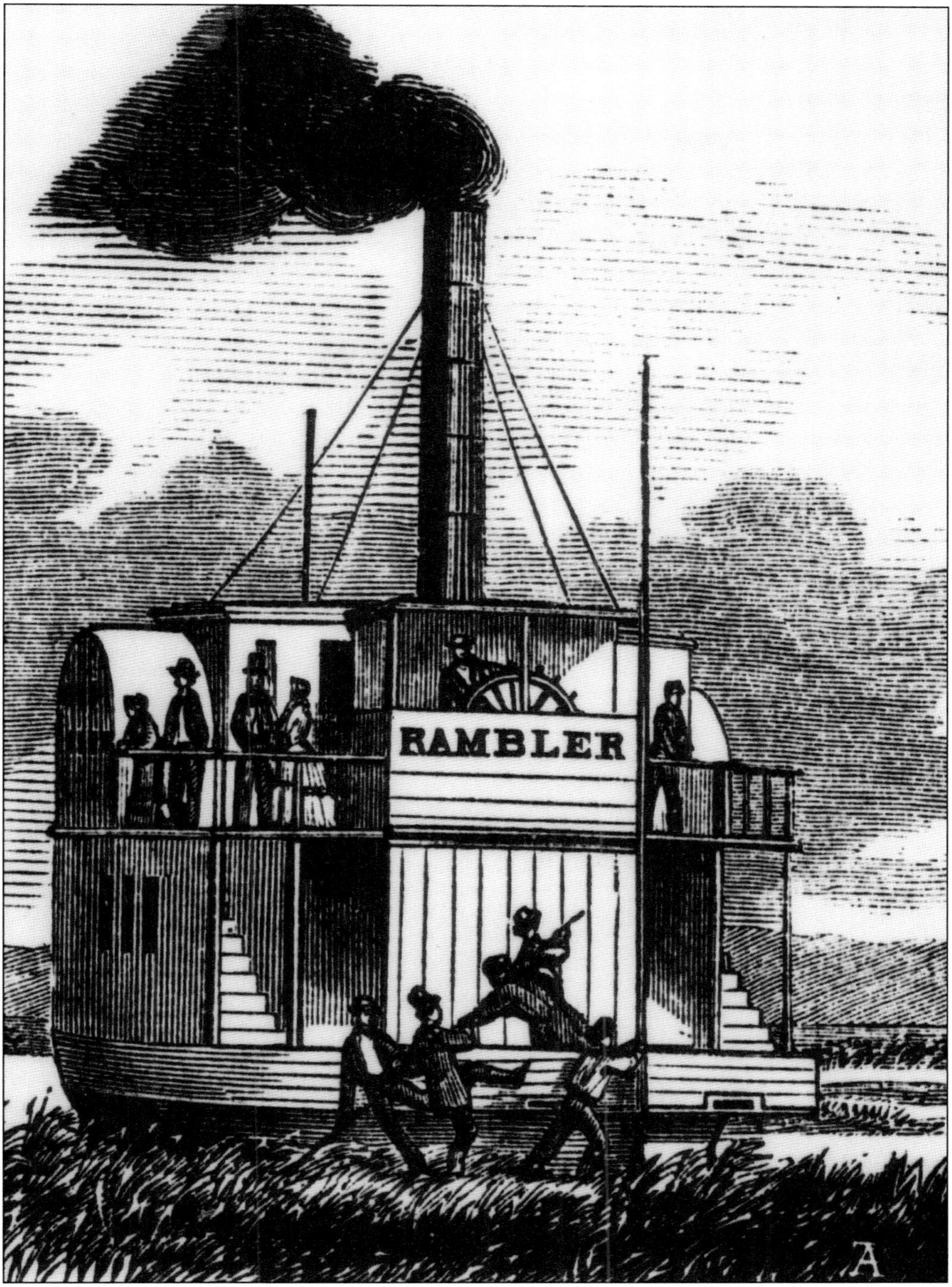


This woodcut of the riverboat *Rambler* is familiar to many riverboat history enthusiasts. Built some time before 1857, she went off documentation before 1868. Basically, she was just another sidewheeler that got stuck, called on male passengers to help push her off with poles, and finished an 1857 voyage. (Courtesy San Francisco Maritime National Historical Park, No. B7.14,121n.)

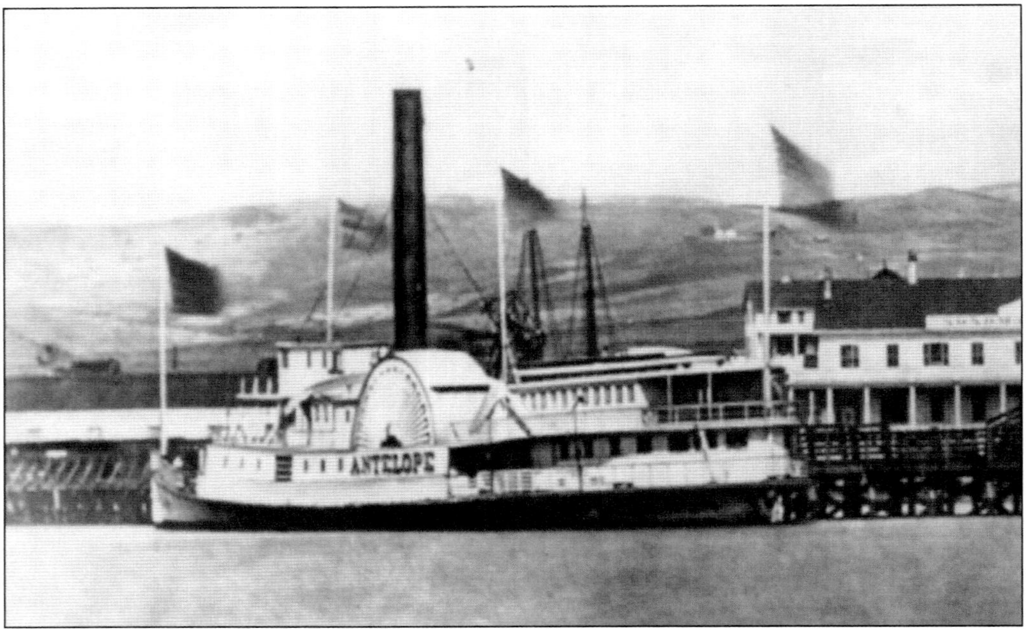


Built on the East Coast in 1846, the *Antelope* steamed around the Horn during the Gold Rush, then on the Sacramento River, earning the sobriquet "Gold Boat" for carrying Wells Fargo's gold. She also carried Pony Express mail. At Donahue Landing on the Petaluma Creek, she is carrying San Francisco & North Pacific Railroad passengers. She was dismantled in 1888. (Courtesy William Knorp collection.)

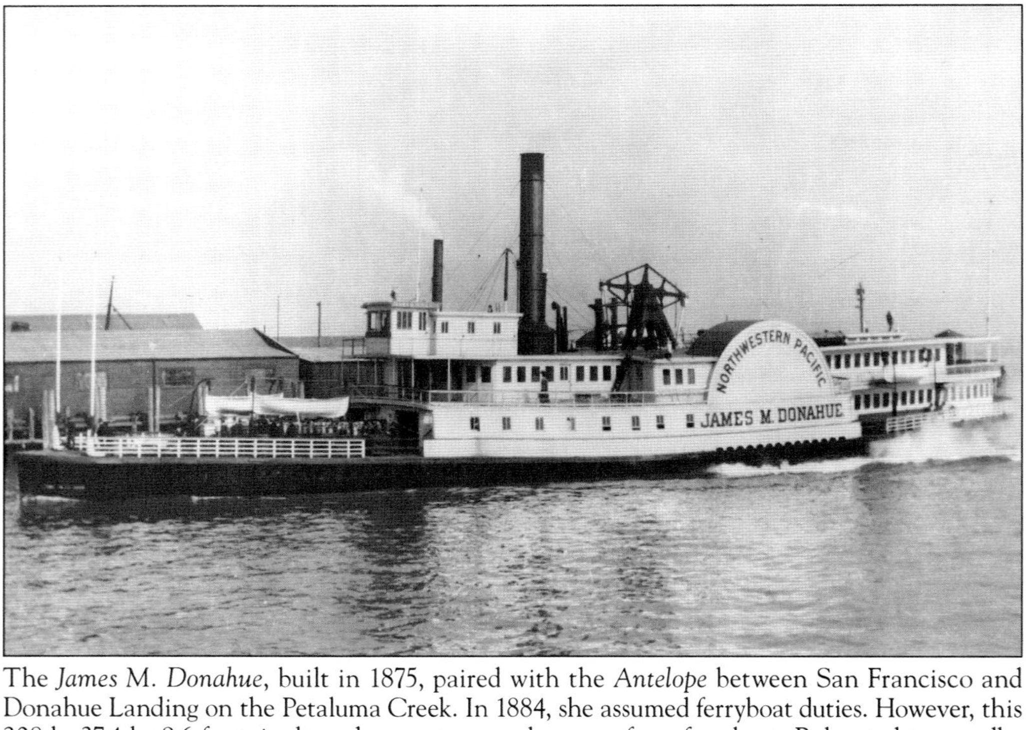


The *James M. Donahue*, built in 1875, paired with the *Antelope* between San Francisco and Donahue Landing on the Petaluma Creek. In 1884, she assumed ferryboat duties. However, this 208-by-37.4-by-9.6-foot single ender was too cumbersome for a ferryboat. Relegated to standby status in 1909, she was retired in 1923. (Wilbur C. Whittaker photograph; author's collection.)

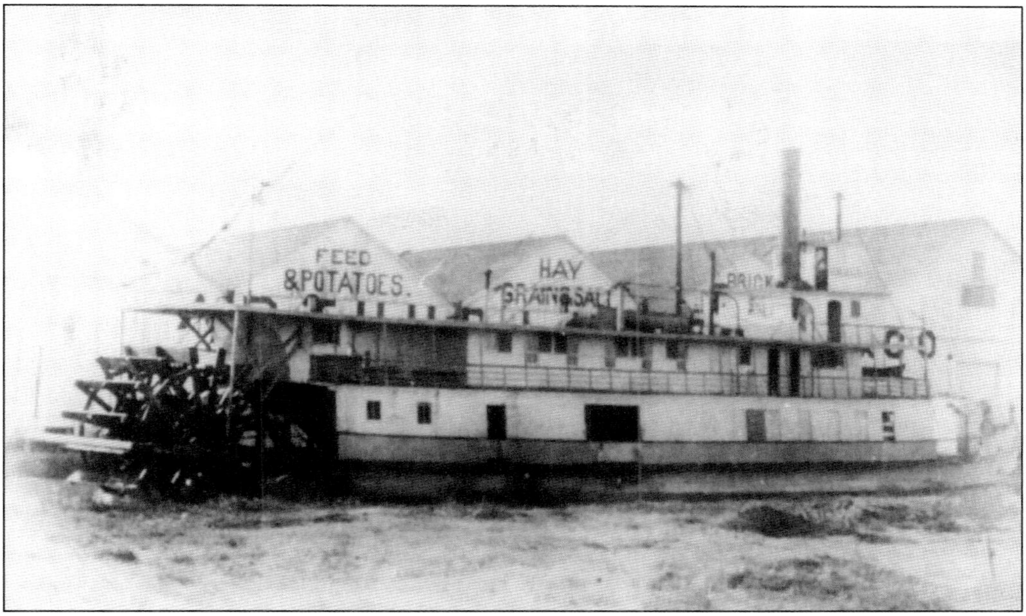


The Petaluma Creek's first steamer, *Gold*, a 292 tonner measuring 134 by 30 by 7 feet with a 240-horsepower engine, was built in 1883 and named for her owner, Capt. N. Gould. In December 1903, the Petaluma & Santa Rosa Railroad purchased her to connect the railroad to San Francisco. She was destroyed by fire on November 8, 1920. (Author's collection.)

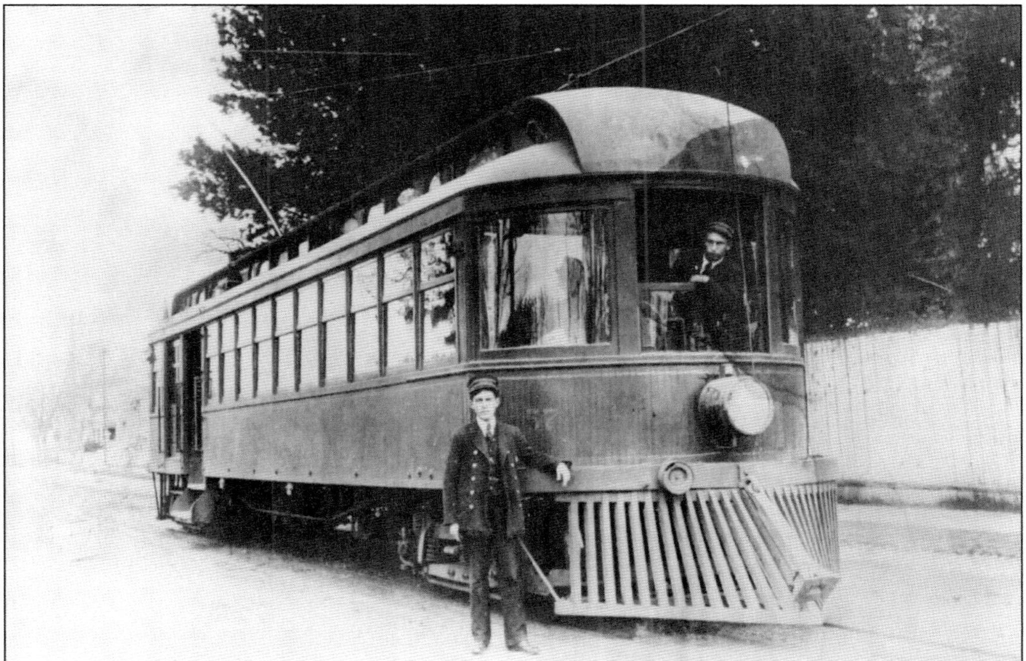

The Petaluma & Santa Rosa Railroad's (P&SR) electric interurbans met its riverboats at Petaluma and brought transferring passengers to Sebastopol, Santa Rosa, Forestville, and Two Rock. Motorman Bill Parks (in window) and conductor Chris Christianson crewed this single-car train in the P&SR's early days. (From Randolph Brandt; author's collection.)

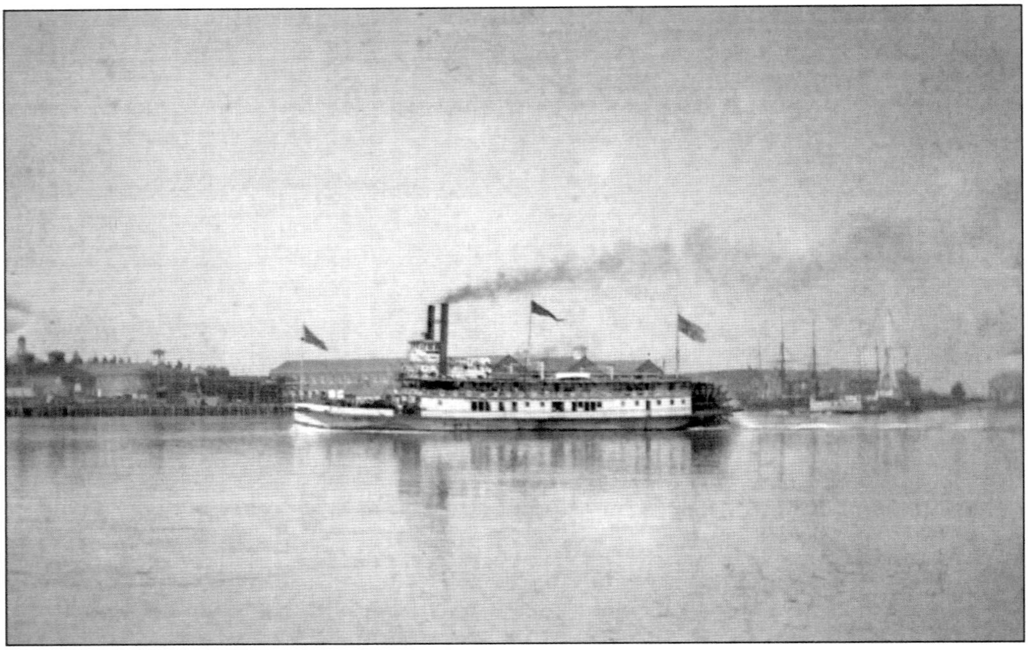

James Turner of Benicia built the 264-ton, 134-by-21-by-5.5-foot *Resolute* in 1884, seen here heading south on the Mare Island Strait. The P&SR bought her in 1922 for $16,625.16, renaming her *Petaluma*. On March 22, 1914, she burned at Petaluma and sank. (Courtesy Vallejo Naval and Historical Museum.)

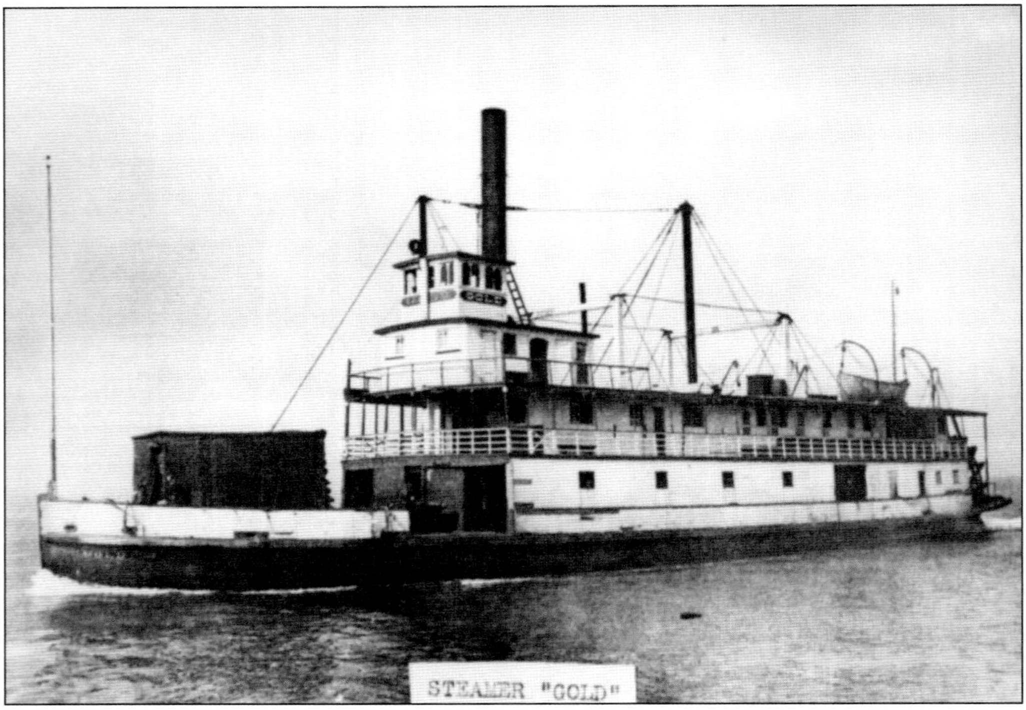


In 1921, the Petaluma & Santa Rosa Railroad bought the 317-ton, 115-by-35-by-6-foot *Fort Bragg* from the California Transportation Co., replacing the *Gold*. After modification, she became *Gold II*, serving until retirement in 1935. She went for scrap in 1940. (Author's collection.)

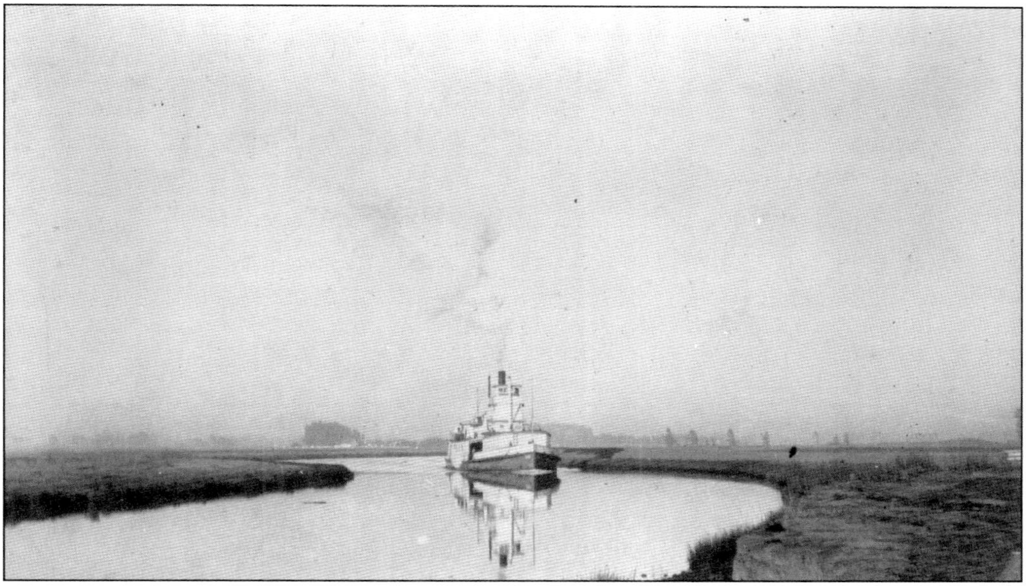

The *Gold II* of the Petaluma & Santa Rosa Railroad steams up the Petaluma Creek from San Francisco. For 16 miles, the creek had a meandering course in places only 60 feet wide and only six feet deep, requiring 95 course changes during a single trip. (Courtesy San Francisco Maritime National Historical Park, No. P80-014.19.)

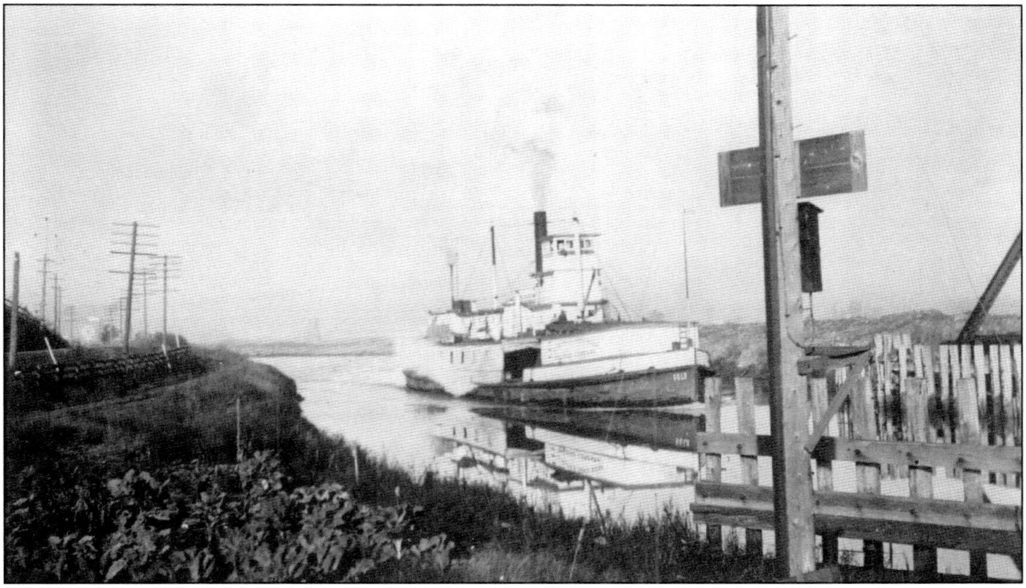

The *Gold II*, built in 1899 at Fort Bragg, California, was originally named *Fort Bragg*. The P&SR purchased her in 1921 and renamed her *Gold II* to replace the *Gold I*, which had burned in 1920. She measured 155 by 35 by 6 feet and rated 317 tons with a 150-horsepower engine. (Courtesy San Francisco Maritime National Historical Park, No. P80-014.25n.)

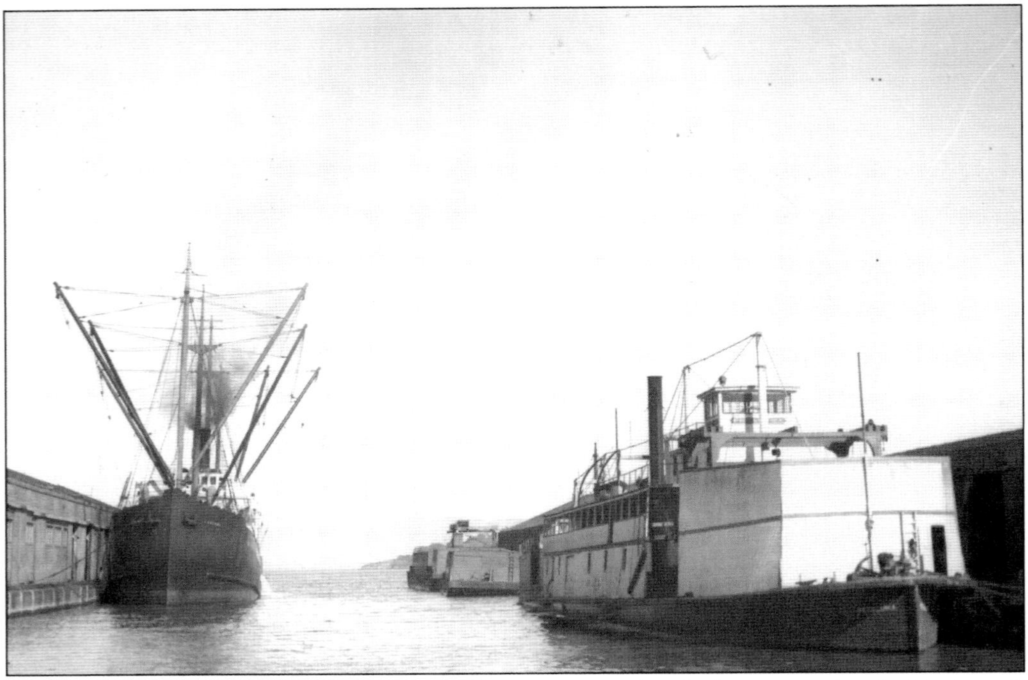

Long after all other California riverboats had been consigned to the history books, the *Petaluma II* of the Petaluma & Santa Rosa Railroad was still in service. She is docked at San Francisco's Pier 3, waiting for a 5:30 p.m. departure for her namesake port. (Courtesy Western Railway Museum Archives, No. 49495.)

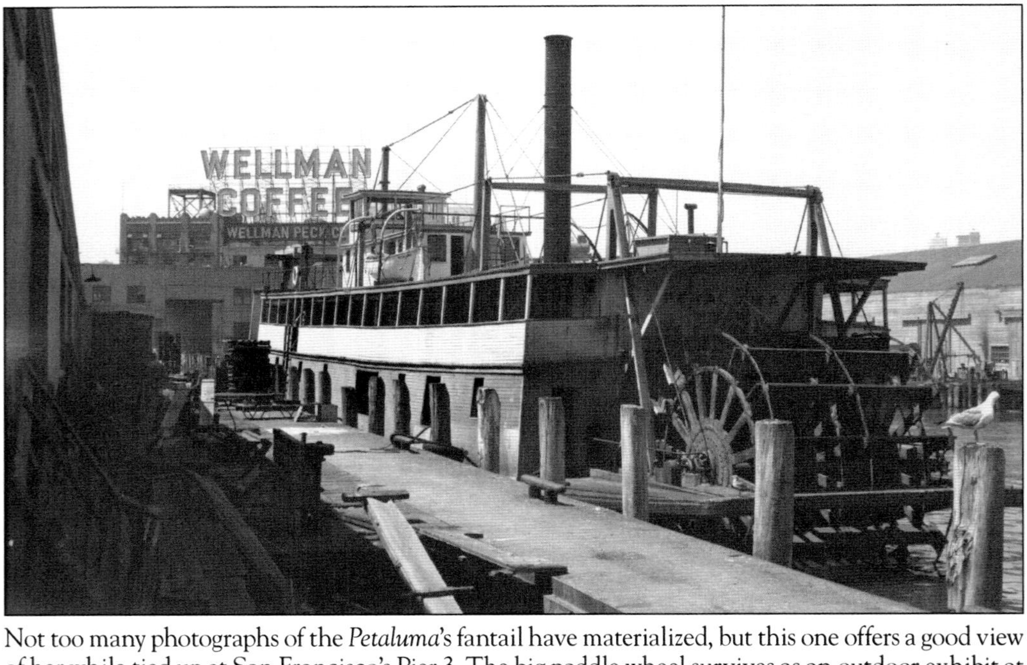


Not too many photographs of the *Petaluma*'s fantail have materialized, but this one offers a good view of her while tied up at San Francisco's Pier 3. The big paddle wheel survives as an outdoor exhibit at the San Francisco Maritime National Historical Park. (Courtesy Richard Schlaich Collection.)

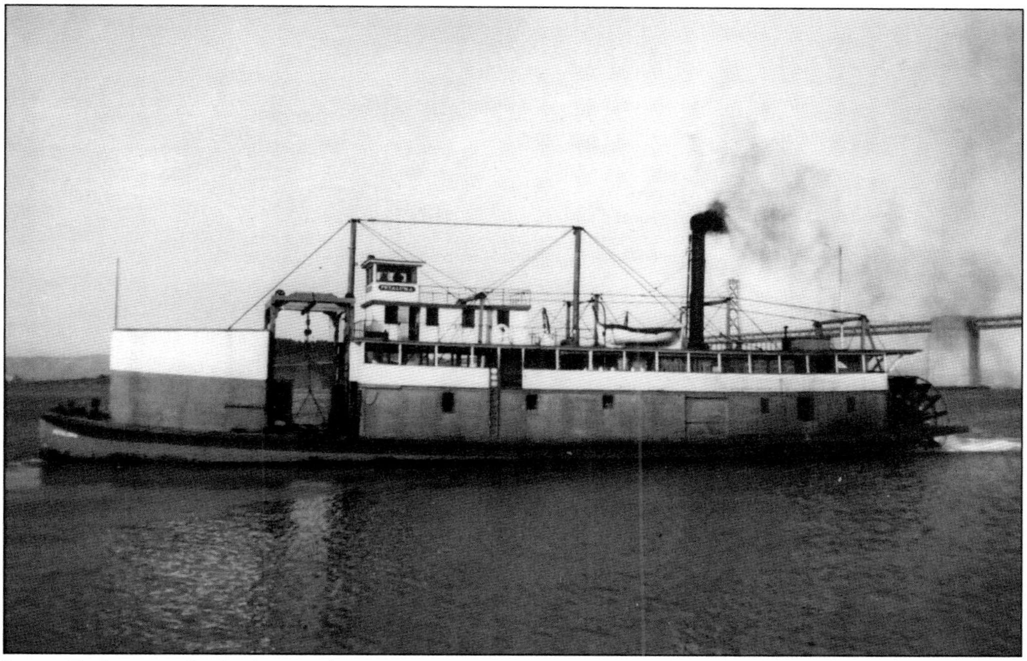

James Robertson built the *Petaluma II* in 1914 as a 141-by-35-foot, 448 tonner carrying passengers and freight. When passenger services ended in 1936, her cabin deck was converted to freight space. Her boiler and stack were abaft, avoiding spoilage of perishables when placed between the boiler and engine. (Author's collection.)

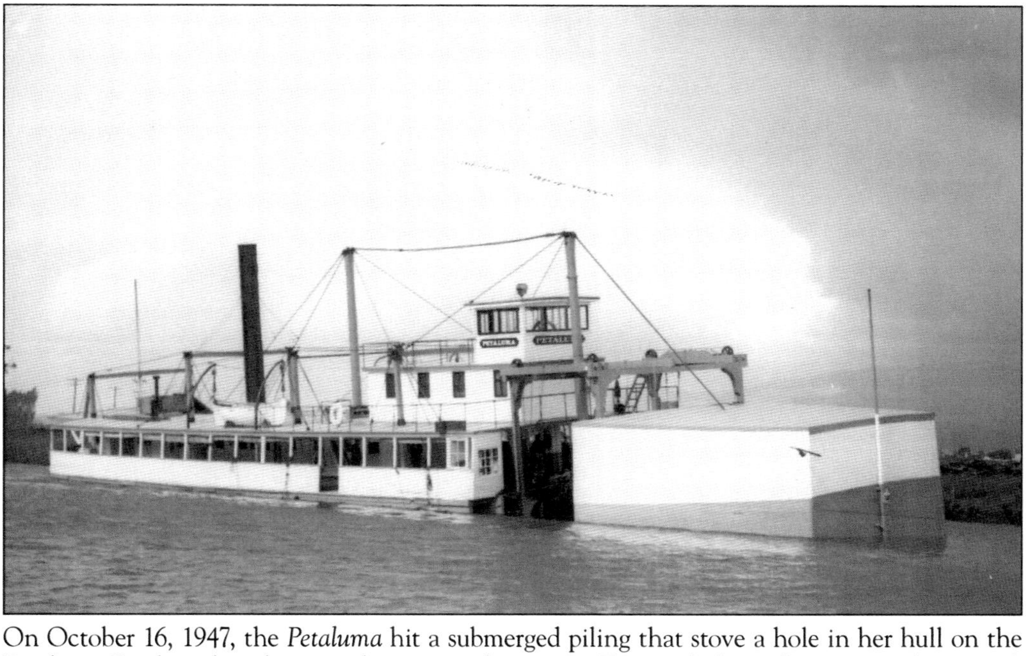

On October 16, 1947, the *Petaluma* hit a submerged piling that stove a hole in her hull on the Petaluma Creek, sinking her into the not-too-deep water. Two weeks later, she was raised, repaired, and back in service. This was the *Petaluma*'s only serious accident. (L.L. Bonney photograph; courtesy Western Railway Museum Archives, No. 49496.)

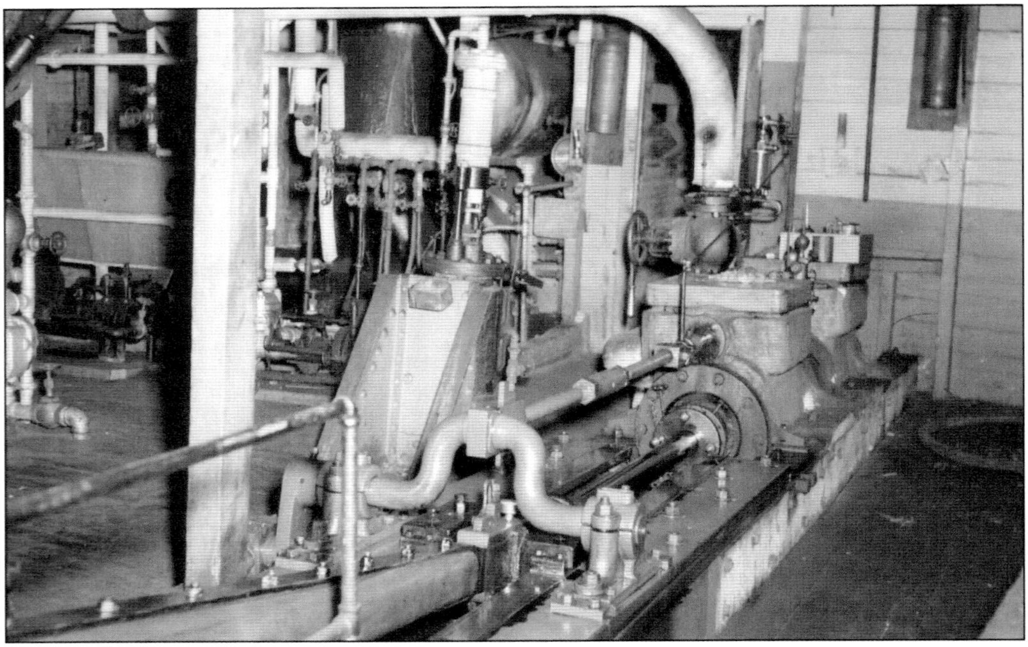

When the first *Petaluma* burned and sank, her steam engine was recovered from the Petaluma Creek and installed in the *Petaluma II*. Thus, the same 250-horsepower engine that went into the *Resolute* in 1884 lasted into the Nuclear Age—66 years later. This is the *Petaluma II*'s engine room in 1950. (Frank Ricci photograph; courtesy San Francisco Maritime National Historical Park, No. B11.20.324.18n.)

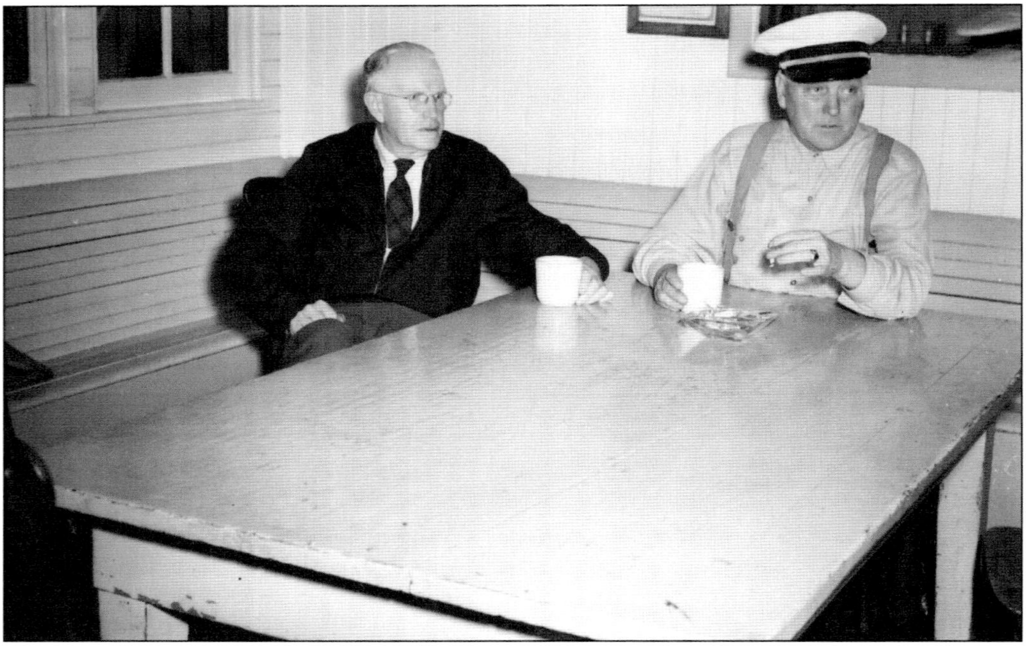

For a riverboat crew, life alternated between hard work and relaxing any way one could. Capt. John H. Urton of the *Petaluma* is having a cup of coffee with a visitor on the texas deck in August 1950. In a few days, California riverboating will be history. (Frank Ricci photograph; courtesy San Francisco Maritime National Historical Park, No. B11.20.324.1n.)

# *Six*

# Riverboats about San Francisco Bay

Primitive roads and lack of railways caused people to look for alternative transportation to San Francisco from San Jose. Thus, the riverboats steamed to the southwestern part of San Francisco Bay, then seven miles up Alviso Creek to Alviso, followed by a five-mile stage ride to San Jose. As the San Francisco & San Jose Railroad would not arrive until January 1864, there was a lively riverboat trade to Santa Clara County. On December 2, 1850, the first *Sacramento* made it up the Alviso Creek with San Jose–bound passengers and freight from San Francisco. As early as 1856, the Napa Transportation Co. was running the *Amelia* and *San Jose* to Alviso, and in 1872, Capt. John Leale was given command of the *Relief* for that run. Other riverboats to Alviso were the *Alviso*, *Express* (Capt. S. Card), *Guadalupe* (Capt. C. Thorn), *Hope*, *Jenny Lind*, *Resolute*, and, as evidence indicates, the *Sonoma*. These boats hauled loads of hay for San Francisco's large equine population, as well as hides, tallow, and quicksilver from the New Almaden mines. The *Relief* carried prodigious loads of fresh strawberries for San Francisco's tables; the riverboats were the preferred mode of transportation as the berries were likely to be crushed en route aboard bouncing buckboards. The railroad put paid to any further riverboat growth on that route as the trains became preferred to the slower steamboats, particularly in the days before refrigeration. These boats also developed a trade on the east side of San Francisco Bay, making landings by steaming up the Alameda Creek to Union City (later changed to Alvarado), Barron's Landing on Mount Eden Creek (three-fourths of a mile south of today's San Mateo-Hayward Bridge), West Berkeley (at the foot of University Avenue), Point Fleming (by the Golden Gate Fields Racetrack), Point Isabel (between Albany and El Cerrito), and just about any other point or inlet to the bay where business could be conducted.

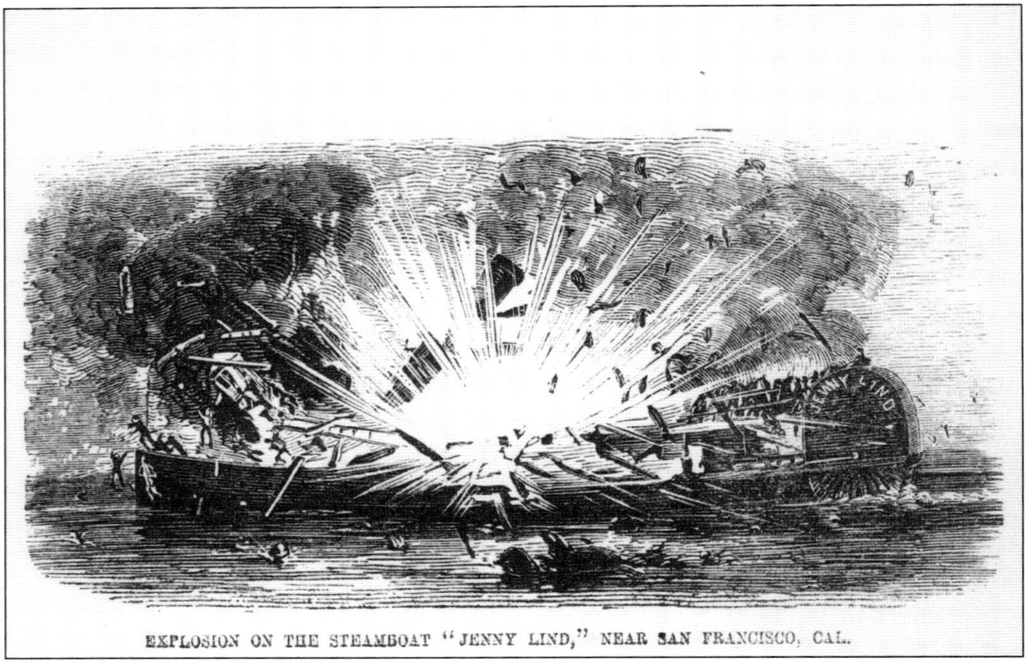


The 61-ton sidewheeler *Jenny Lind*, built in 1850, worked the San Francisco–Alviso run. On April 11, 1853, at 12:30 p.m., the *Jenny Lind* was on Alviso Slough when a dining room pipe exploded, killing 31 of her 125 passengers. The artist erroneously illustrated her a sternwheeler. (Courtesy California State Library.)

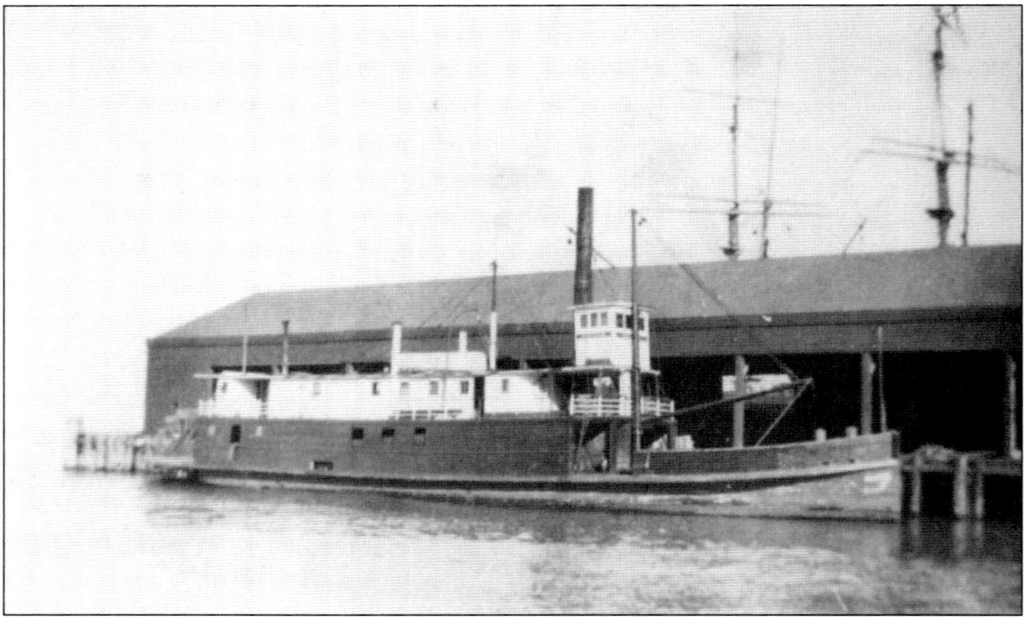

The *Alviso*, built in 1895, made trips up Alviso Slough. However, Alviso Landing had declined, and she went to the upper Sacramento River. On December 15, 1920, she and the *Weitchpec* burned at Bryte, a fire likely started by down-and-outers wintering in the boats' cabins. (Author's collection.)

A riverboat is tied up at Alviso in this c. 1905 image. The vessel has a cabin deck and carries a load of happy passengers dressed in Sunday best. It is unusual for passengers to be on the hurricane deck, and if they were not by the wheelhouse, the vessel's identity would be visible. (Courtesy San Francisco Maritime National Historical Park, No. B11.30,961pl.)

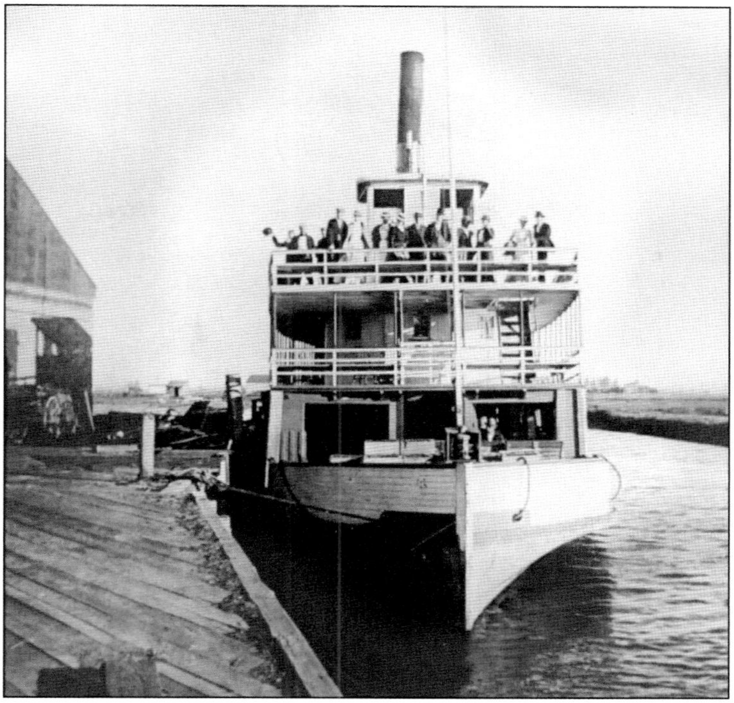

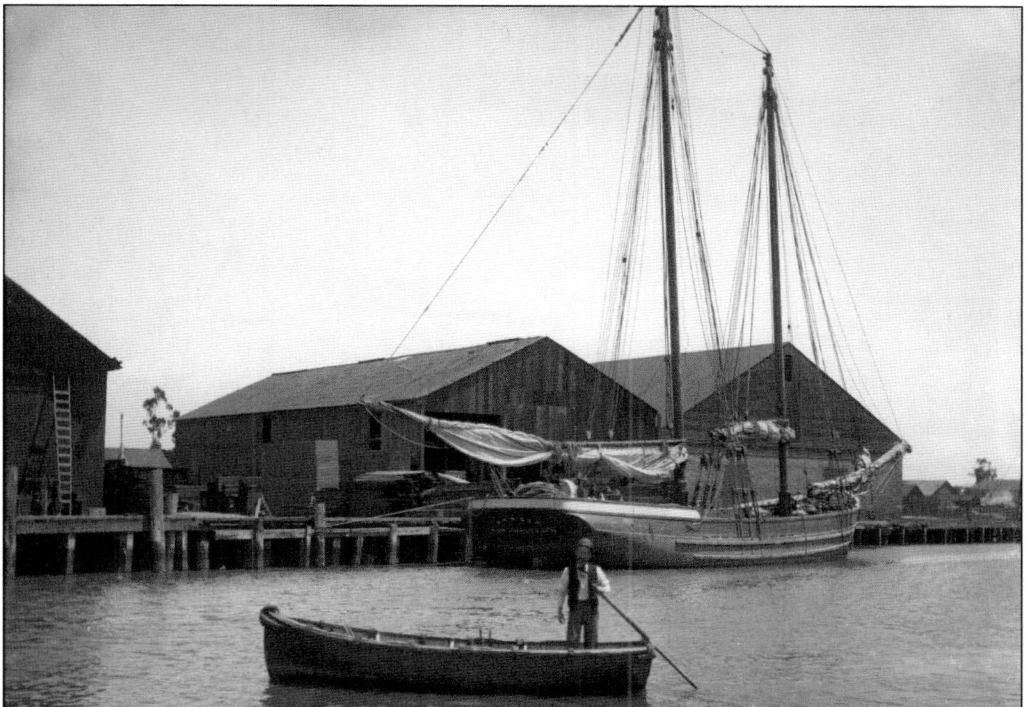

The scow schooner *Portia* is tied up at Alviso while a man is sculling a rowboat. In some places in the bay region, such as Alviso Slough, scow schooners were very effective competition to the riverboats due to smaller crew sizes and lack of fuel costs. (Courtesy Randolph Brandt Collection, San Francisco Maritime National Historical Park, No. B19,246pl.)

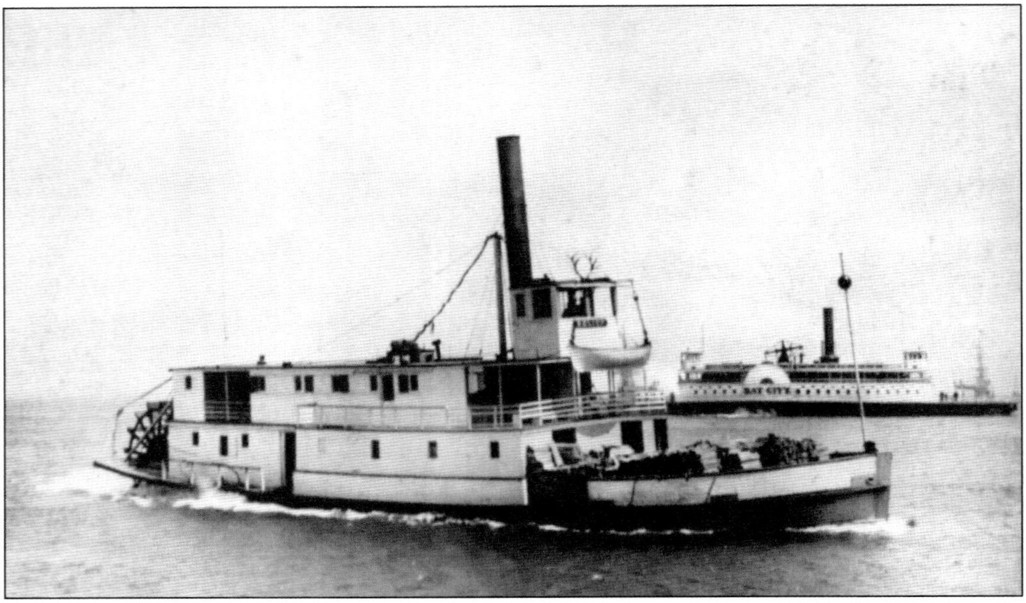

This 145-ton, 99-foot-long sternwheeler is the *Relief* c. 1882. In the background is the South Pacific Coast Railroad ferryboat *Bay City*, also headed for San Francisco. Built in 1864, the *Relief* went off documentation by 1895 after having worked Alviso Slough and other bay ports. (Courtesy San Francisco Maritime National Historical Park, No. B7.8,677n.)

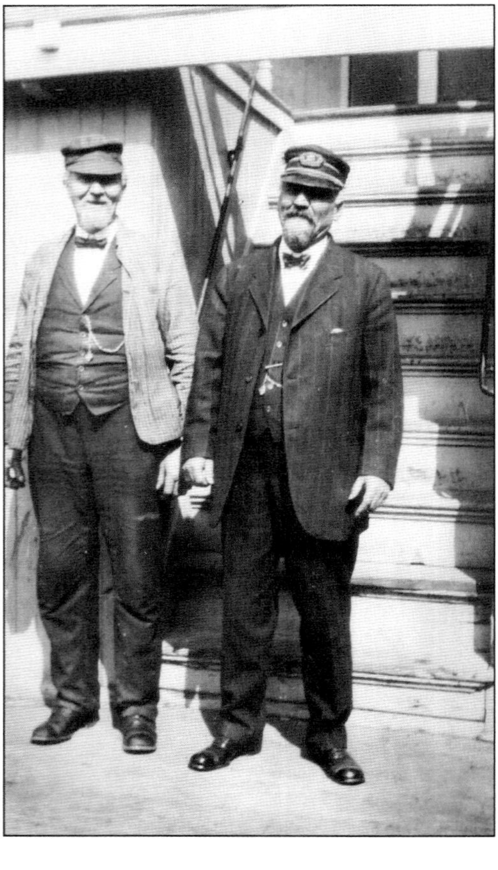

At right is Capt. John Leale, the most famous of Northern California's inland steamboat masters. He commanded the *Relief* on Alviso Slough, as well as the *Constance*, *Reform*, and *Onward*. Leale retired in 1914 after 32 years on Southern Pacific ferryboats. (Courtesy California State Library.)

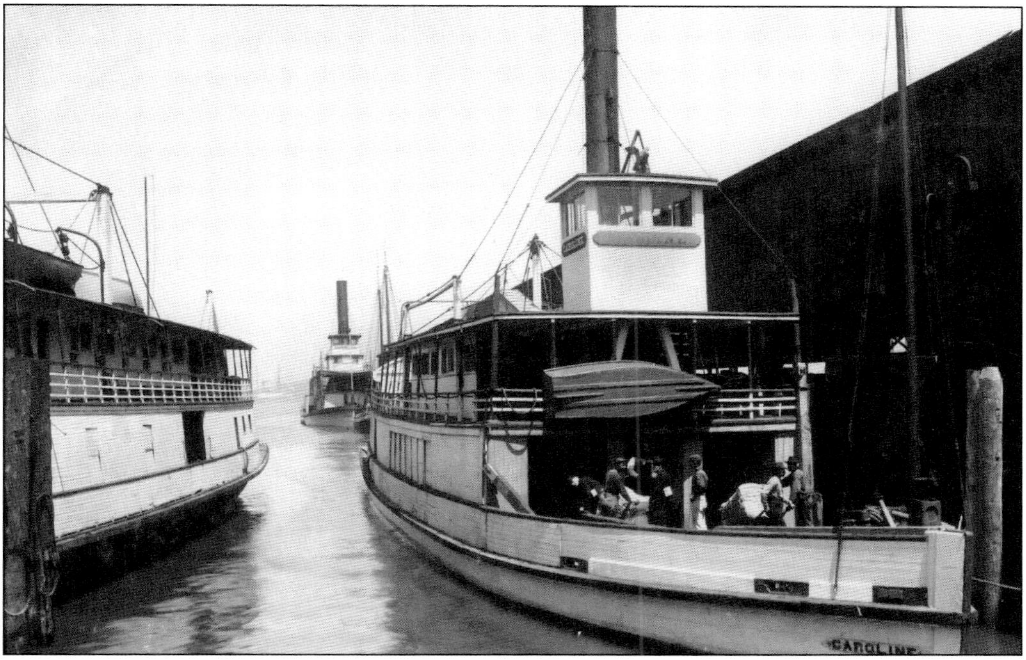

The 104-foot-long, 182.56-ton *Caroline* was built in 1868 at Union City. She was sold in 1882 to Capt. William Leale, and then worked the smaller creeks and rivers emptying into San Francisco Bay as charters or weekly trips between San Francisco and San Quentin Prison. (Courtesy San Francisco Maritime National Historical Park, No. P78-461.02x.)

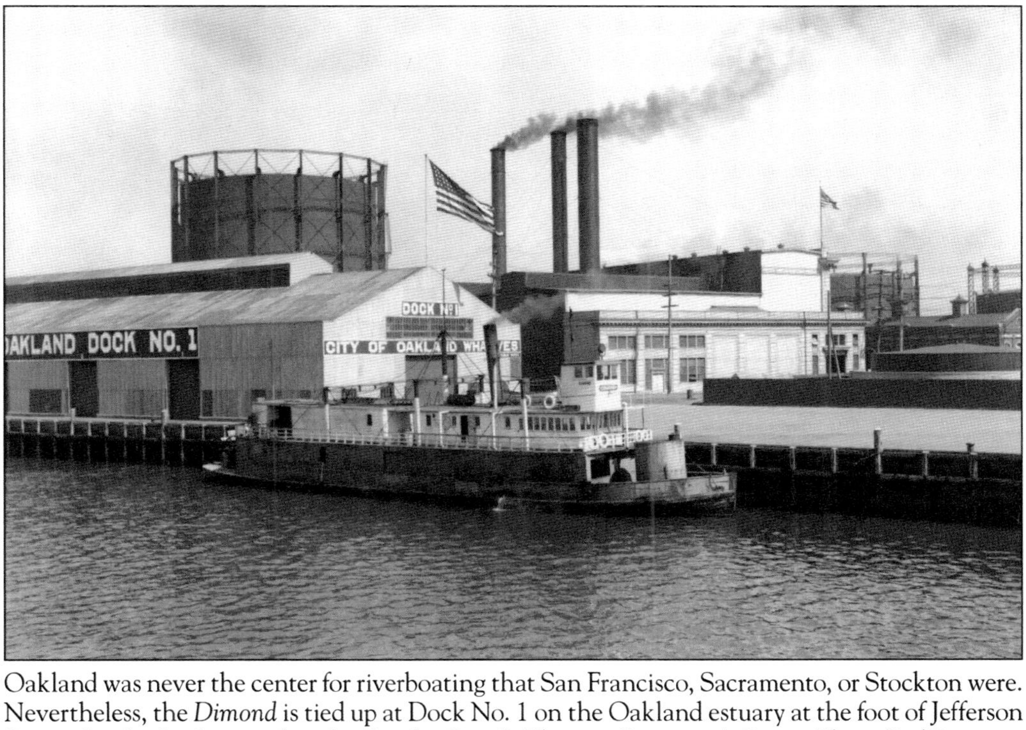


Oakland was never the center for riverboating that San Francisco, Sacramento, or Stockton were. Nevertheless, the *Dimond* is tied up at Dock No. 1 on the Oakland estuary at the foot of Jefferson Street. In the background is the Pacific Gas & Electric Company's Power Plant C. (Courtesy Richard Schlaich Collection.)

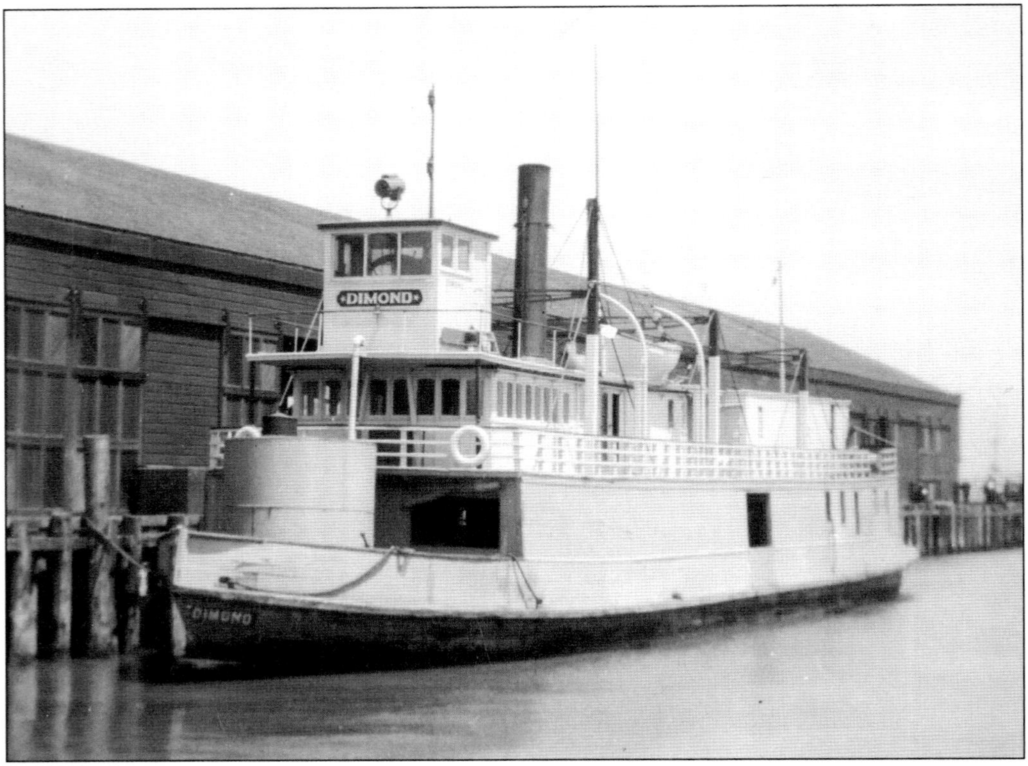


San Francisco–built in 1898 as the *Mary Lucy*, her owner, the California Salt Co., renamed her *Dimond* in 1900. *Dimond* measured 120 by 25.6 by 5 feet, rated 225 gross tons, and had a 10-man crew. She probably was a salt freighter before going off documentation in 1920. (Courtesy Western Railway Museum Archives, No. 49509.)

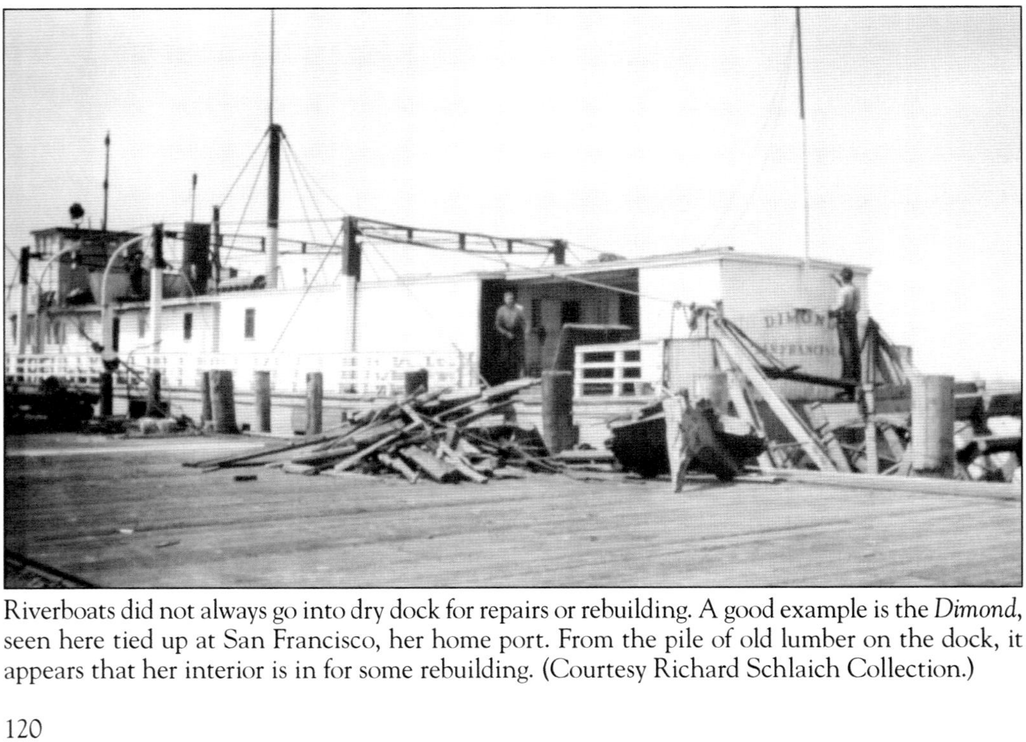

Riverboats did not always go into dry dock for repairs or rebuilding. A good example is the *Dimond*, seen here tied up at San Francisco, her home port. From the pile of old lumber on the dock, it appears that her interior is in for some rebuilding. (Courtesy Richard Schlaich Collection.)

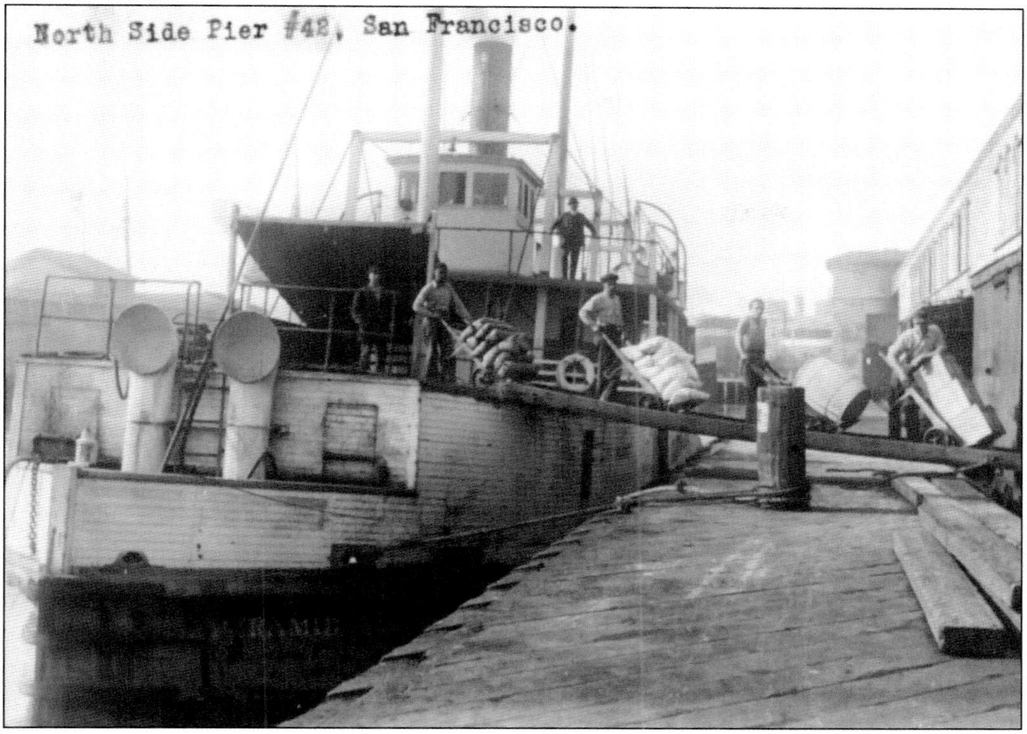


Here the *Pyramid*, ex-*Sunol*, is at San Francisco's Pier 42. She came in at 294 tons and measured 135 by 27.5 by 7.8 feet. Leslie Salt Co. bought her in 1924 and renamed her *Pyramid*. In 1946, she was beached on the Napa River, vacated and left to rot. (Courtesy Western Railway Museum Archives, No. 49510.)

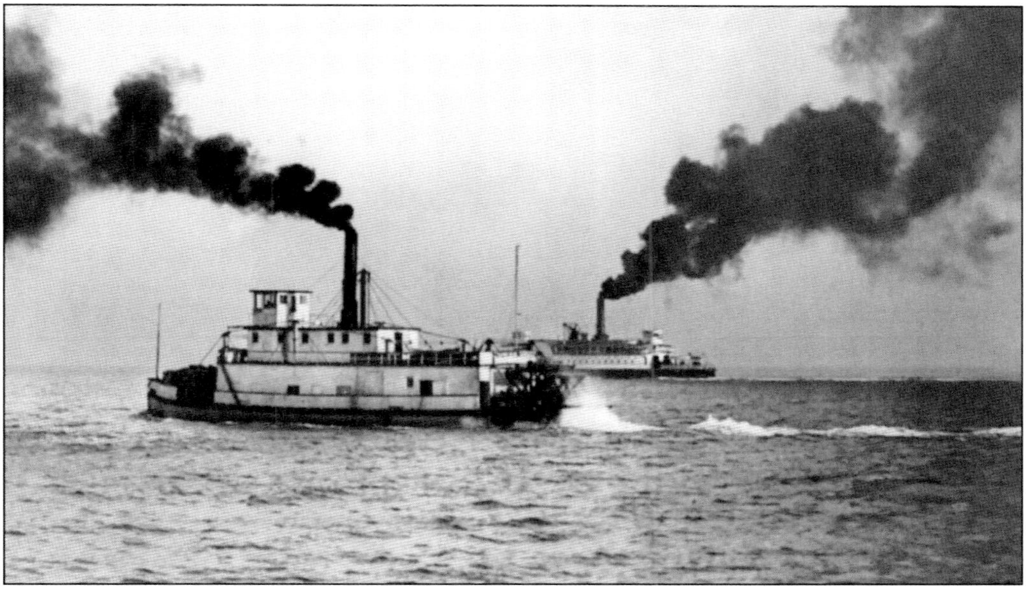

The *Frank Silva* is steaming eastward across San Francisco Bay c. 1890. Behind her appears to be the South Pacific Coast Railroad ferryboat *Encinal* heading to Alameda. The *Frank Silva* is a freighter, having no cabin deck for passengers. Both vessels are poster children for clean air laws. (Courtesy San Francisco Maritime National Historical Park, No. P89-089.002n.)

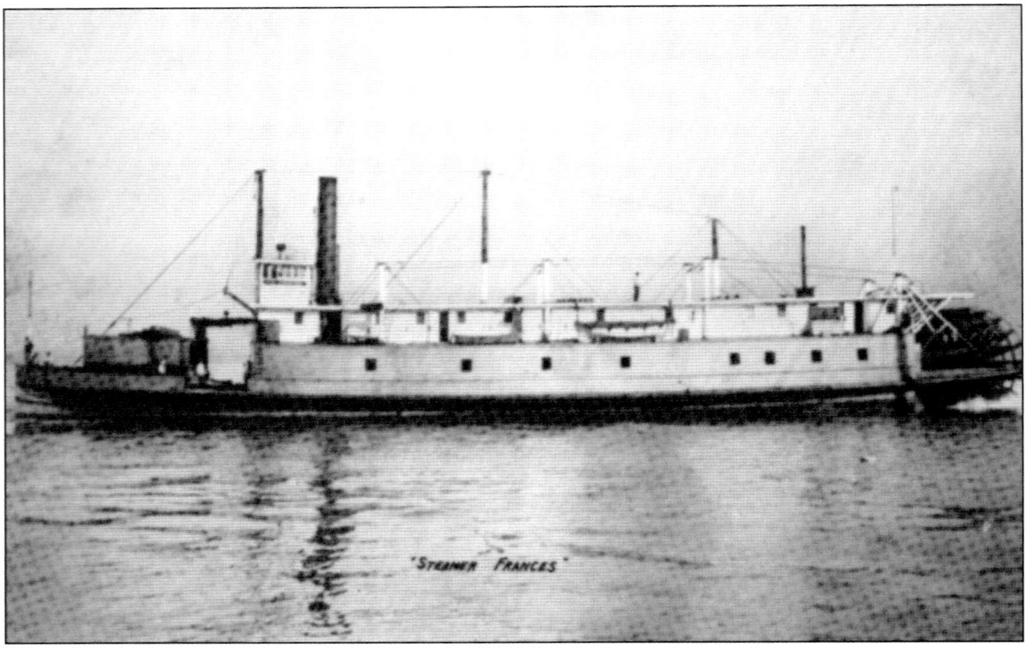


The *Frances*, built in 1905 as a 174-foot-long, 698.44 tonner, was abandoned in 1941. (Courtesy San Francisco Maritime National Historical Park, No. P82-100.6pl.)

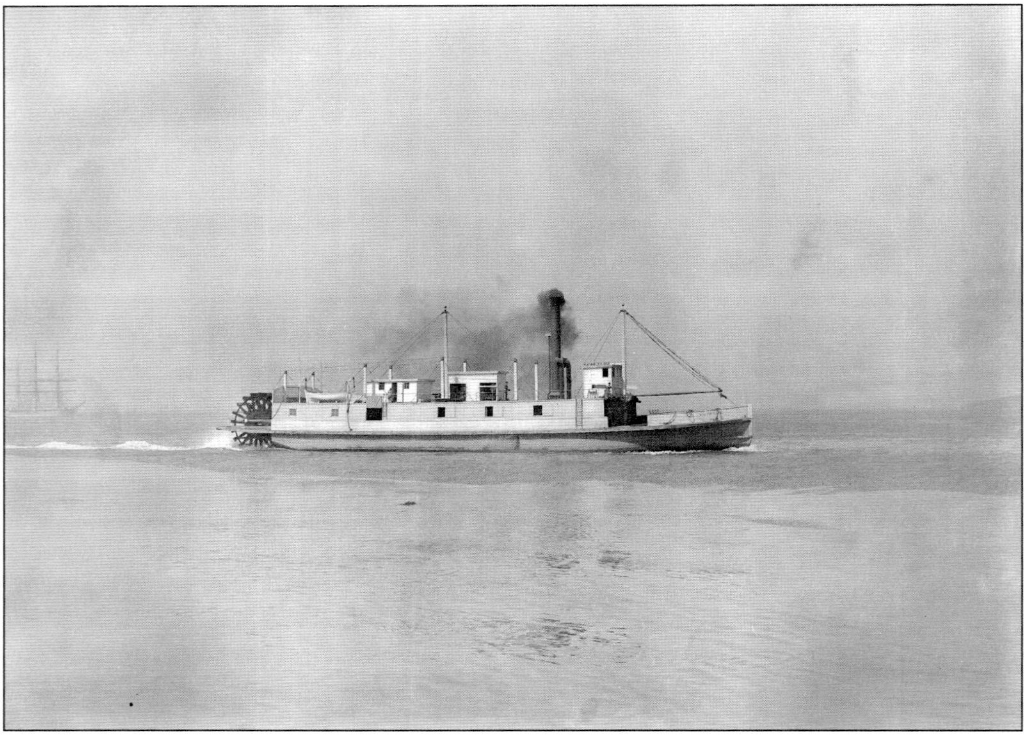

Shown here steaming across San Francisco Bay is the freighter *Potrero*, a stranger to history books until now. Taken from a glass plate negative, the picture reveals that she worked in the days of sailing ships well before clean air laws. (Courtesy San Francisco Maritime National Historical Park, No. P83-142A.4343.)

# *Seven*

# FINISHED WITH ENGINES

The chapter title is the final entry in a riverboat's log that signifies a final voyage. The engines were shut down, never to run again, regardless of her fate, whether it be scrapping, burning, or abandonment. In the early 1920s, the riverboat industry in California seemed healthy, offering the cheapest transportation in California. After 1922, riverboating began showing signs of age and the lack of ability to compete with publicly funded roads, highways, and bridges. In 1927, the *Fort Sutter* and *Capital City* were relegated to Stockton in favor of the two new *Deltas* on the Sacramento River. The Broderick fire on August 28, 1932, cost the Sacramento River 13 tugs, barges, and riverboats. In December, the *J. D. Peters* made the last Stockton–San Francisco run. Between 1927 and 1928, the Carquinez Bridge opened, the Yolo Causeway was widened, and the Tower Bridge at Sacramento replaced the old M Street Bridge across the Sacramento River. By 1938, the San Francisco-Oakland Bay Bridge and the Golden Gate Bridge were completed. These were all publicly funded projects, and the privately owned riverboats simply could not compete. In 1941, the *Delta King* and *Delta Queen* made their final trips to San Francisco. After World War II, only the *Petaluma II* was an active riverboat, and there is reasonable speculation that she might have been retired earlier had it not been for wartime transportation demands. Indeed, six riverboats and a few old ferryboats actually had their careers extended thanks to wartime needs. After V-J Day, it was all over. Attempts to preserve and reuse the *Fort Sutter* and *Petaluma* ultimately failed. The *Delta King* found herself in Kitimat, British Columbia, as a beached dormitory for construction workers. She was towed back to the bay area in 1959 to begin a 30-year saga fraught with one career-threatening episode after another, before finding a new life as a Sacramento hotel in 1989. The *Delta Queen* is now a floating restaurant in Memphis, Tennessee.

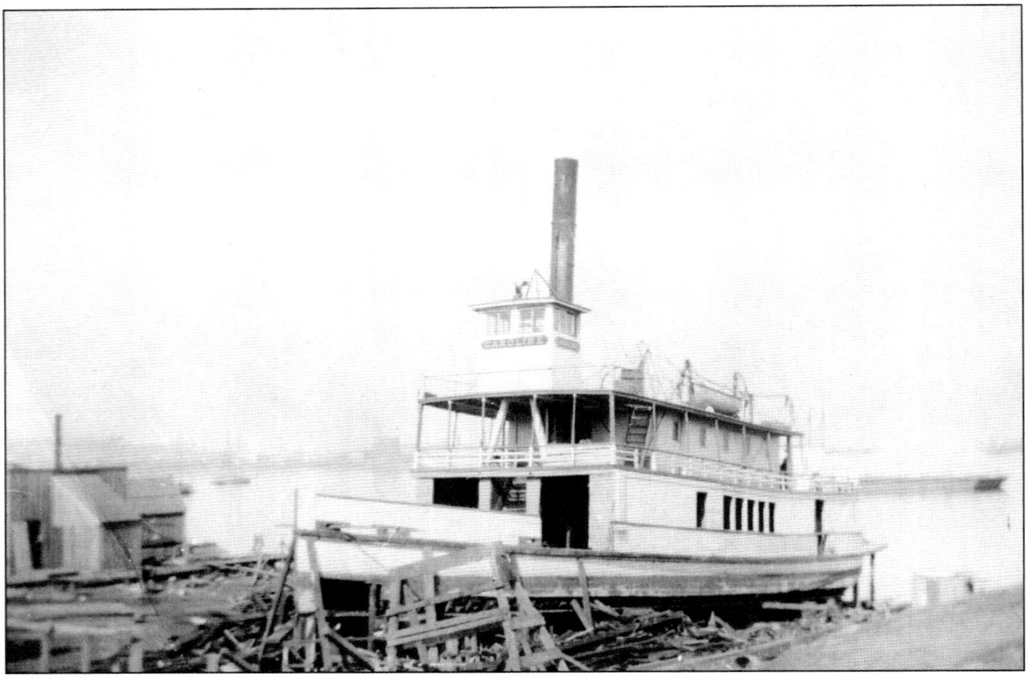

In 1917, after 49 years of service, the old and tired *Caroline* was beached in Sausalito where she caught fire and burned to her waterline, resulting in a reported $20,000 loss. Owner-captain William Leale died the following year in San Francisco. (Author's collection.)

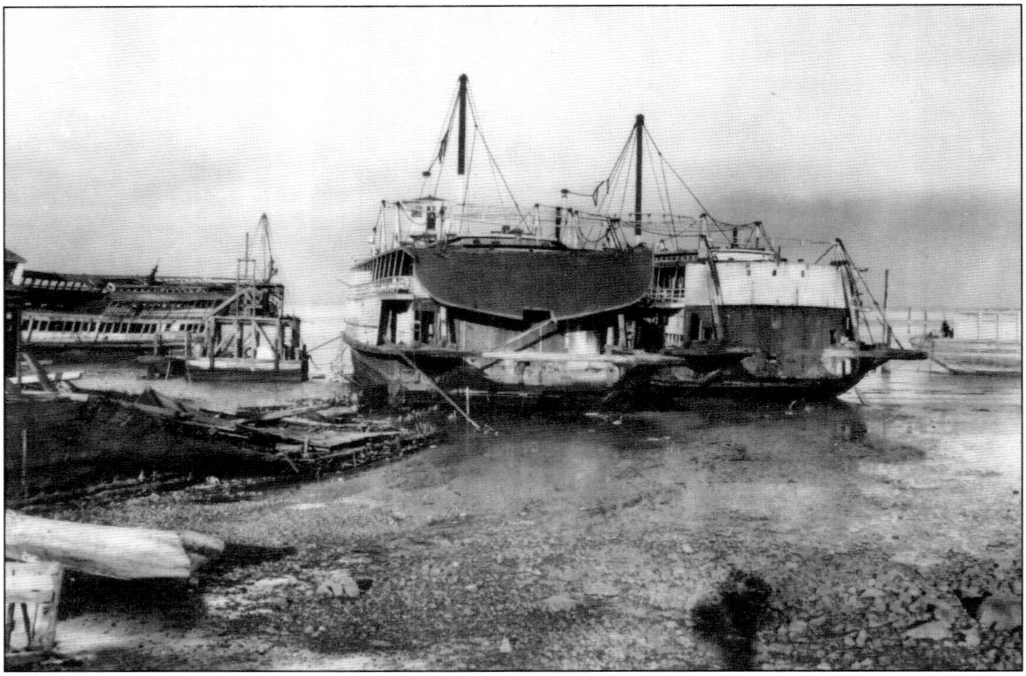

Ex-Southern Pacific riverboats *Modoc* (left) and *Apache* (right) lie abandoned with other derelicts at Hunters Point in San Francisco in 1928. This scene makes one grateful for the efforts to preserve the *Delta King* at Sacramento and the ferryboats *Eureka* at San Francisco and *Berkeley* at San Diego. (Courtesy California State Library.)

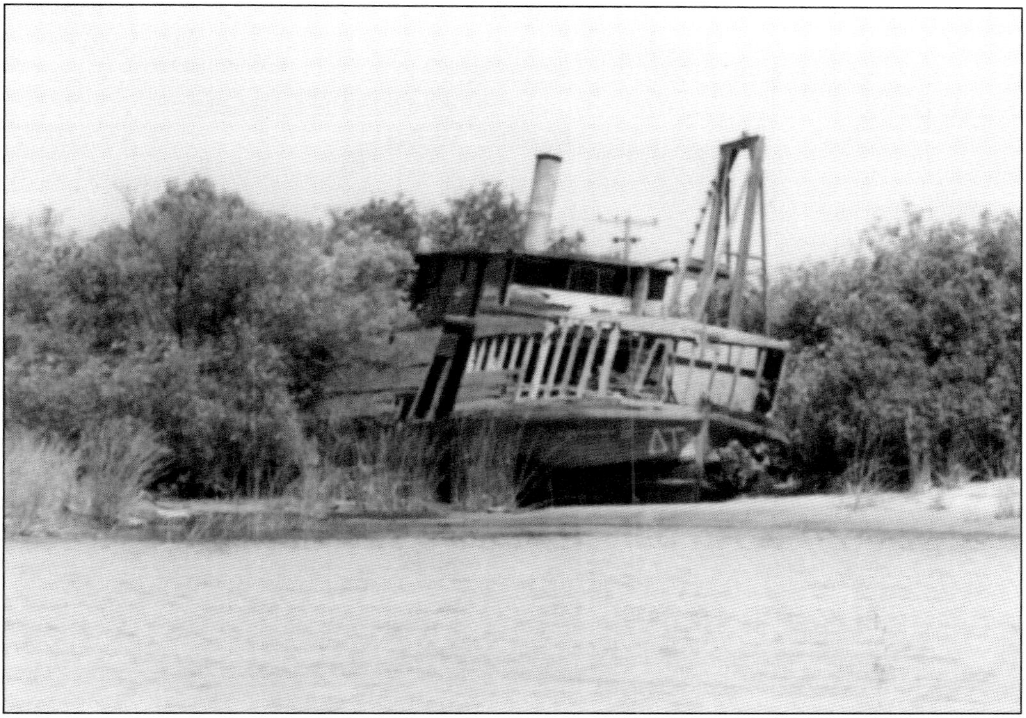

Page 58 of *Ferries of San Francisco Bay* shows what the photographer believed was an abandoned ferryboat. In 1938, a levee broke, flooding Mandeville Island. Three idled riverboats, the *J. D. Peters*, *Navajo*, and *Reform*, were run through the break, their paddle wheels forcing floodwater off the island, saving rich Delta farmlands. The stranded riverboats later became workers' bunkhouses. (Paul Wamsley photograph; author's collection.)

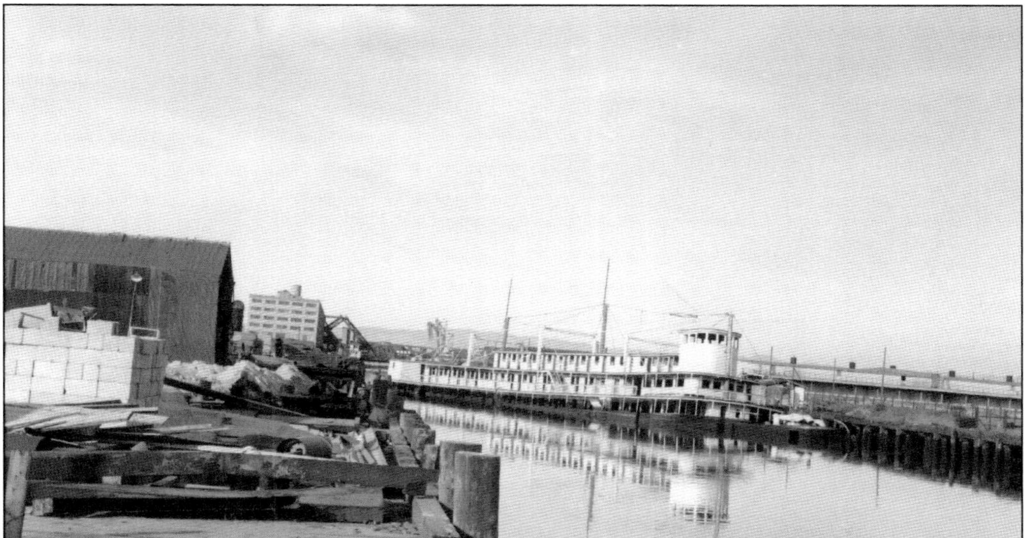

The *Port of Stockton*'s final decades were unjust. Downgraded in 1927 to the Stockton runs by the new *Delta King* and *Delta Queen*, she went to the Stockton–Sacramento run after 1932. During World War II, she ferried troops around San Francisco Bay. Unneeded and unloved, she sank at Stockton in 1952. (Courtesy Western Railway Museum Archives, No. 50346.)

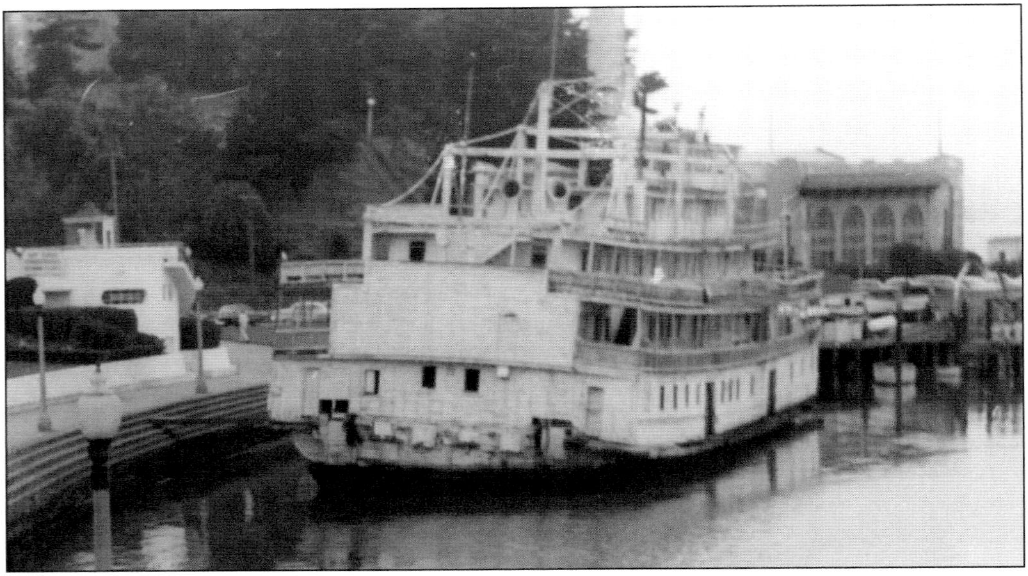

The *Fort Sutter* was once her owner's pride. However, by 1956, the years had taken their toll. Considered an eyesore by neighbors and badly in need of repairs, she had sat for three years at San Francisco's Aquatic Park while other vessels were being readied for the nearby new maritime museum. (Tom Gray photograph; courtesy Tom Gray.)

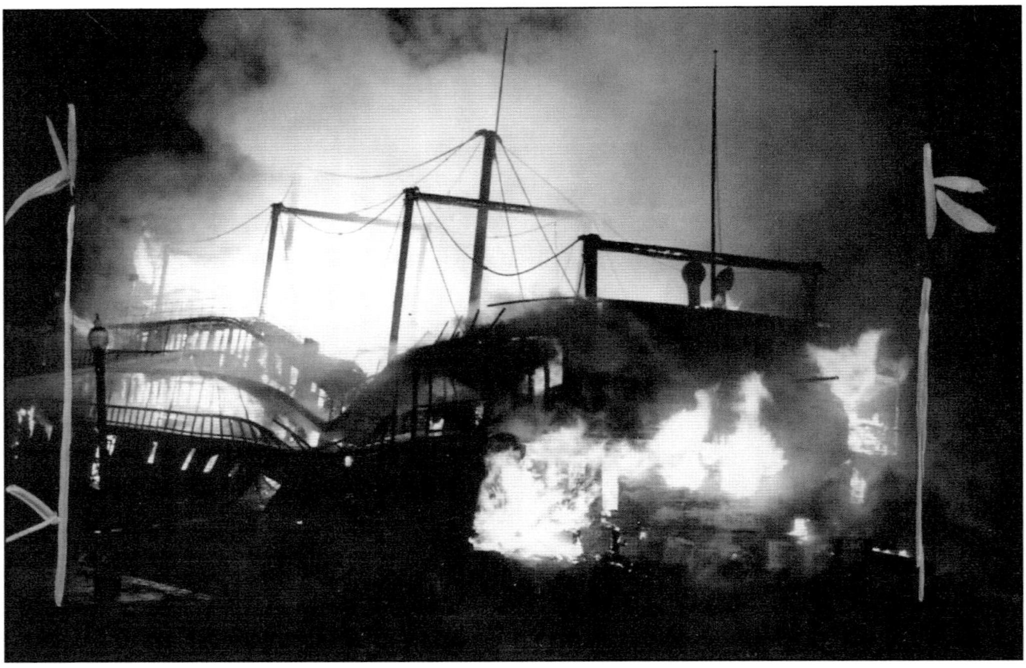

On the night of May 2, 1959, the *Fort Sutter* went up in flames under suspicious circumstances. It was never fully investigated by authorities, so the cause will probably never be known for sure. What is known is that it was the finale for this relic of a bygone age. (Courtesy San Francisco Maritime National Historical Park, No. P82-019a.4,445x.)

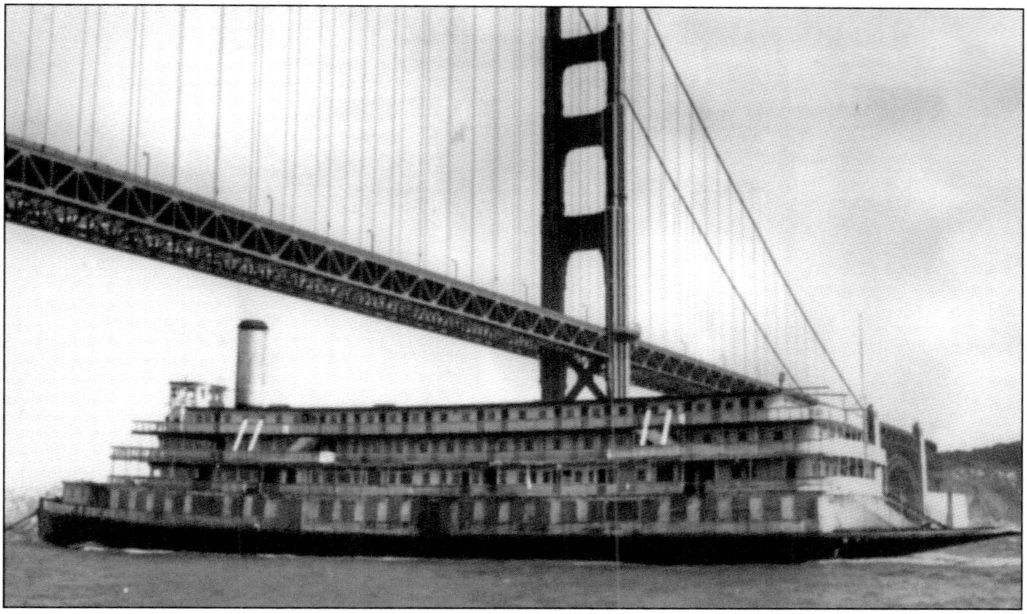

It is about 5:00 p.m. on April 28, 1959, and the *Delta King* is being towed under the Golden Gate Bridge by the tug *Lloyd B. Gore* after a four-day trip from British Columbia where she spent seven years as a landlocked dormitory for construction workers. (Courtesy San Francisco Maritime National Historical Park, No. P82-019a.1851pl.)

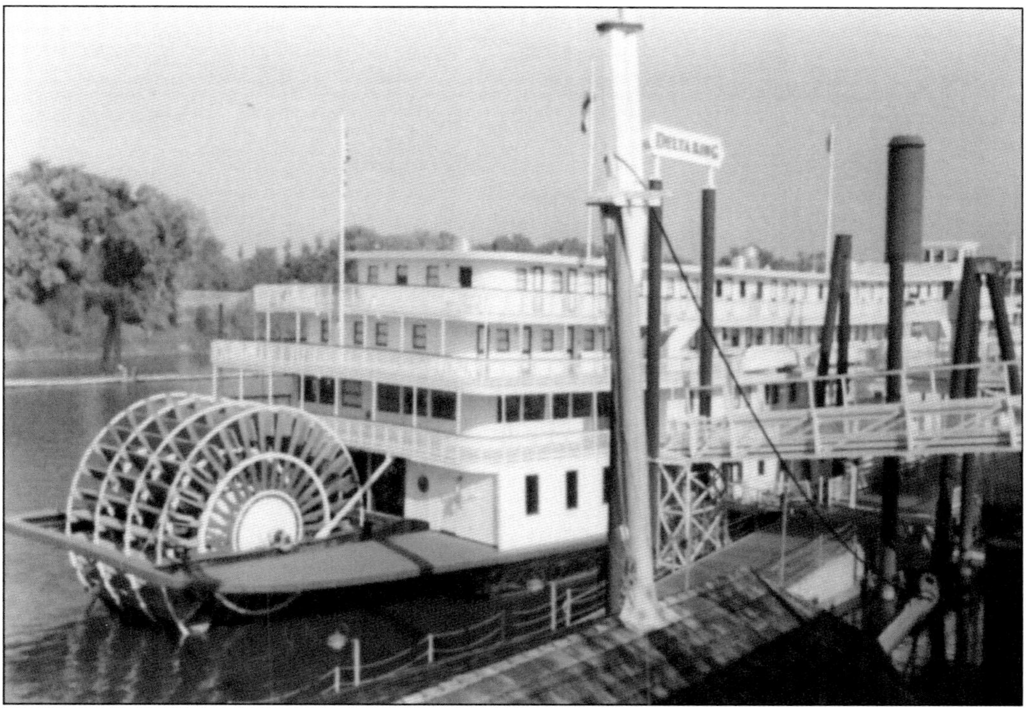

On October 13, 1989, the *Delta King* was in her new life as a floating hotel in Sacramento. Of over 300 riverboats that once served the Golden State's inland waterways, only the *Delta King* is afloat in California. Sister ship *Delta Queen* is a floating restaurant in Memphis, Tennessee. (Paul C. Trimble photograph.)